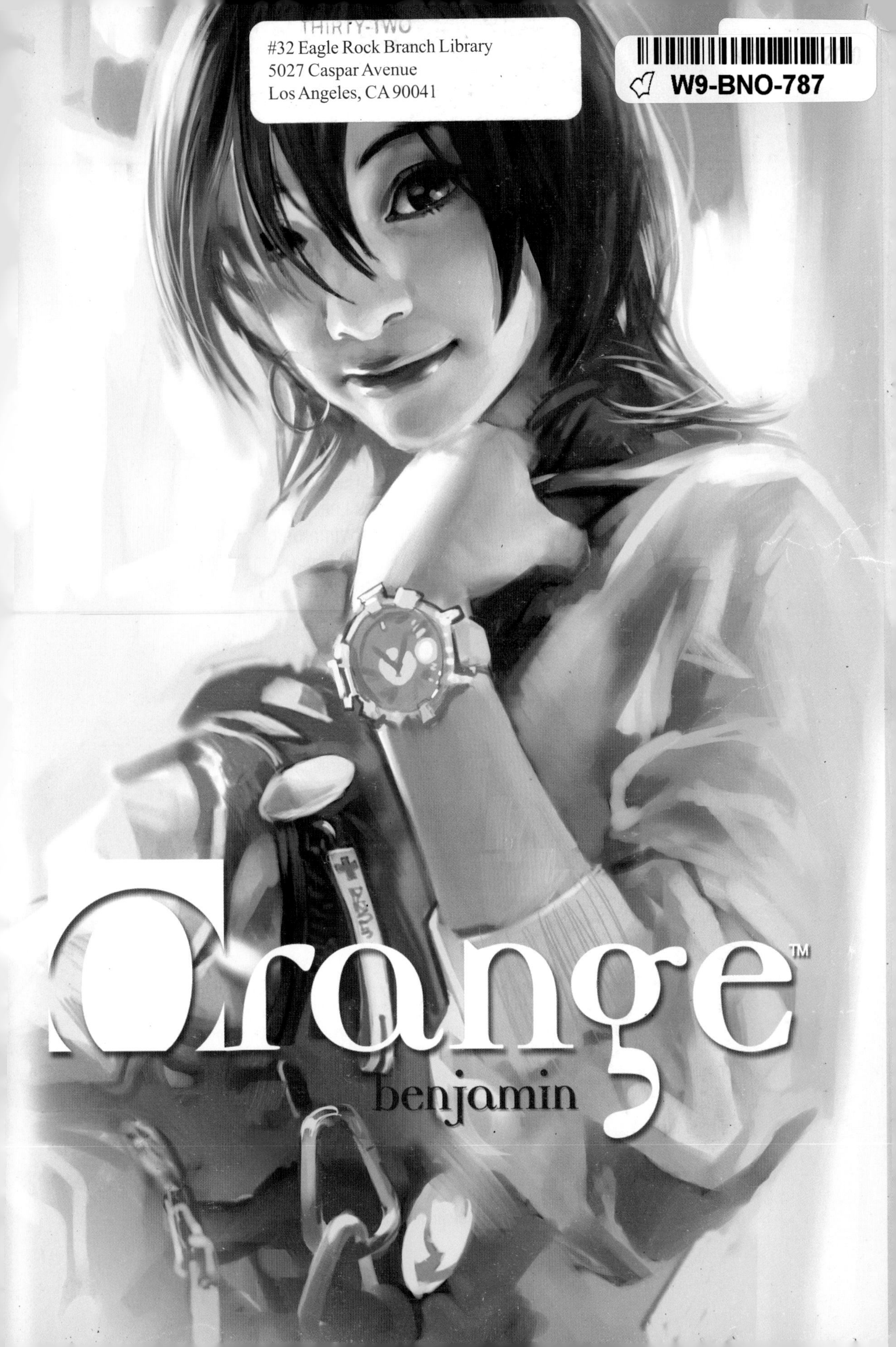
Orange™
benjamin

# *Orange*
## Created by Benjamin

Translation - Edward Gauvin
Lettering - Star Print Brokers
Production Artist - Vicente Rivera, Jr.
Graphic Designer - Louis Csontos

Senior Editor - Bryce P. Coleman
Pre-Production Supervisor - Vicente Rivera, Jr.
Pre-Production Specialist - Lucas Rivera
Managing Editor - Vy Nguyen
Senior Designer - Louis Csontos
Senior Designer - James Lee
Senior Editor - Jenna Winterberg
Associate Publisher - Marco F. Pavia
President and C.O.O. - John Parker
C.E.O. and Chief Creative Officer - Stu Levy

A 🐸 **TOKYOPOP**® Manga

TOKYOPOP and 🐸 are trademarks or registered trademarks of TOKYOPOP Inc.

TOKYOPOP Inc.
5900 Wilshire Blvd. Suite 2000
Los Angeles, CA 90036

E-mail: info@TOKYOPOP.com
Come visit us online at www.TOKYOPOP.com

ISBN: 978-1-4278-1463-0

First TOKYOPOP printing: February 2009
10  9  8  7  6  5  4  3  2
Printed in the USA

# Orange™

## benjamin

TOKYOPOP®

**HAMBURG // LONDON // LOS ANGELES // TOKYO**

# Orange™
## benjamin

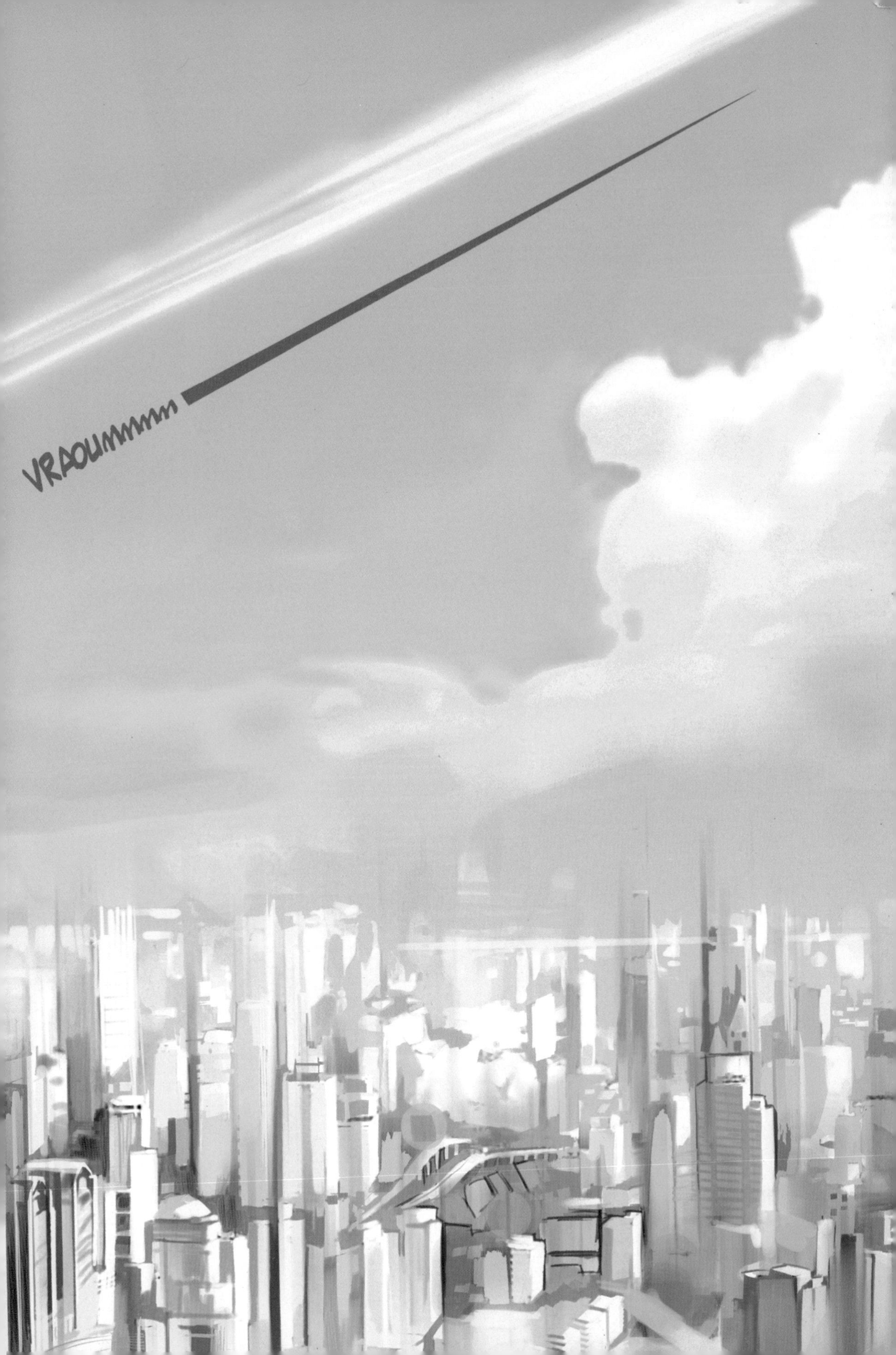
VRAOUMMMMM

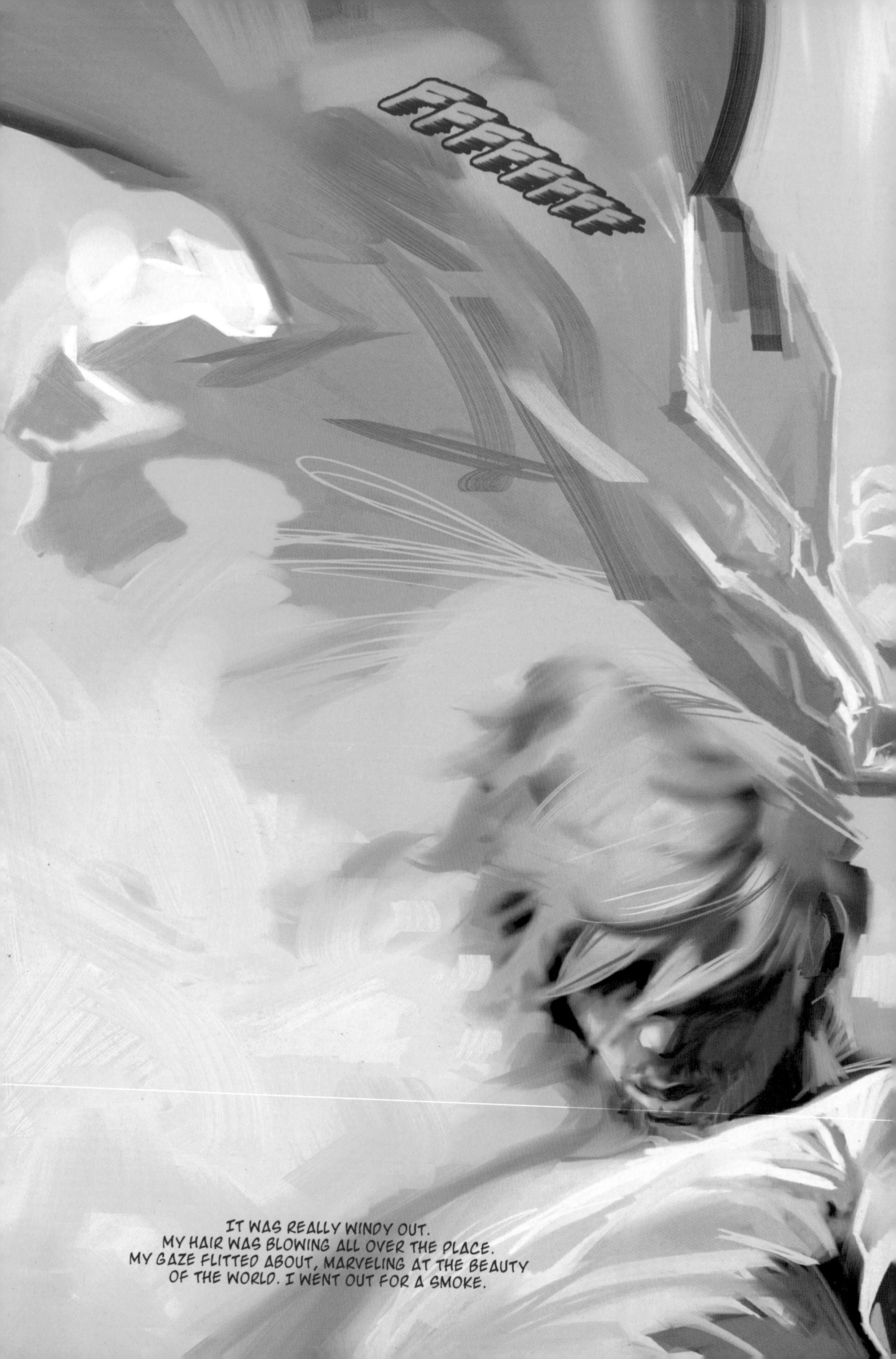
FFFFFFFF
IT WAS REALLY WINDY OUT.
MY HAIR WAS BLOWING ALL OVER THE PLACE.
MY GAZE FLITTED ABOUT, MARVELING AT THE BEAUTY
OF THE WORLD. I WENT OUT FOR A SMOKE.

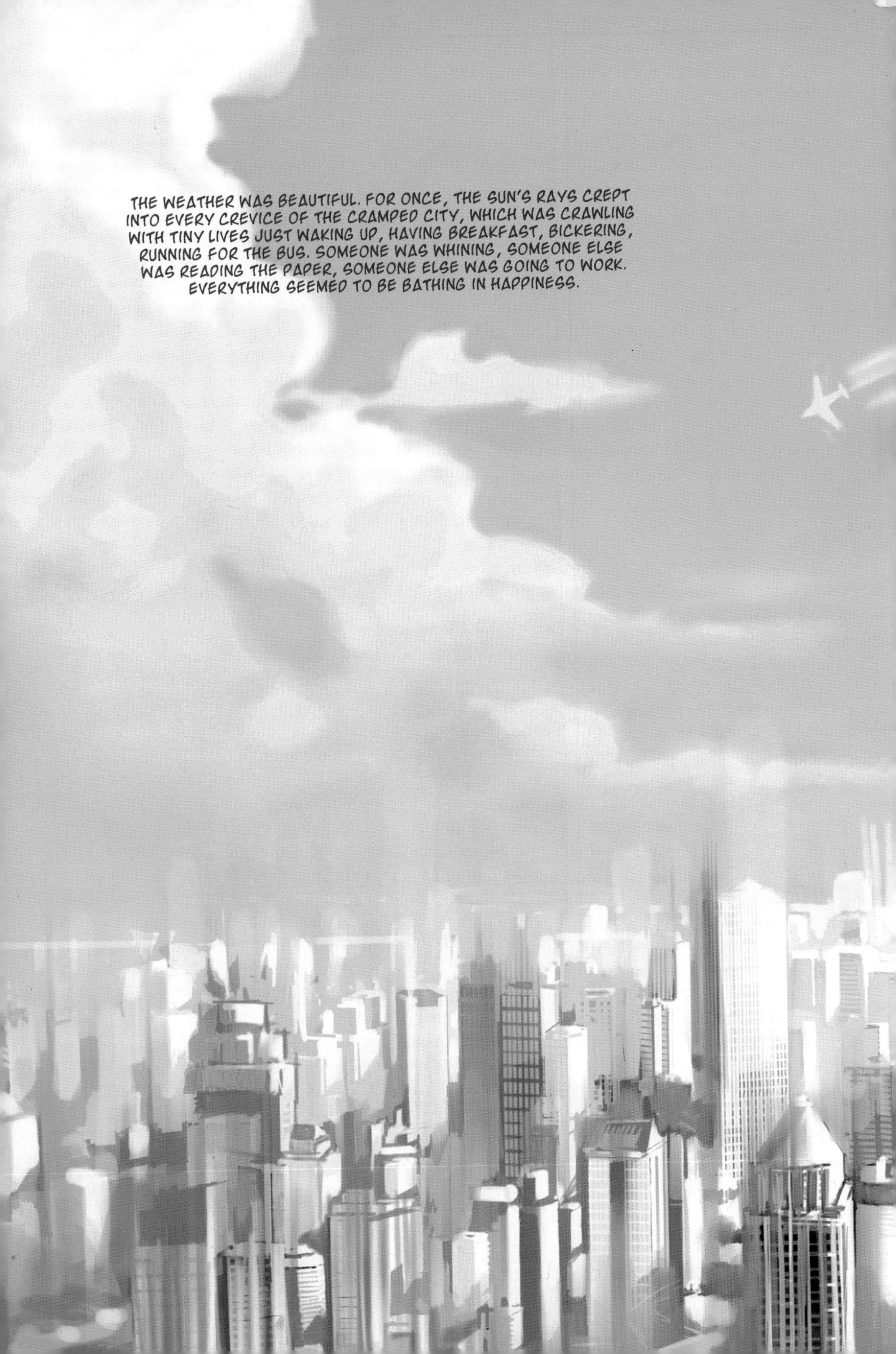
THE WEATHER WAS BEAUTIFUL. FOR ONCE, THE SUN'S RAYS CREPT INTO EVERY CREVICE OF THE CRAMPED CITY, WHICH WAS CRAWLING WITH TINY LIVES JUST WAKING UP, HAVING BREAKFAST, BICKERING, RUNNING FOR THE BUS. SOMEONE WAS WHINING, SOMEONE ELSE WAS READING THE PAPER, SOMEONE ELSE WAS GOING TO WORK. EVERYTHING SEEMED TO BE BATHING IN HAPPINESS.

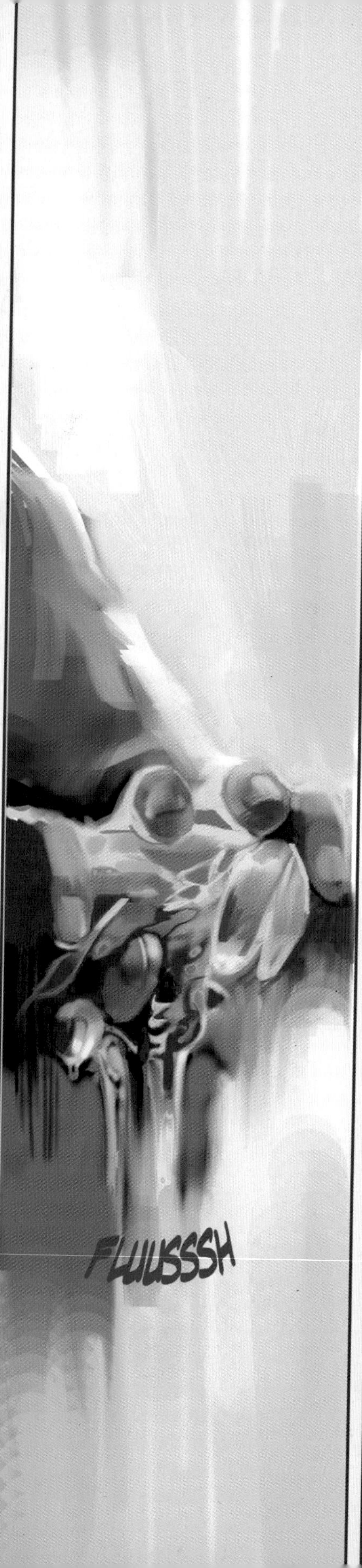
FLUUSSSH

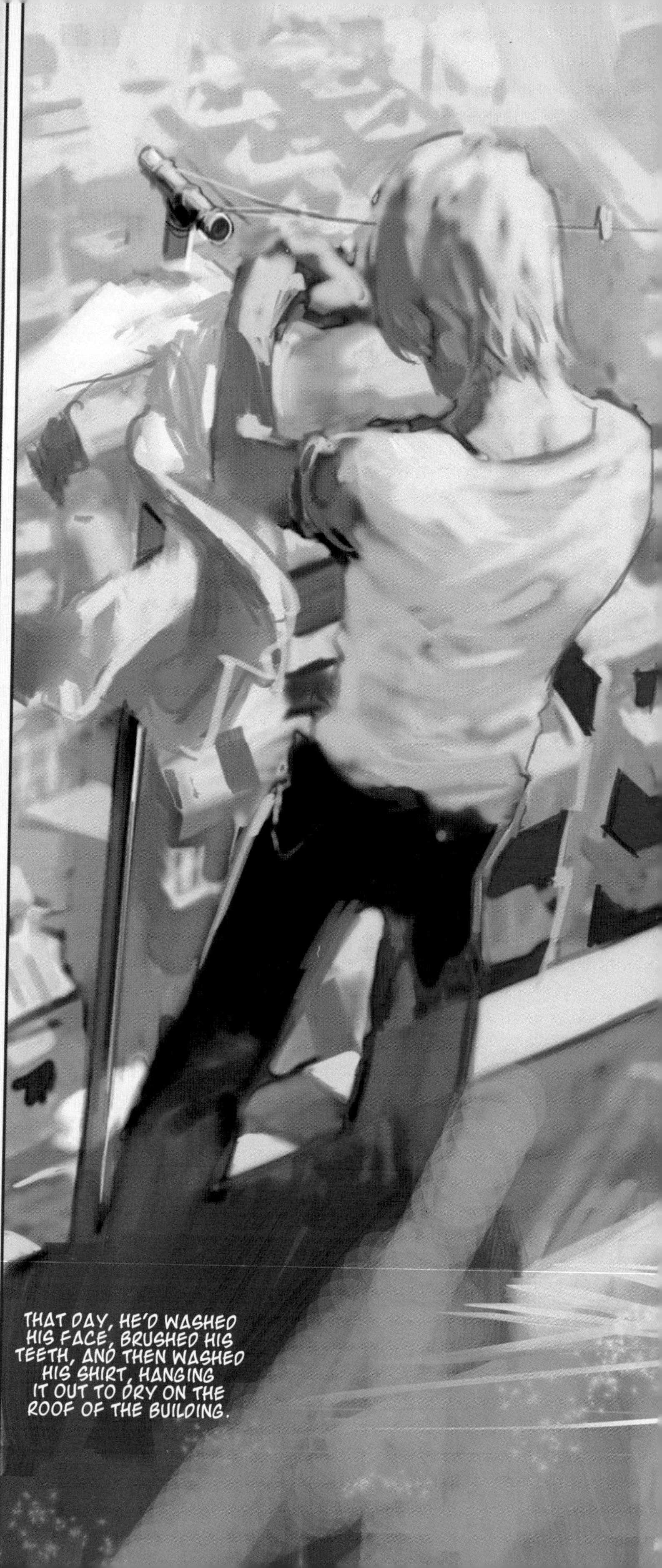
THAT DAY, HE'D WASHED HIS FACE, BRUSHED HIS TEETH, AND THEN WASHED HIS SHIRT, HANGING IT OUT TO DRY ON THE ROOF OF THE BUILDING.

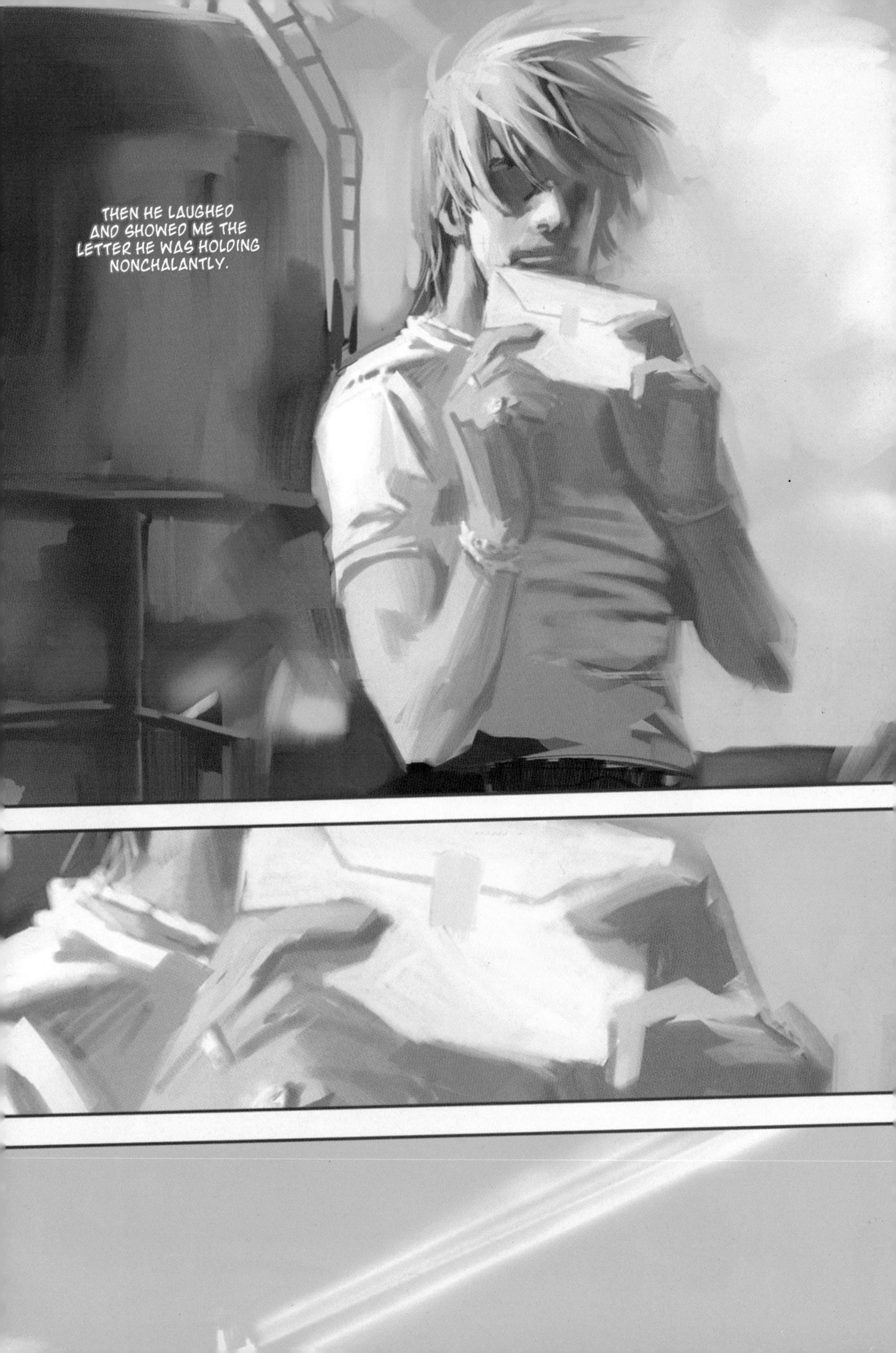
THEN HE LAUGHED AND SHOWED ME THE LETTER HE WAS HOLDING NONCHALANTLY.

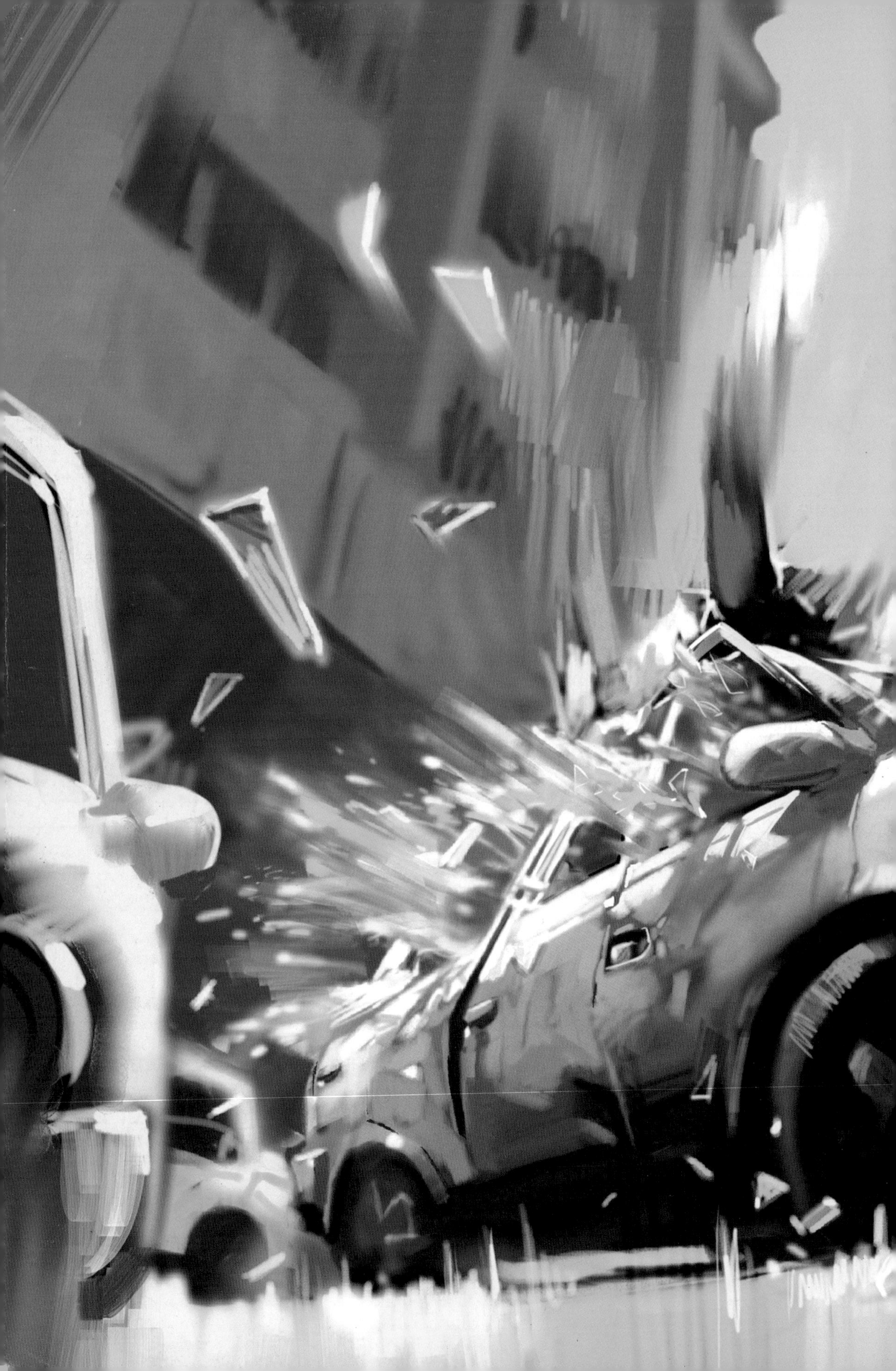

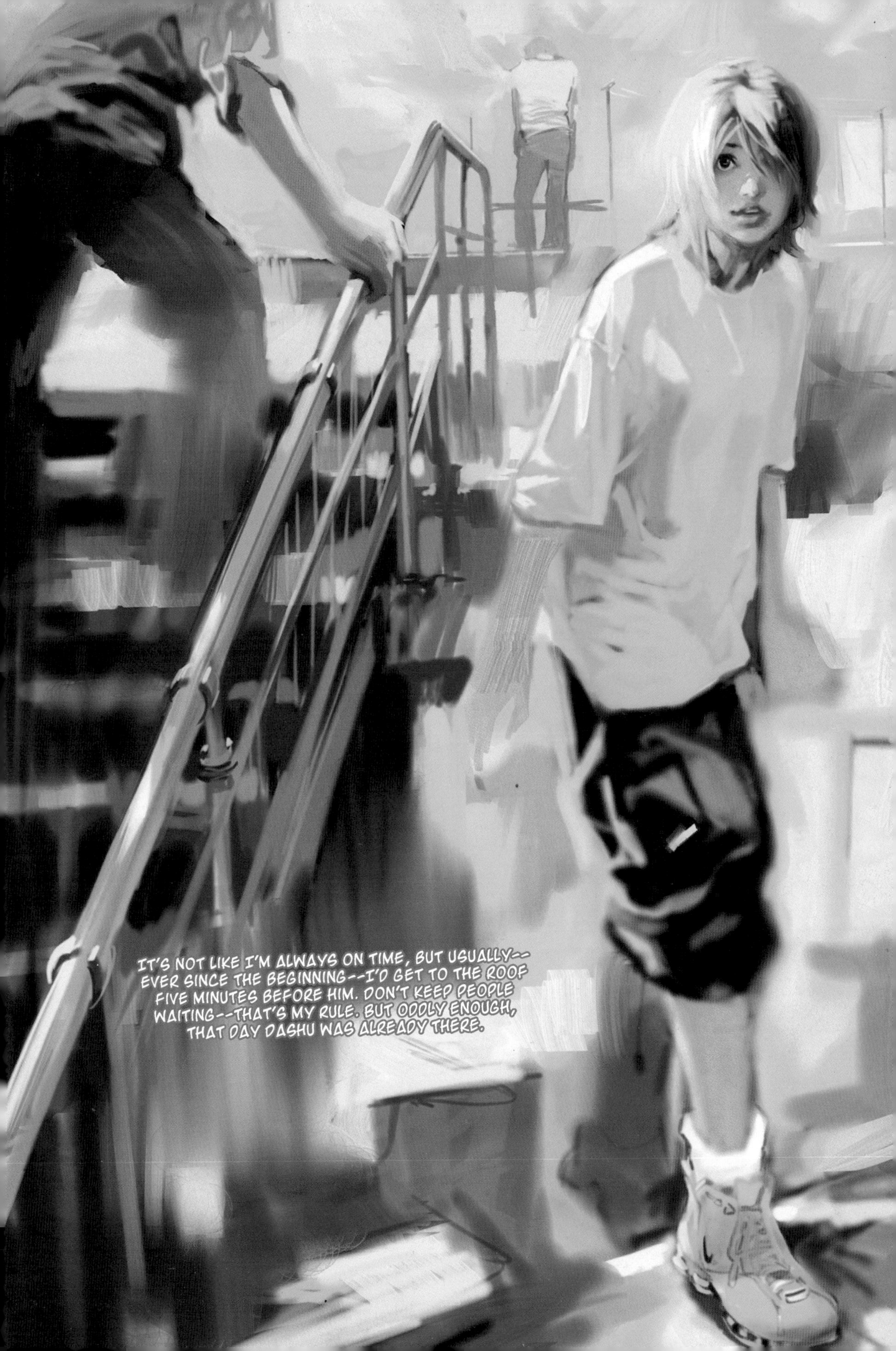
IT'S NOT LIKE I'M ALWAYS ON TIME, BUT USUALLY--
EVER SINCE THE BEGINNING--I'D GET TO THE ROOF
FIVE MINUTES BEFORE HIM. DON'T KEEP PEOPLE
WAITING--THAT'S MY RULE. BUT ODDLY ENOUGH,
THAT DAY DASHU WAS ALREADY THERE.

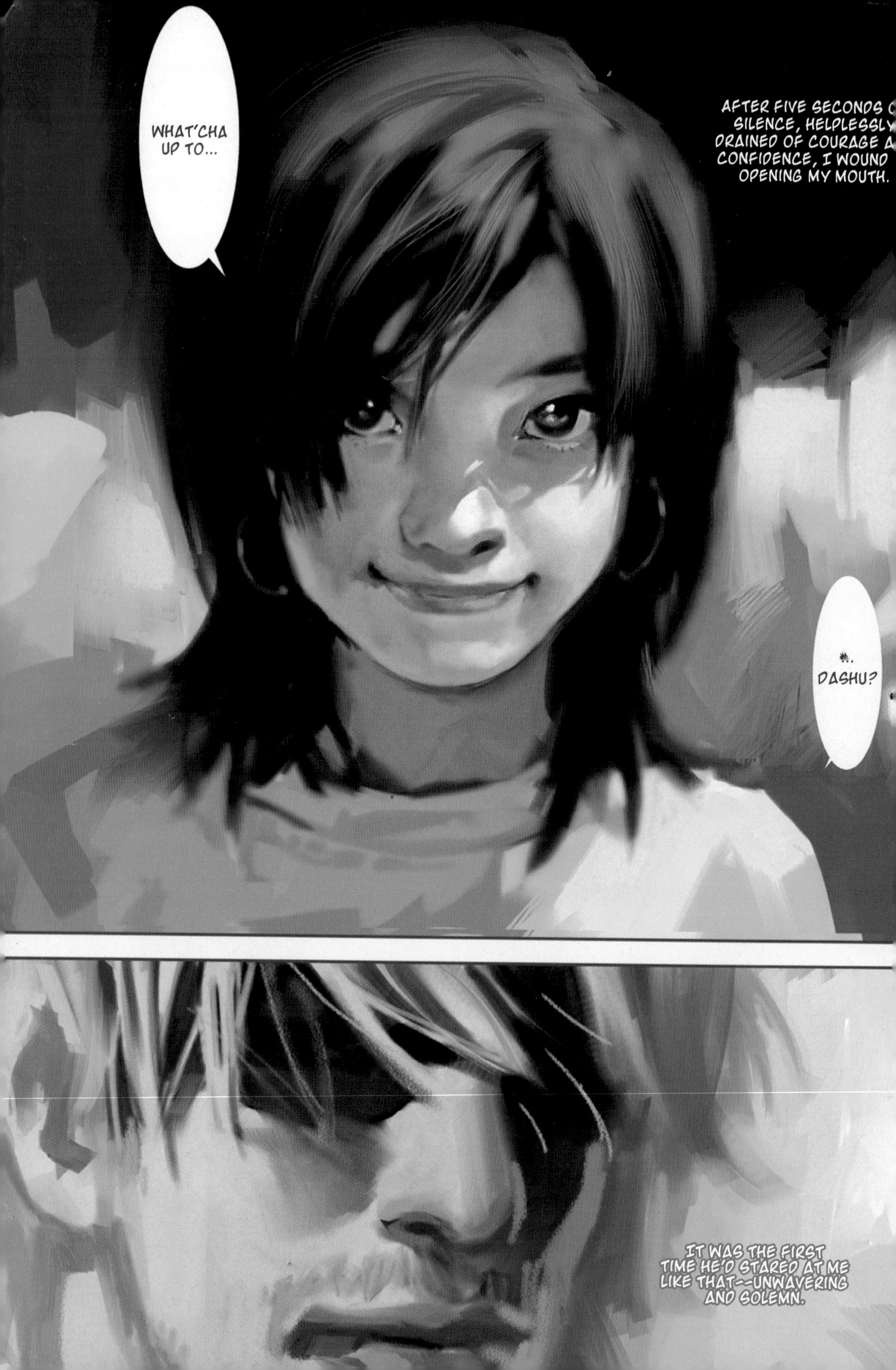
WHAT'CHA UP TO...
AFTER FIVE SECONDS O SILENCE, HELPLESSLY DRAINED OF COURAGE A CONFIDENCE, I WOUND OPENING MY MOUTH.
... DASHU?
IT WAS THE FIRST TIME HE'D STARED AT ME LIKE THAT--UNWAVERING AND SOLEMN.

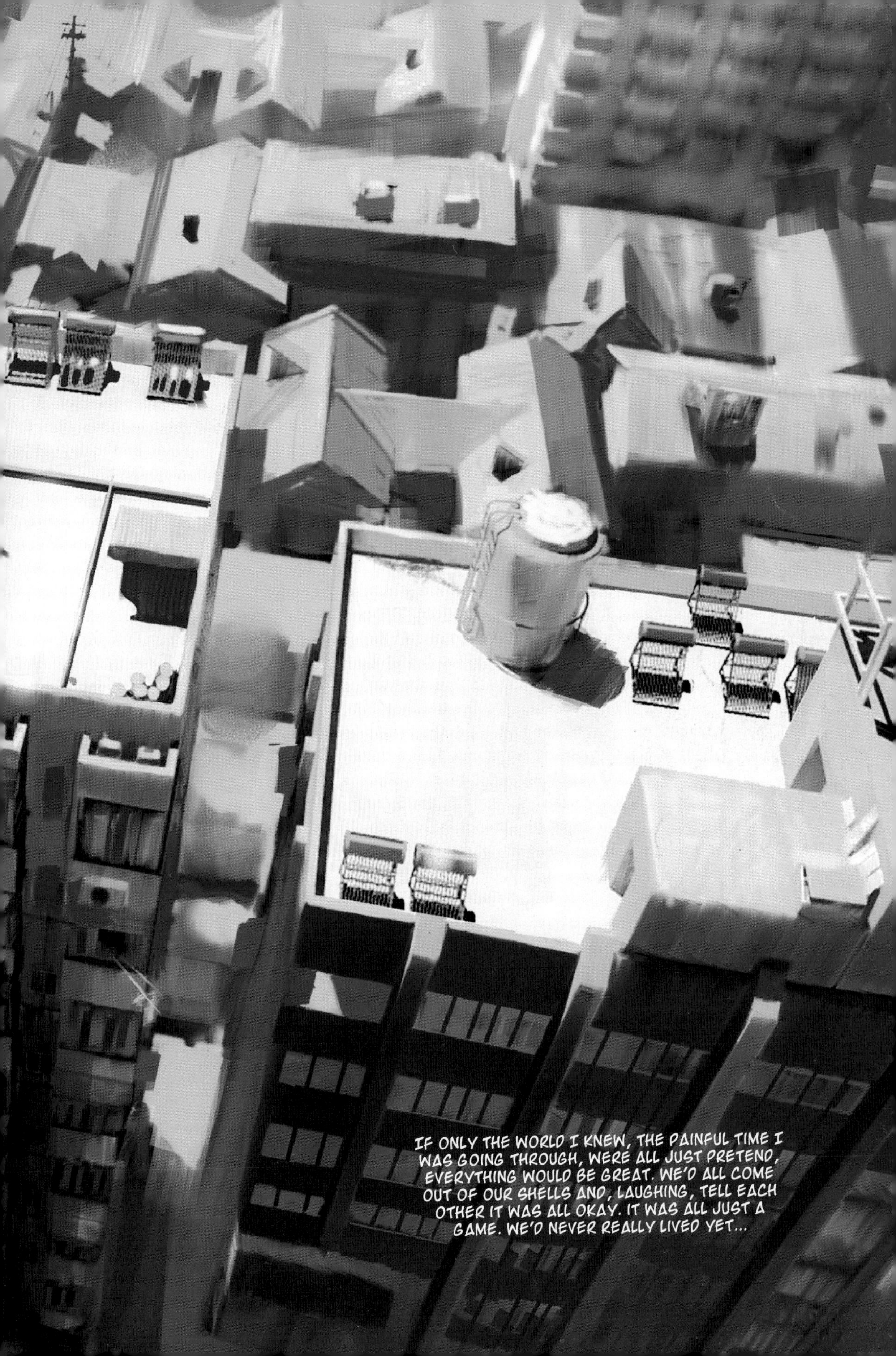
IF ONLY THE WORLD I KNEW, THE PAINFUL TIME I WAS GOING THROUGH, WERE ALL JUST PRETEND, EVERYTHING WOULD BE GREAT. WE'D ALL COME OUT OF OUR SHELLS AND, LAUGHING, TELL EACH OTHER IT WAS ALL OKAY. IT WAS ALL JUST A GAME. WE'D NEVER REALLY LIVED YET...

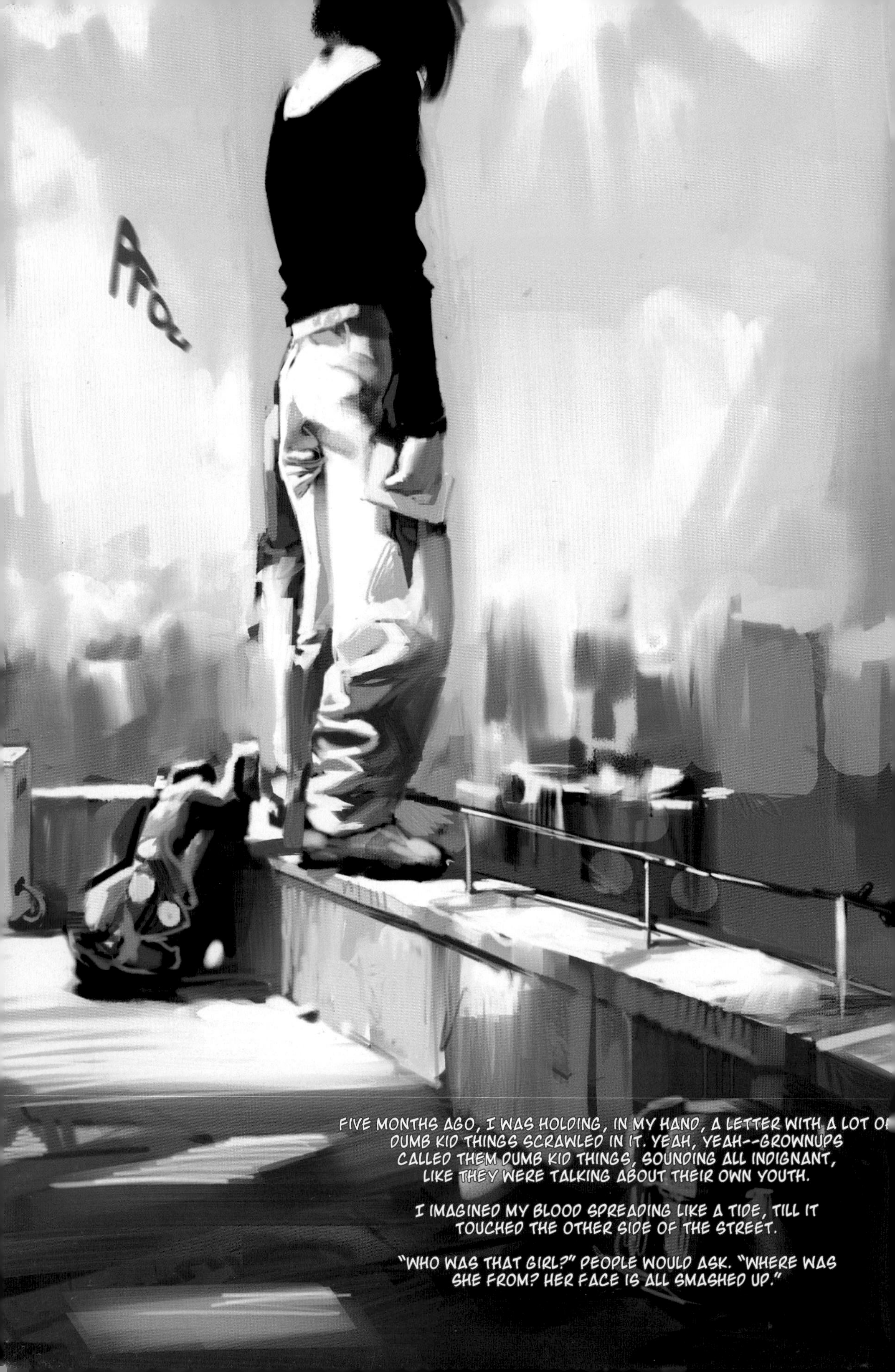
FIVE MONTHS AGO, I WAS HOLDING, IN MY HAND, A LETTER WITH A LOT O
DUMB KID THINGS SCRAWLED IN IT. YEAH, YEAH--GROWNUPS CALLED THEM DUMB KID THINGS, SOUNDING ALL INDIGNANT, LIKE THEY WERE TALKING ABOUT THEIR OWN YOUTH.
I IMAGINED MY BLOOD SPREADING LIKE A TIDE, TILL IT TOUCHED THE OTHER SIDE OF THE STREET.
"WHO WAS THAT GIRL?" PEOPLE WOULD ASK. "WHERE WAS SHE FROM? HER FACE IS ALL SMASHED UP."

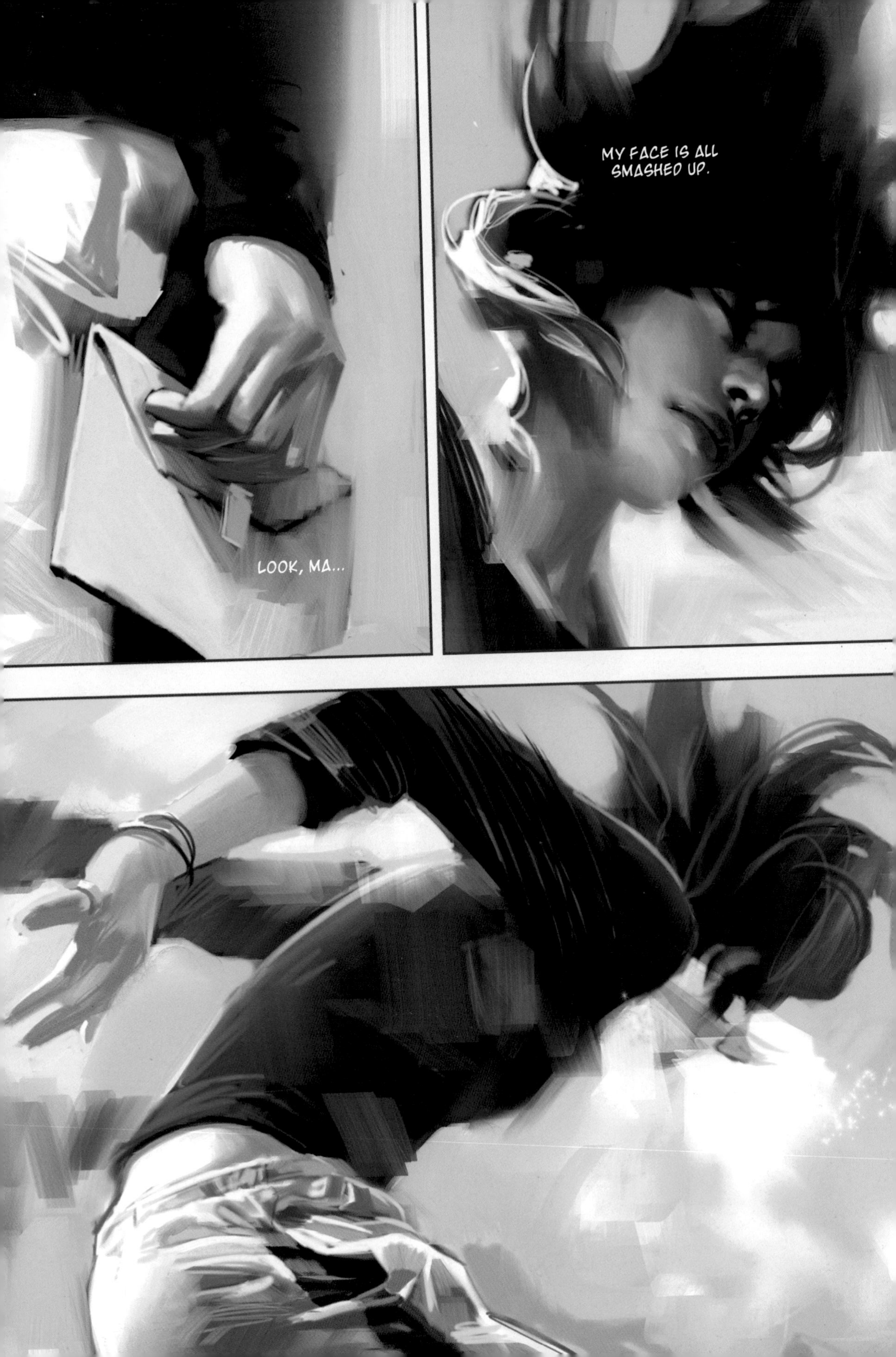
LOOK, MA...
MY FACE IS ALL SMASHED UP.

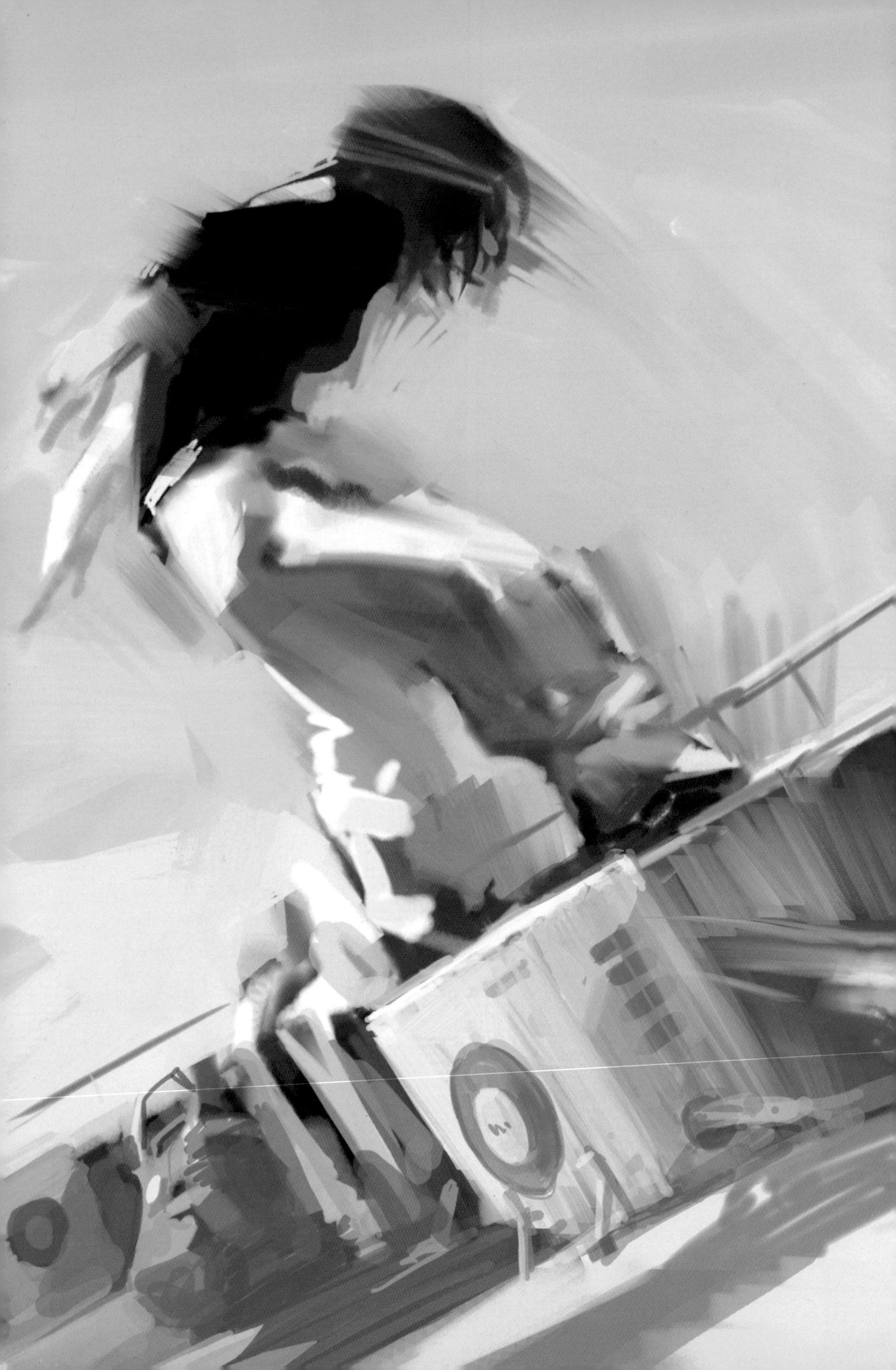

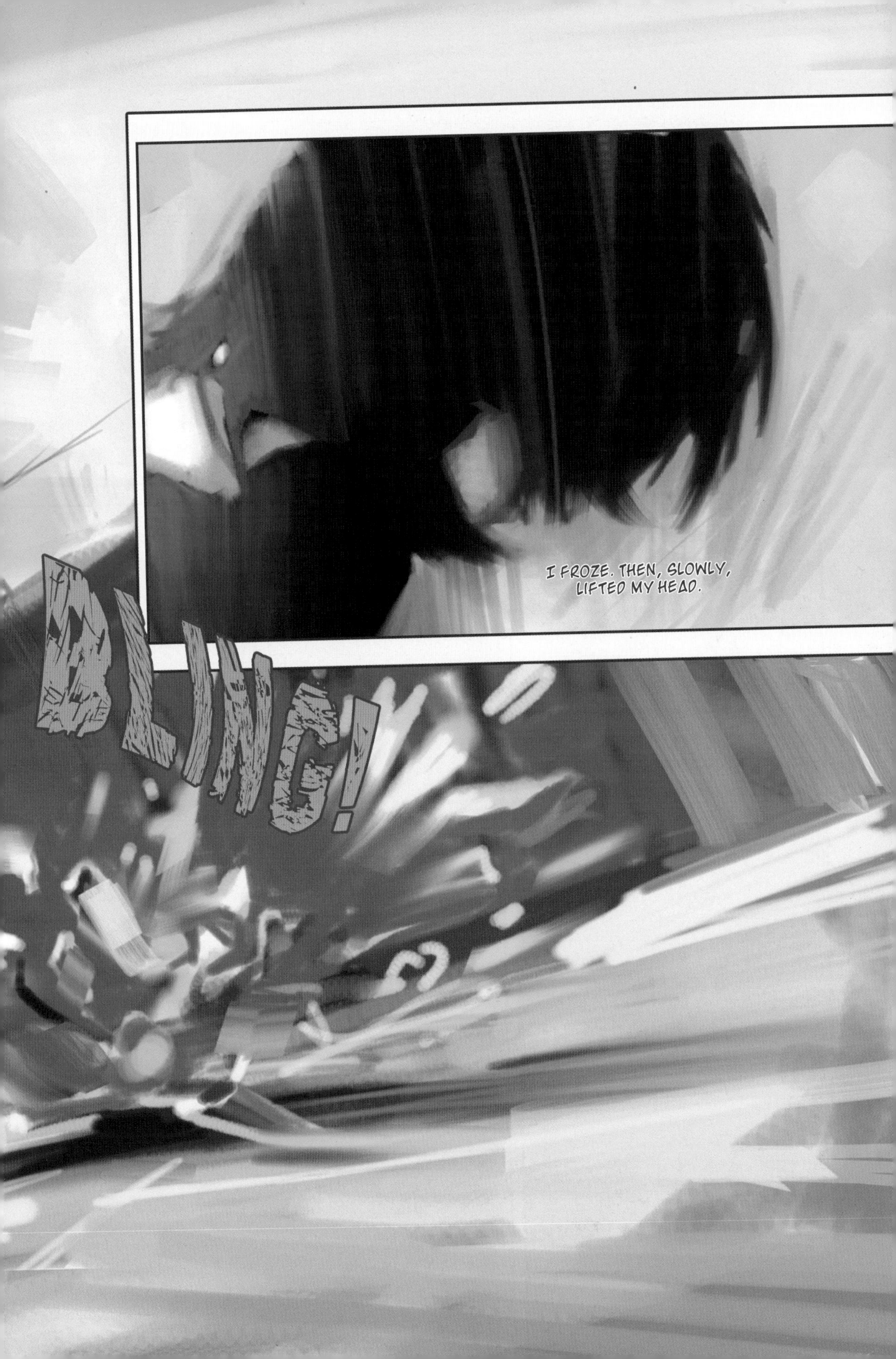
I FROZE. THEN, SLOWLY,
LIFTED MY HEAD.
BLING!

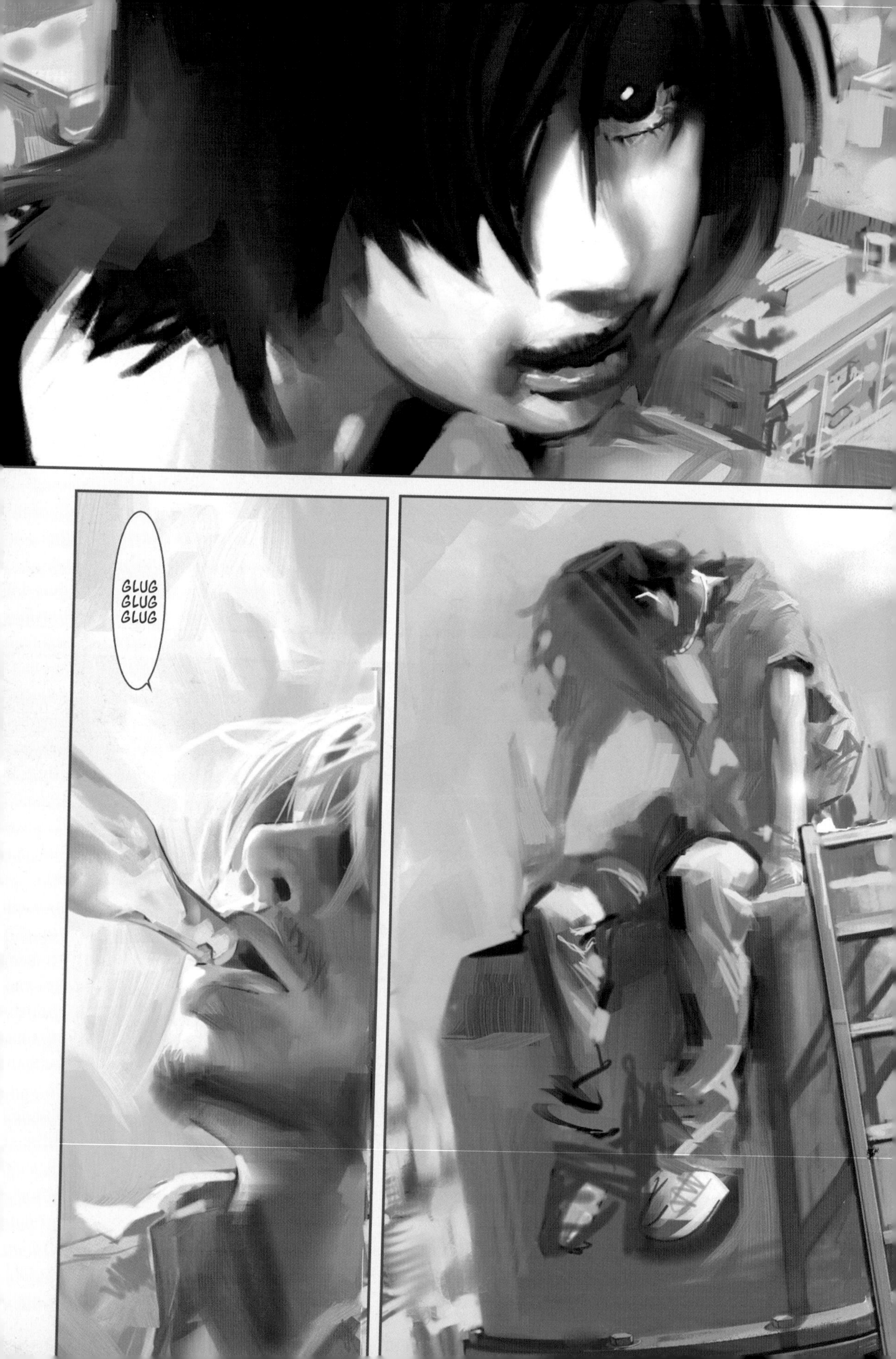
GLUG GLUG GLUG

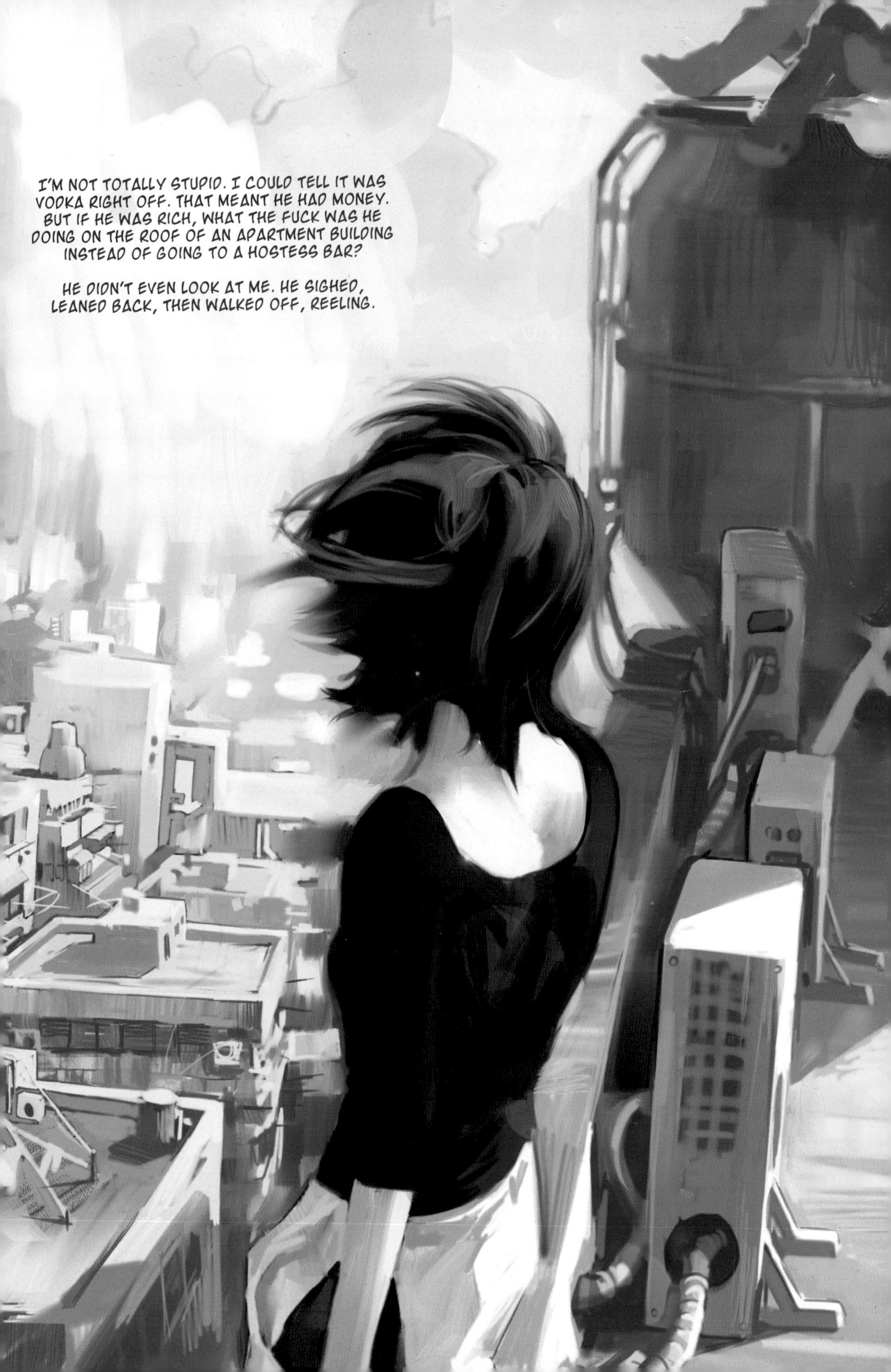
I'M NOT TOTALLY STUPID. I COULD TELL IT WAS VODKA RIGHT OFF. THAT MEANT HE HAD MONEY. BUT IF HE WAS RICH, WHAT THE FUCK WAS HE DOING ON THE ROOF OF AN APARTMENT BUILDING INSTEAD OF GOING TO A HOSTESS BAR?
HE DIDN'T EVEN LOOK AT ME. HE SIGHED, LEANED BACK, THEN WALKED OFF, REELING.

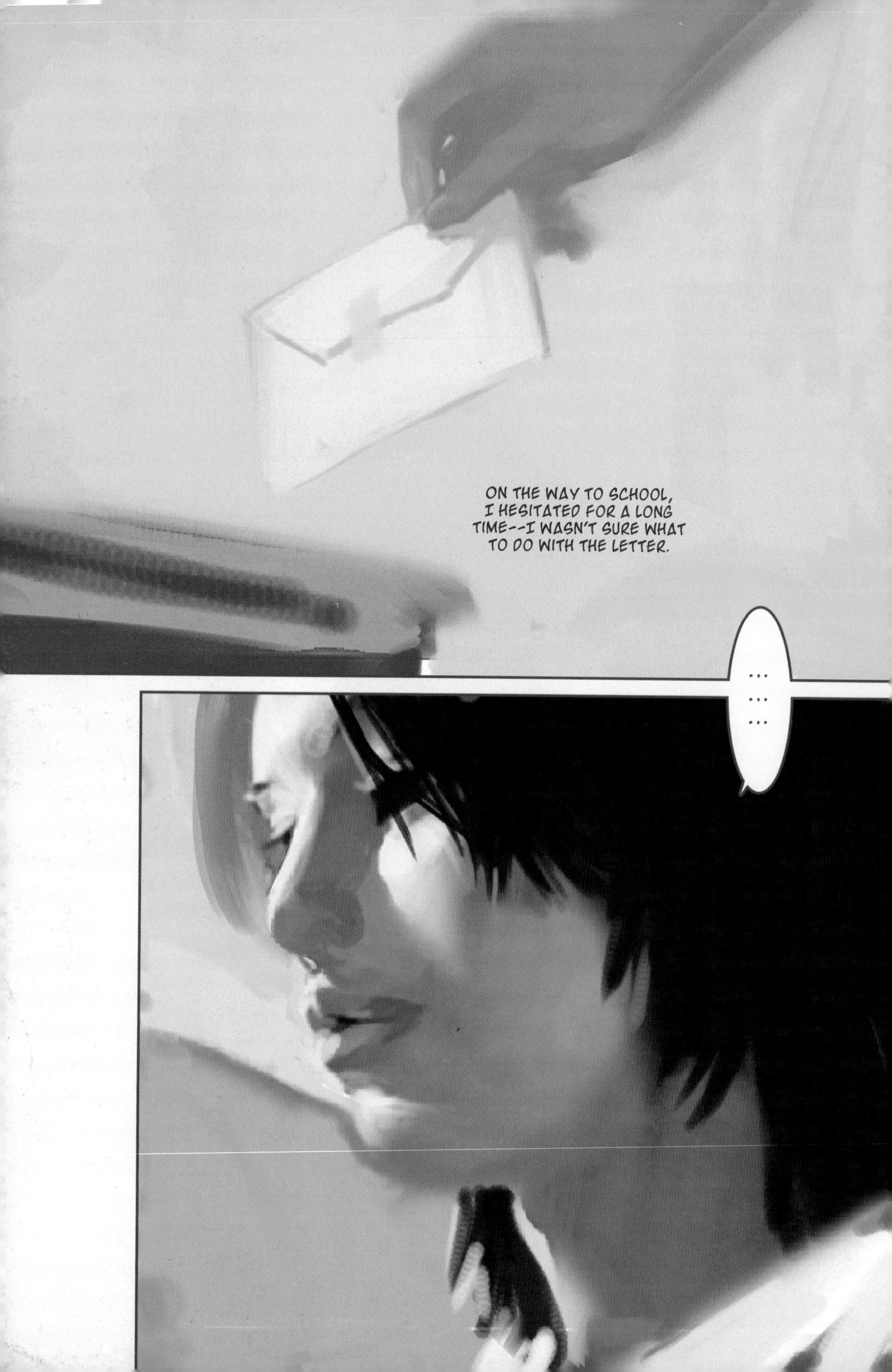
ON THE WAY TO SCHOOL,
I HESITATED FOR A LONG
TIME--I WASN'T SURE WHAT
TO DO WITH THE LETTER.
...
...
...

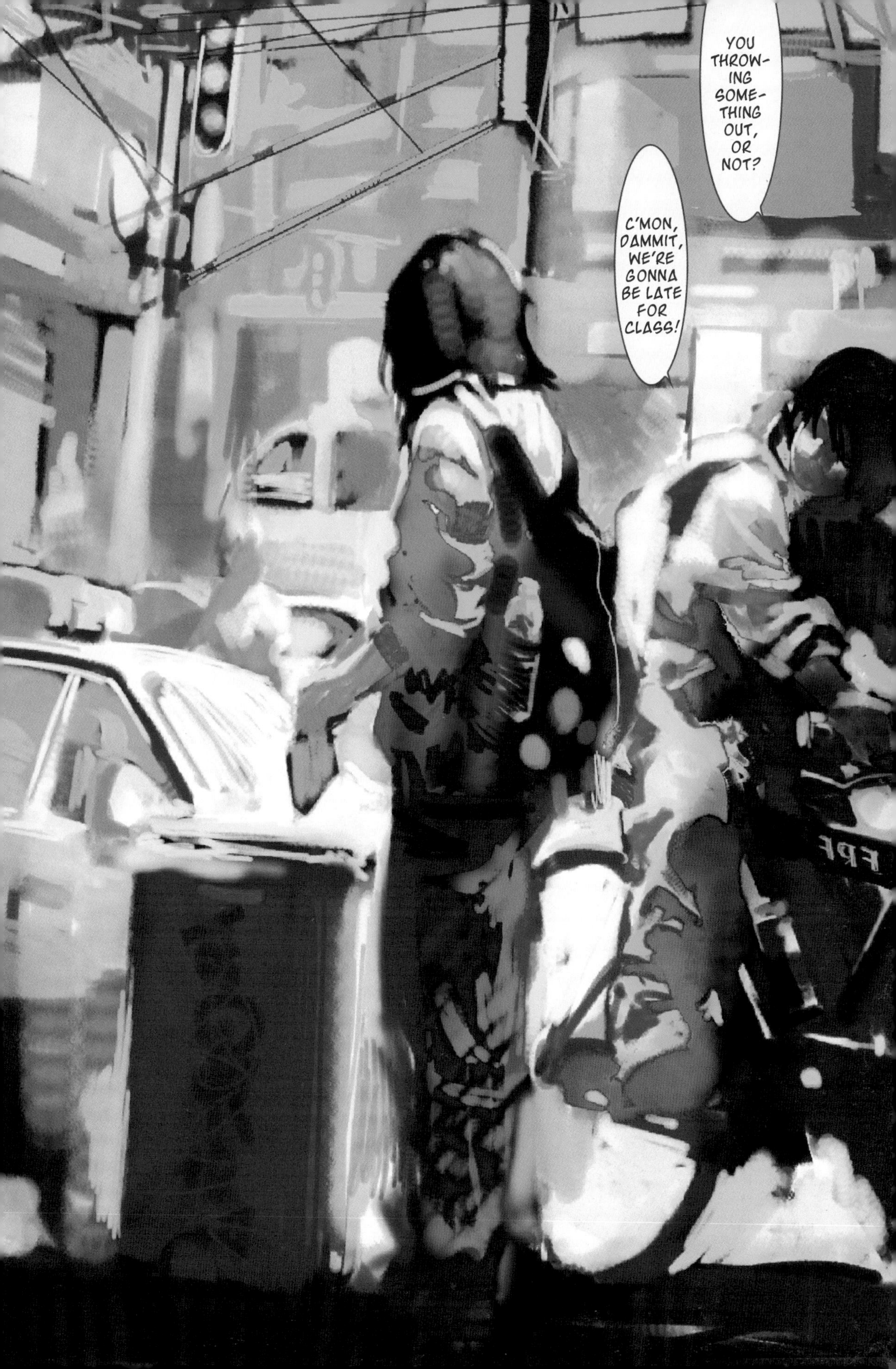
YOU THROWING SOMETHING OUT, OR NOT?
C'MON, DAMMIT, WE'RE GONNA BE LATE FOR CLASS!

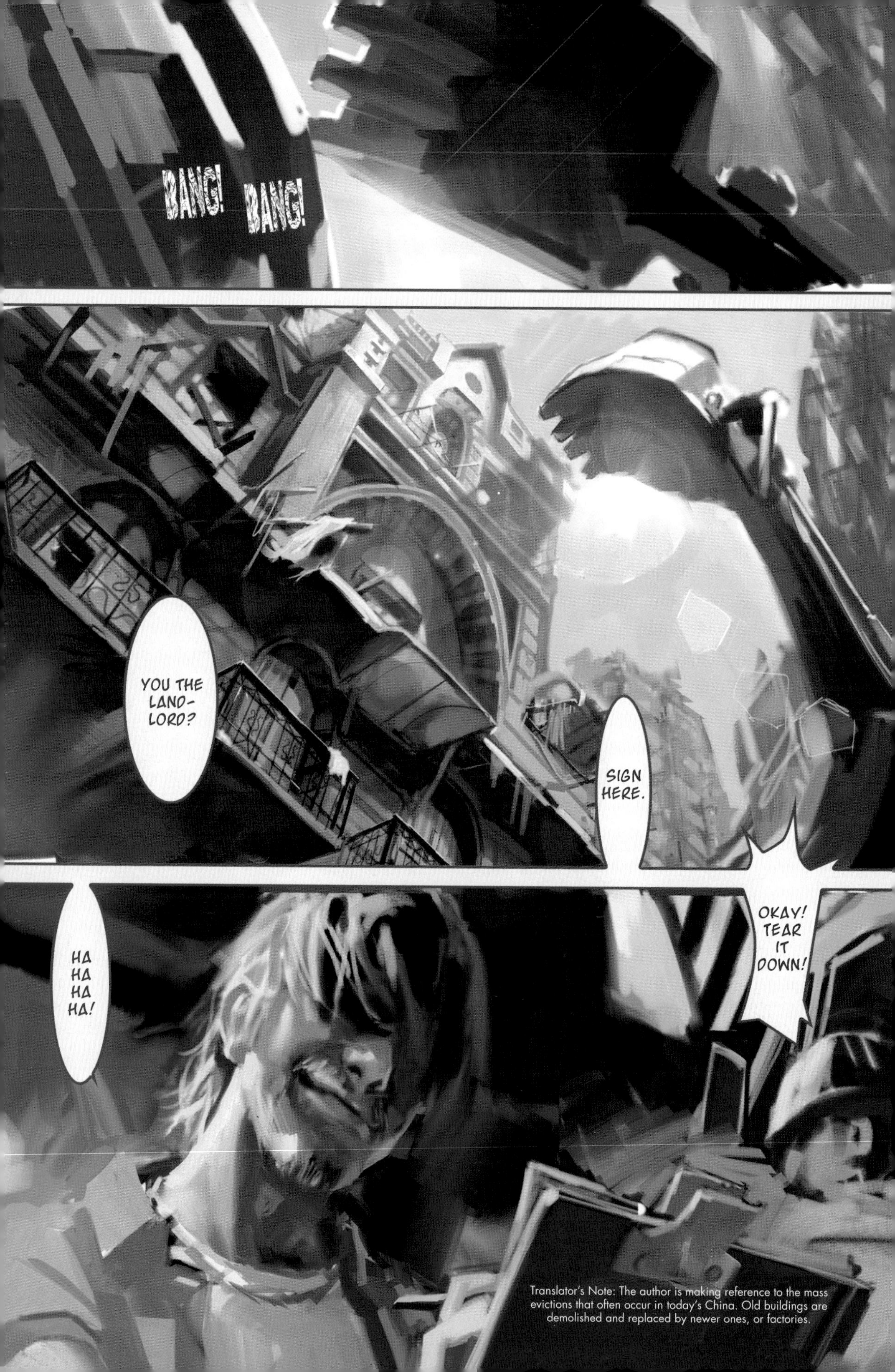
BANG! BANG!
YOU THE LAND-LORD?
SIGN HERE.
HA HA HA HA!
OKAY! TEAR IT DOWN!

Translator's Note: The author is making reference to the mass evictions that often occur in today's China. Old buildings are demolished and replaced by newer ones, or factories.

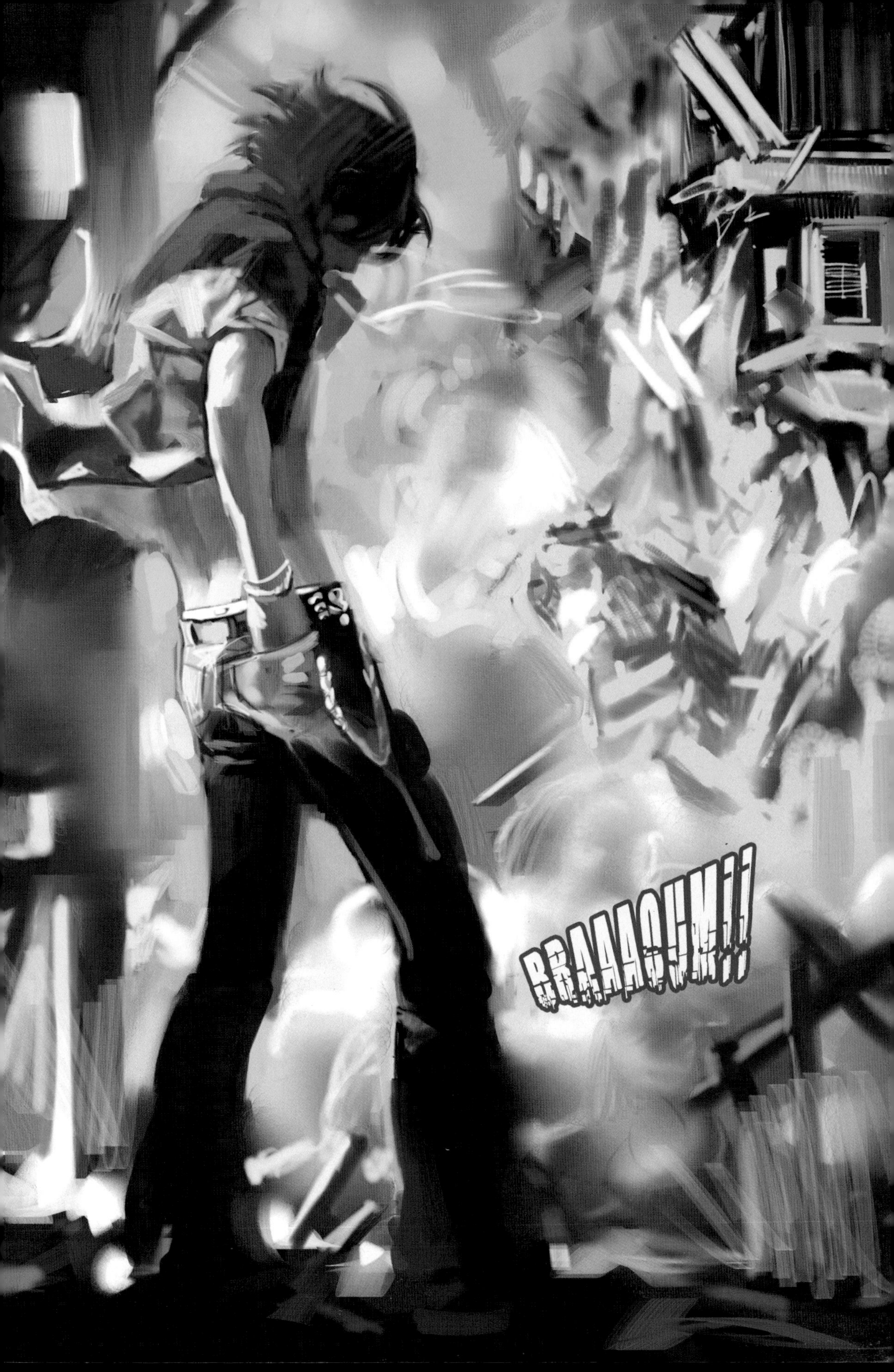
BRAAAAOUM!!

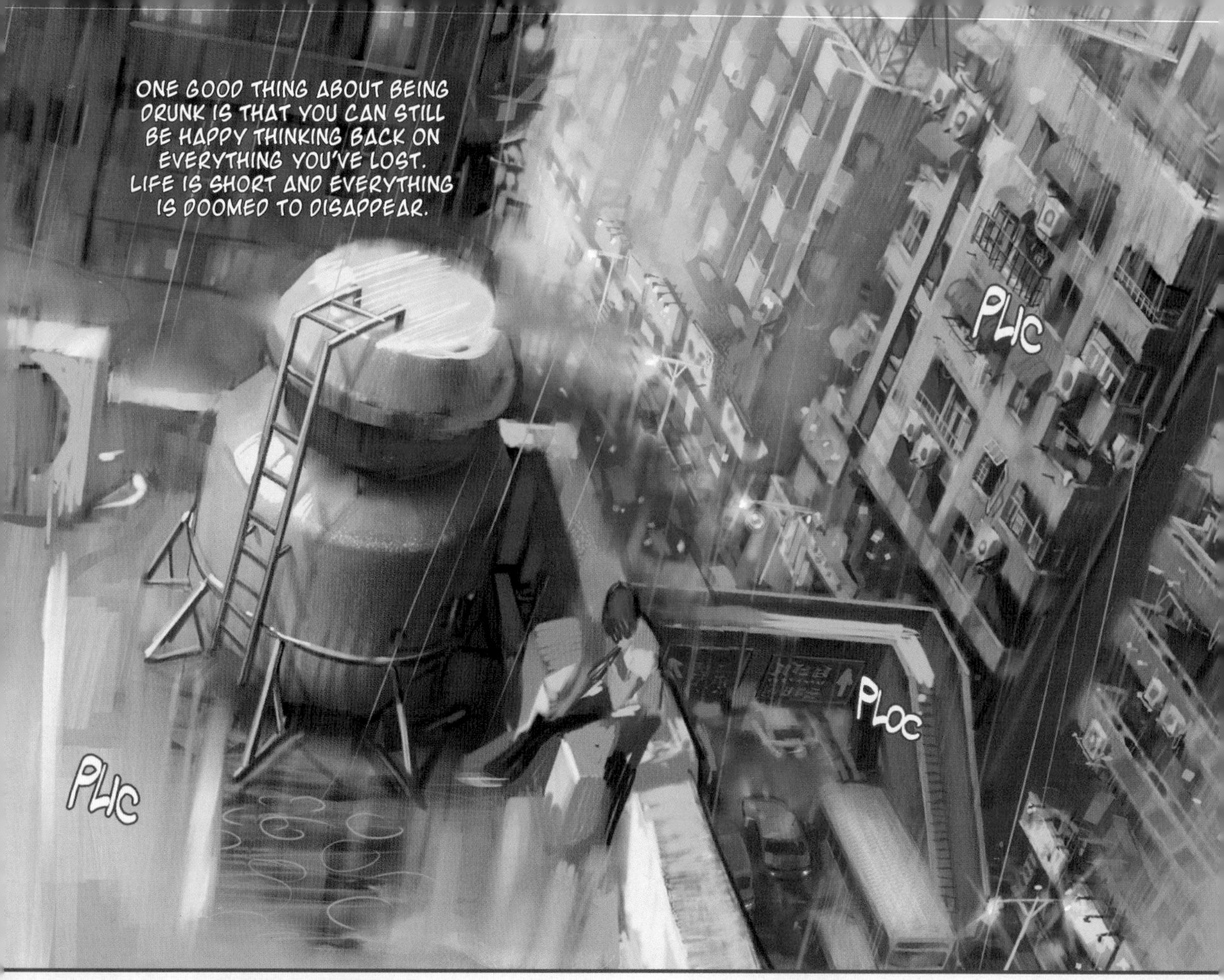
ONE GOOD THING ABOUT BEING DRUNK IS THAT YOU CAN STILL BE HAPPY THINKING BACK ON EVERYTHING YOU'VE LOST. LIFE IS SHORT AND EVERYTHING IS DOOMED TO DISAPPEAR.
PLIC
PLOC
PLIC
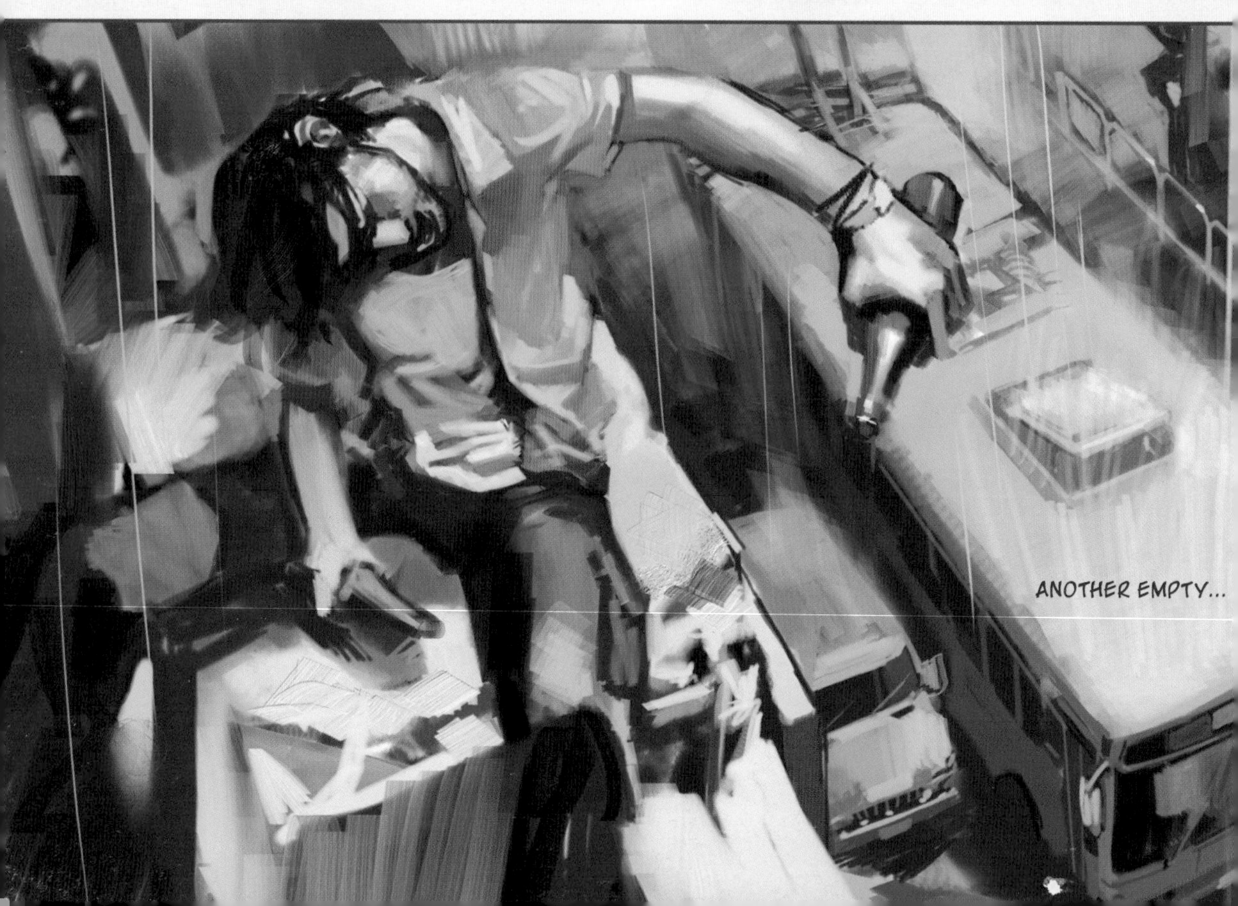
ANOTHER EMPTY...

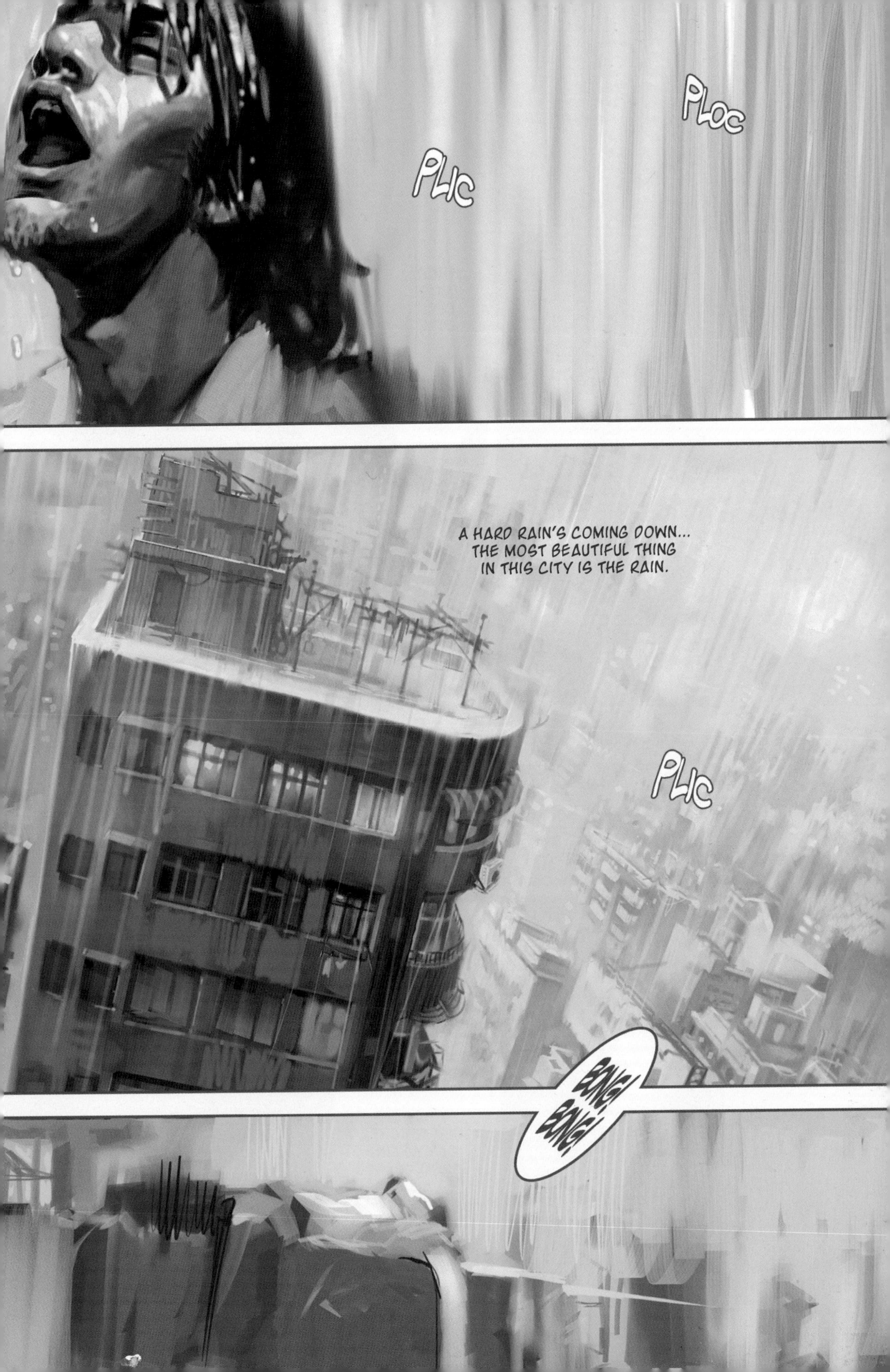
PLOC
PLIC
A HARD RAIN'S COMING DOWN... THE MOST BEAUTIFUL THING IN THIS CITY IS THE RAIN.
PLIC
BONG! BONG!

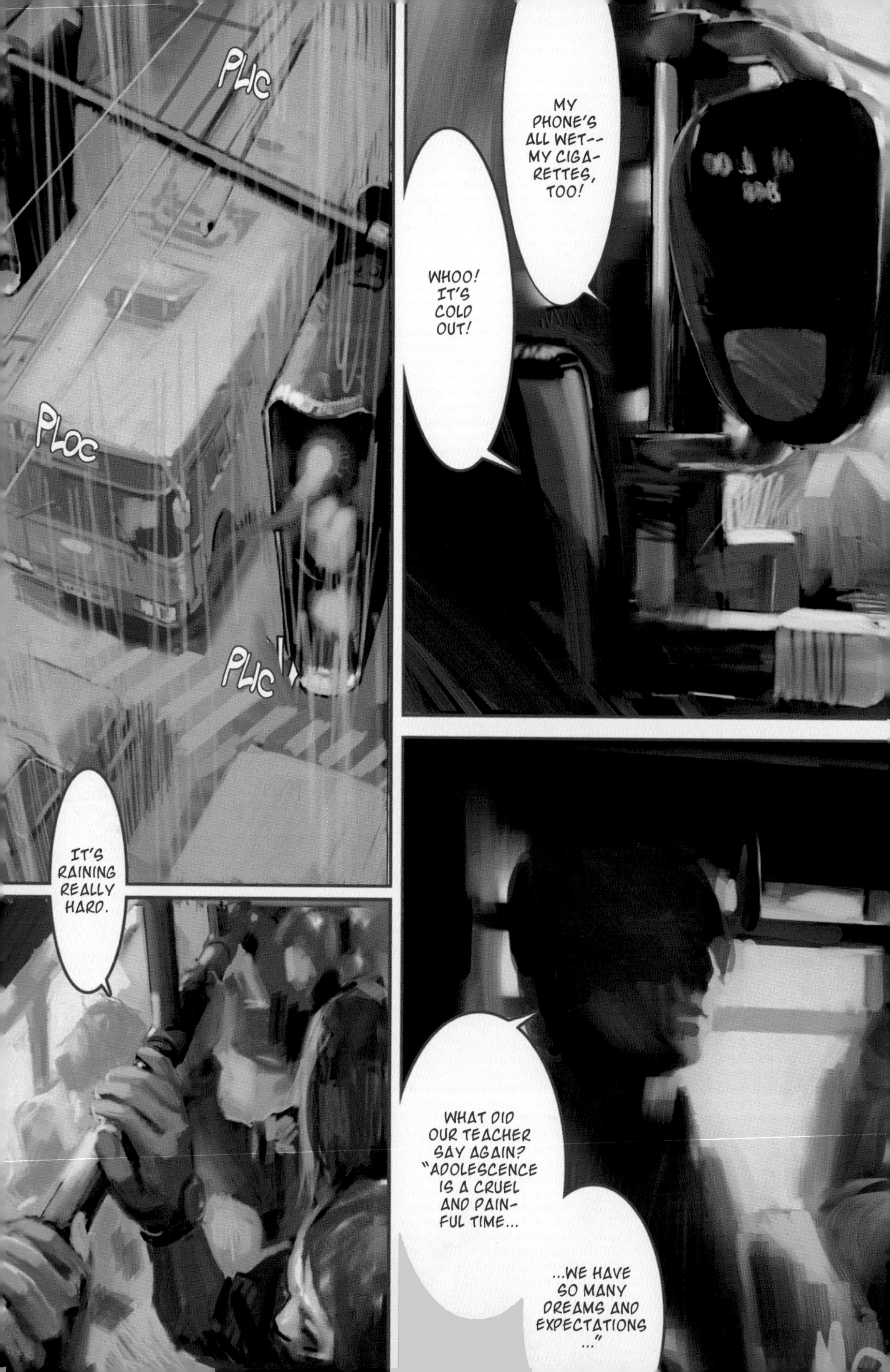
PLIC
PLOC
PLIC
IT'S RAINING REALLY HARD.
MY PHONE'S ALL WET--MY CIGA-RETTES, TOO!
WHOO! IT'S COLD OUT!
WHAT DID OUR TEACHER SAY AGAIN? "ADOLESCENCE IS A CRUEL AND PAIN-FUL TIME...
...WE HAVE SO MANY DREAMS AND EXPECTATIONS..."

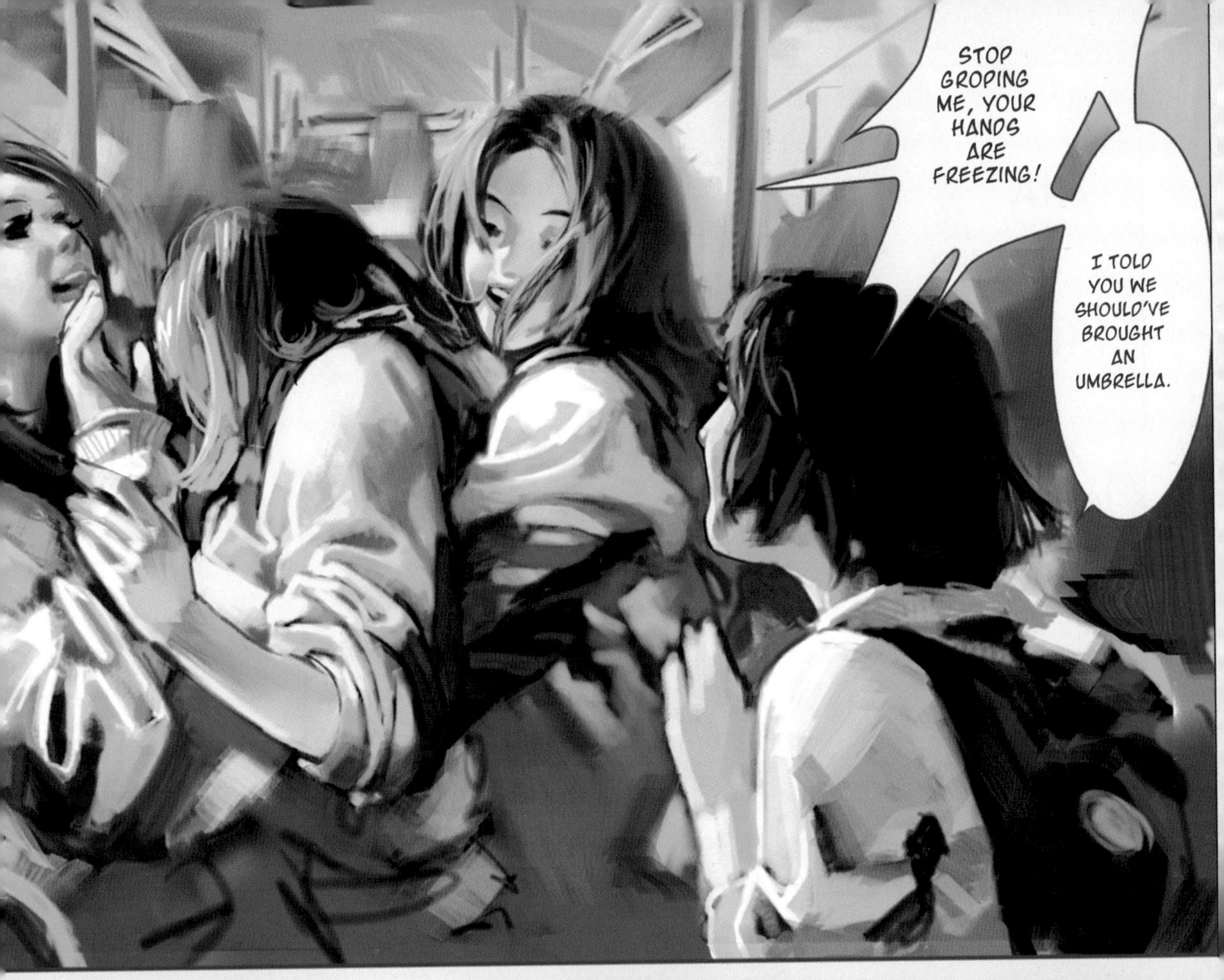
STOP GROPING ME, YOUR HANDS ARE FREEZING!
I TOLD YOU WE SHOULD'VE BROUGHT AN UMBRELLA.

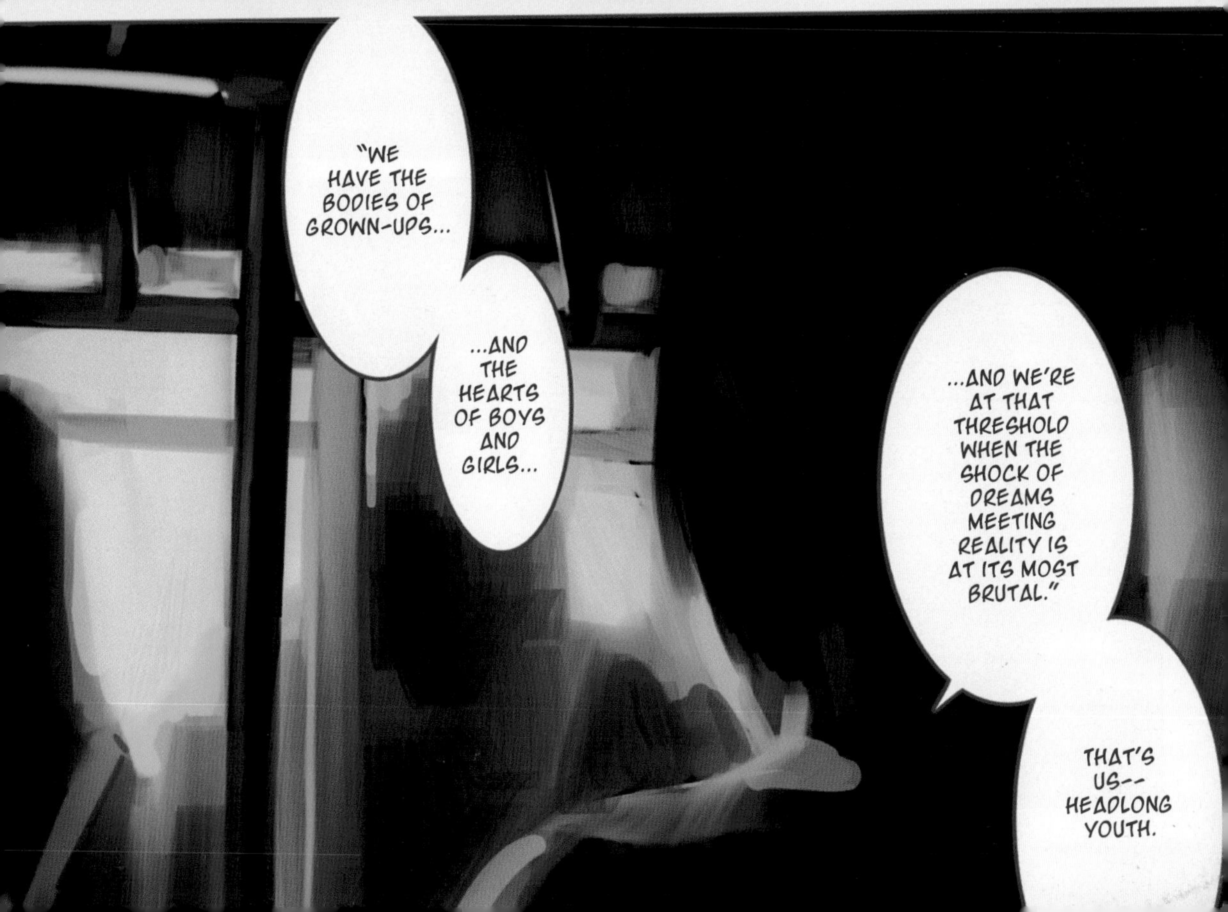
"WE HAVE THE BODIES OF GROWN-UPS...
...AND THE HEARTS OF BOYS AND GIRLS...
...AND WE'RE AT THAT THRESHOLD WHEN THE SHOCK OF DREAMS MEETING REALITY IS AT ITS MOST BRUTAL."
THAT'S US-- HEADLONG YOUTH.

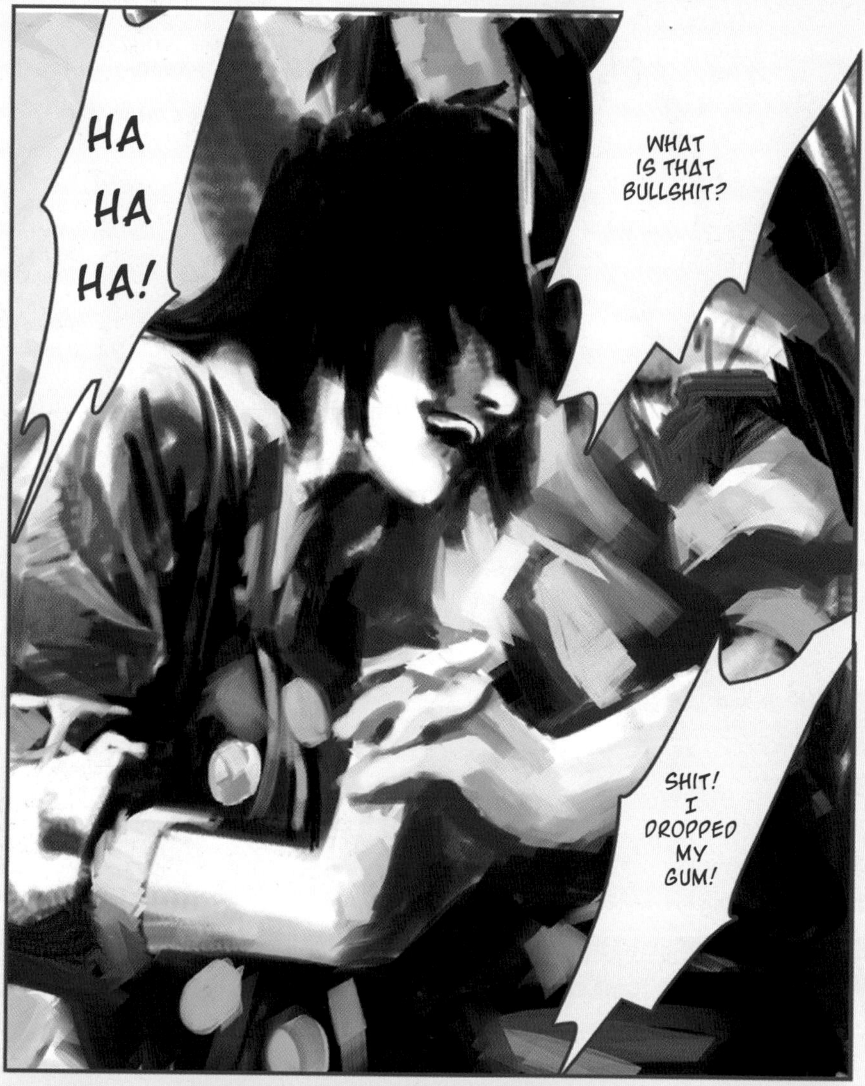
HA
HA
HA!
WHAT IS THAT BULLSHIT?
SHIT! I DROPPED MY GUM!

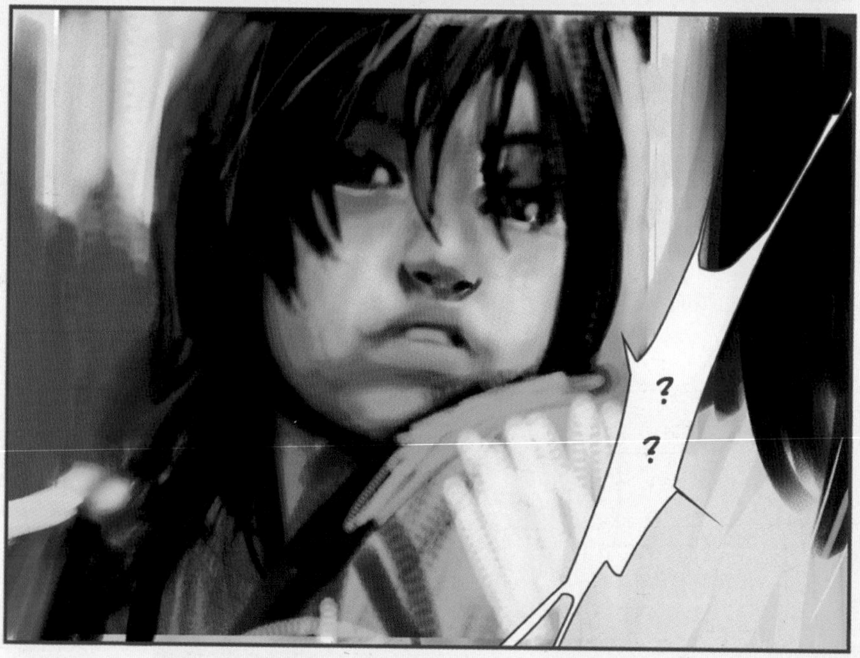
?
?

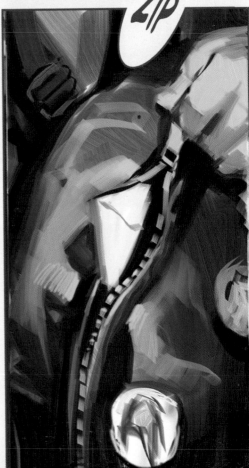

SUDDENLY, THERE HE WAS.
SOAKED, COMPLETELY HAMMERED,
UNSTEADY ON HIS FEET. THE BUS WAS PACKED,
BUT THERE WAS A CLEAR SPACE AROUND HIM.

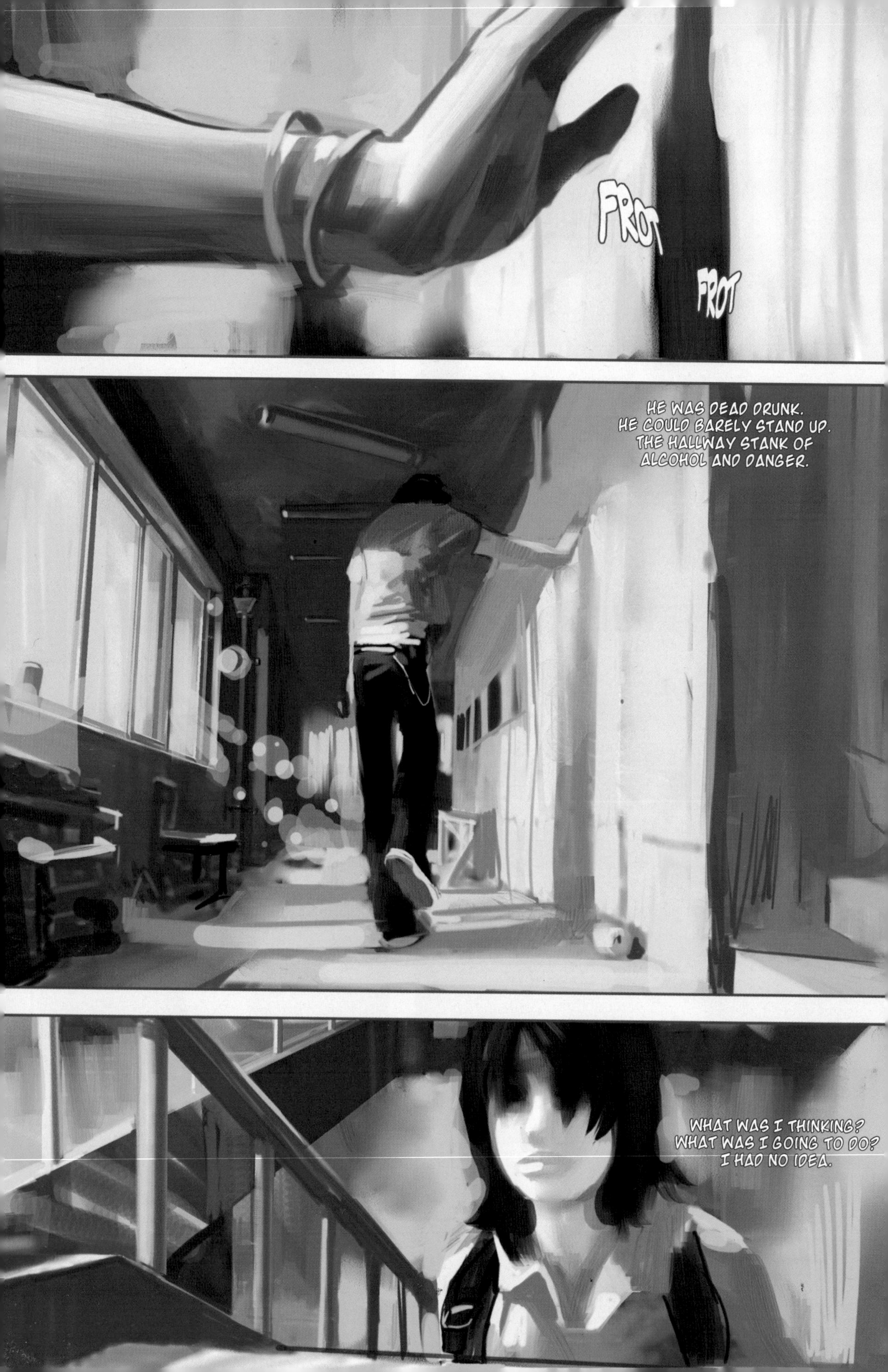
FROT
FROT
HE WAS DEAD DRUNK. HE COULD BARELY STAND UP. THE HALLWAY STANK OF ALCOHOL AND DANGER.
WHAT WAS I THINKING? WHAT WAS I GOING TO DO? I HAD NO IDEA.

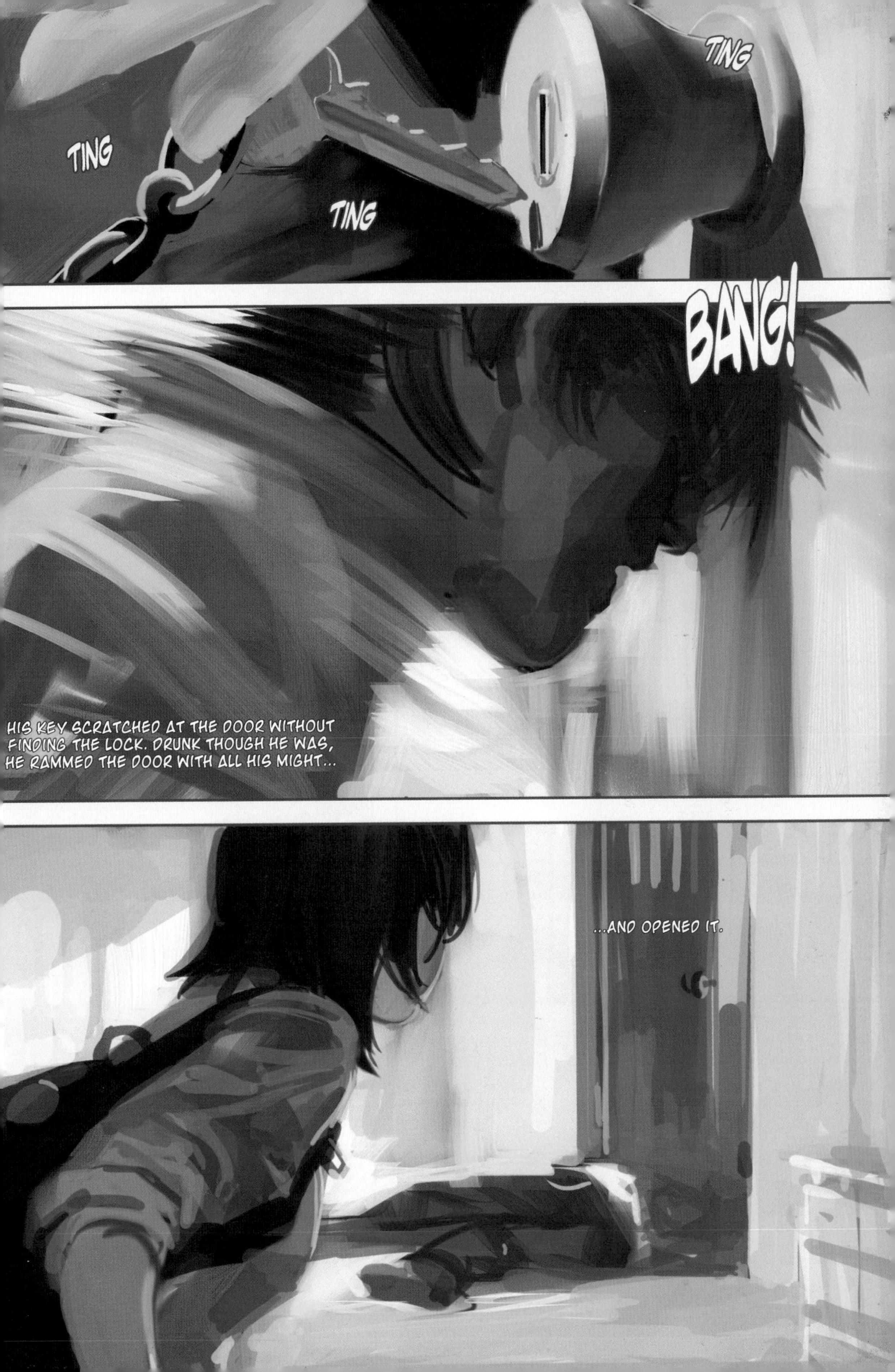
TING
TING
TING
BANG!
HIS KEY SCRATCHED AT THE DOOR WITHOUT FINDING THE LOCK. DRUNK THOUGH HE WAS, HE RAMMED THE DOOR WITH ALL HIS MIGHT...
...AND OPENED IT.

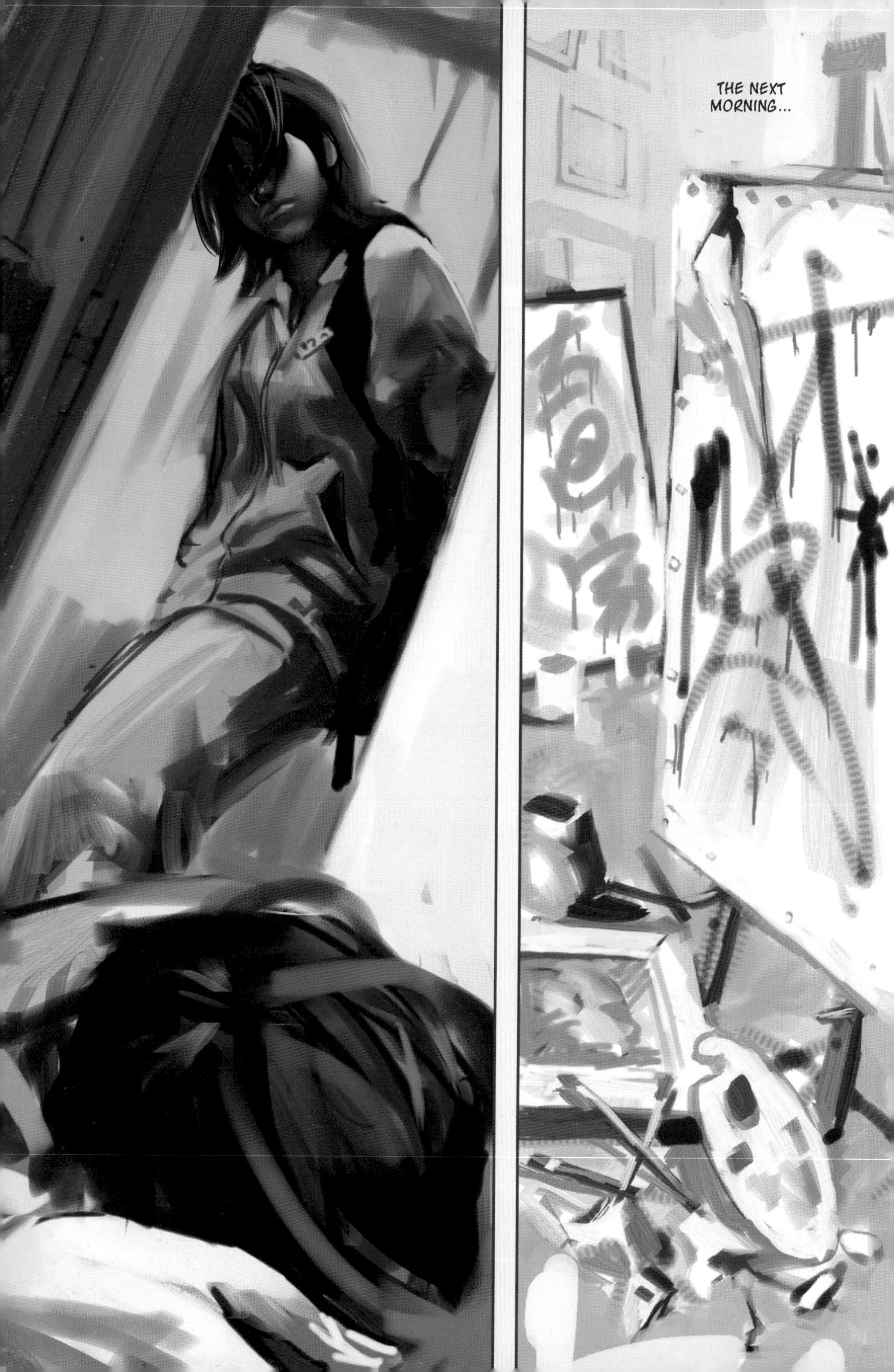
THE NEXT MORNING...

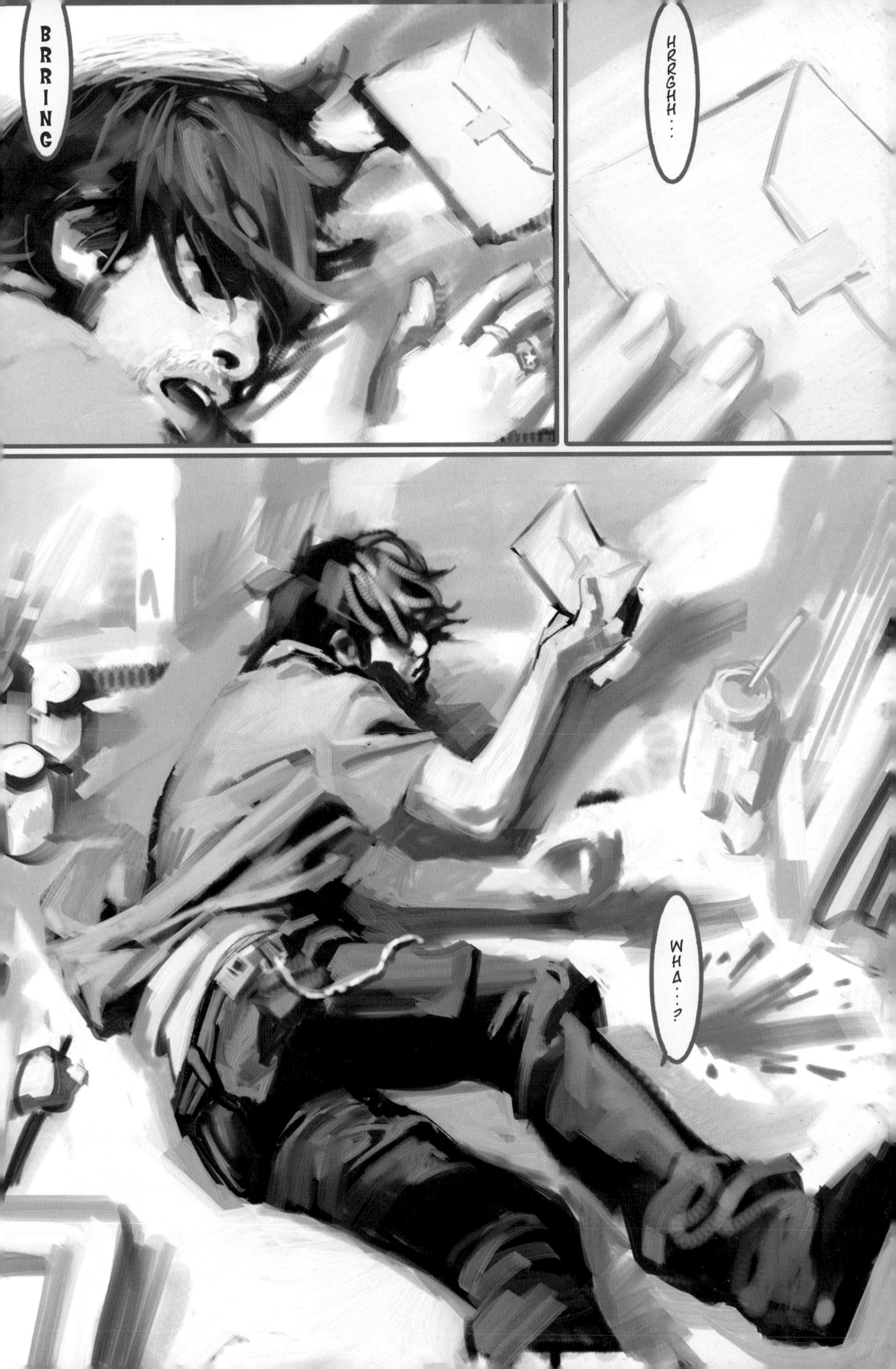
BRRRING
HRRGHH...
WHA...?

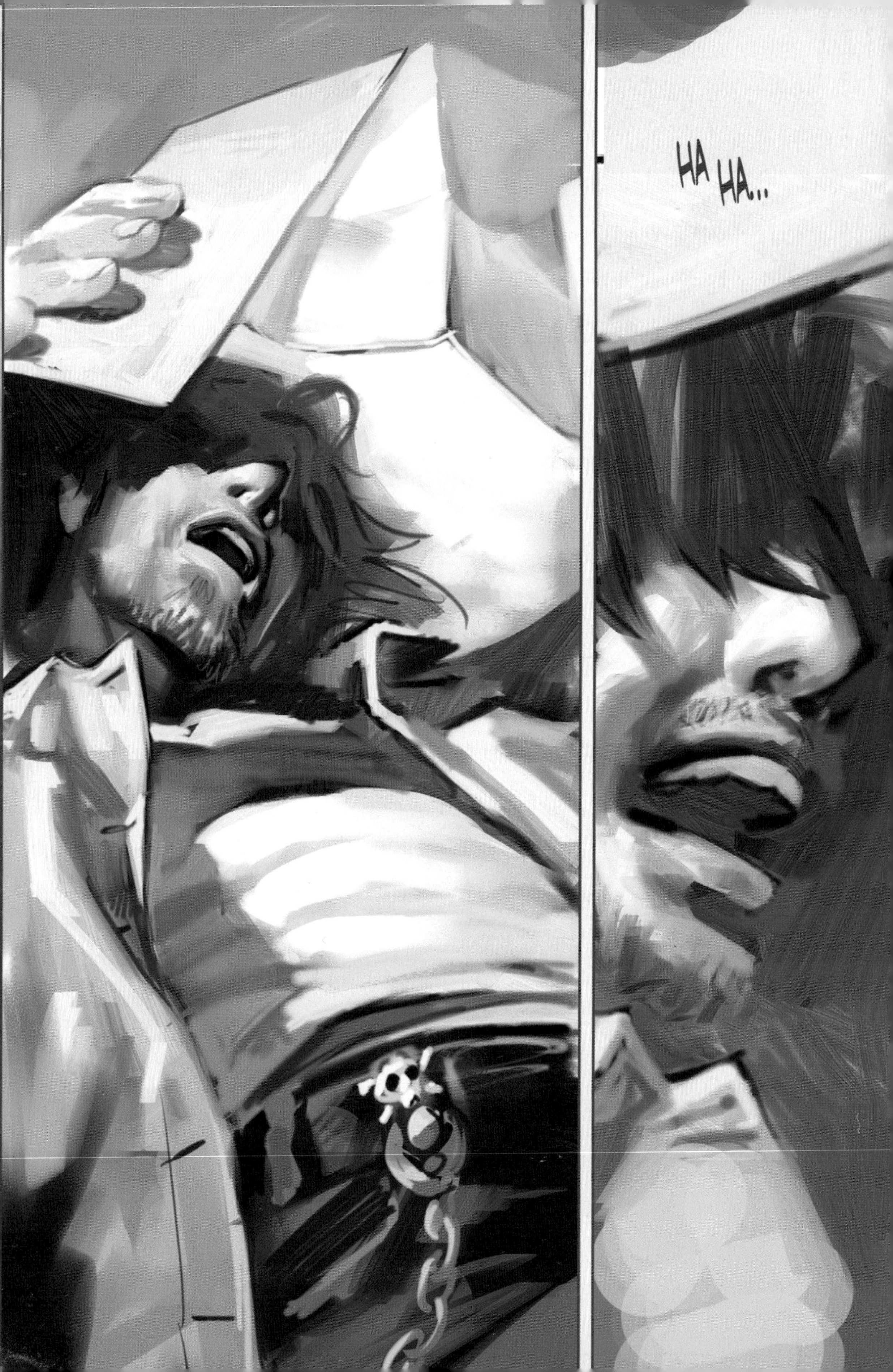
HA HA...

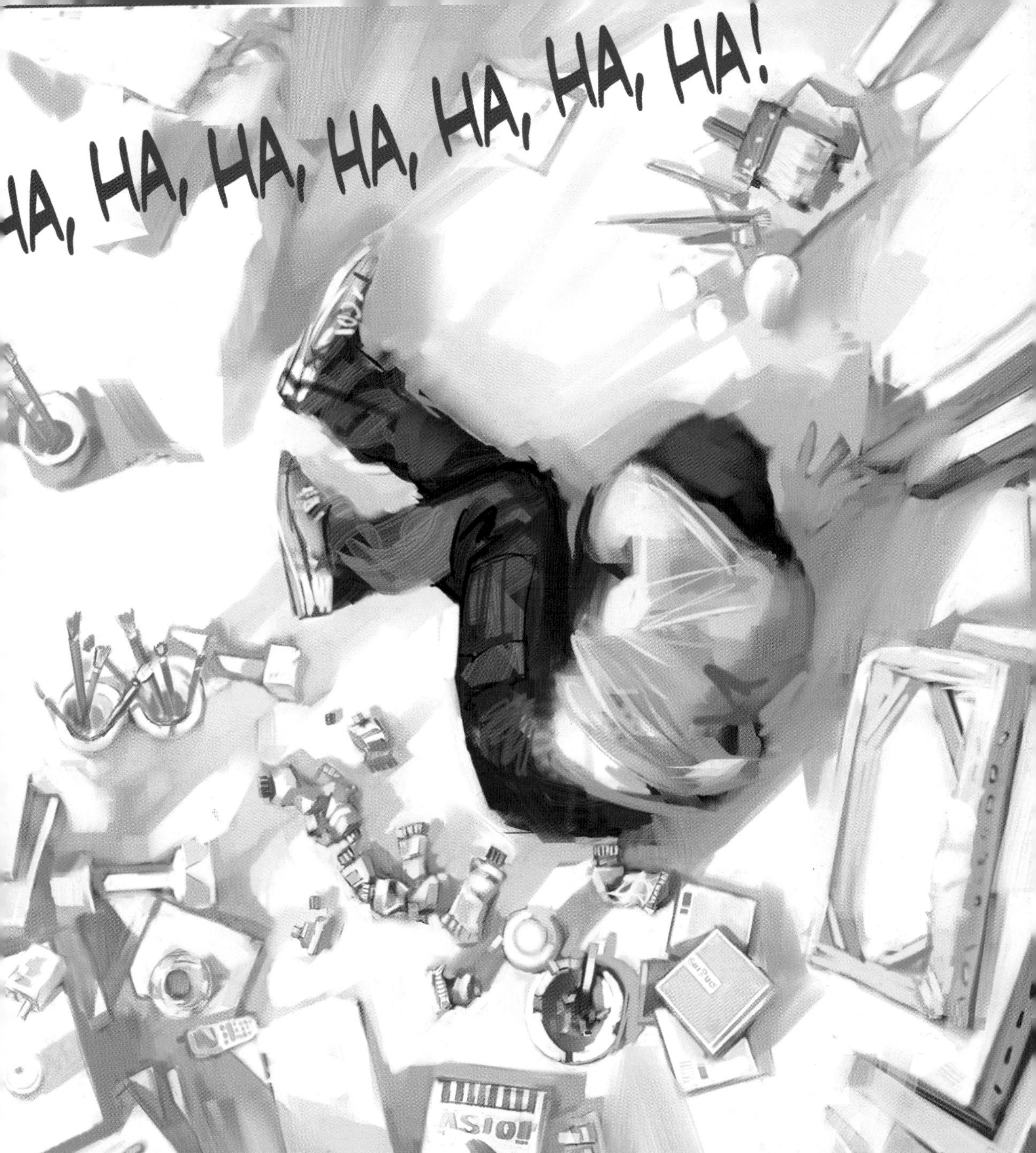
HA, HA, HA, HA, HA, HA, HA!

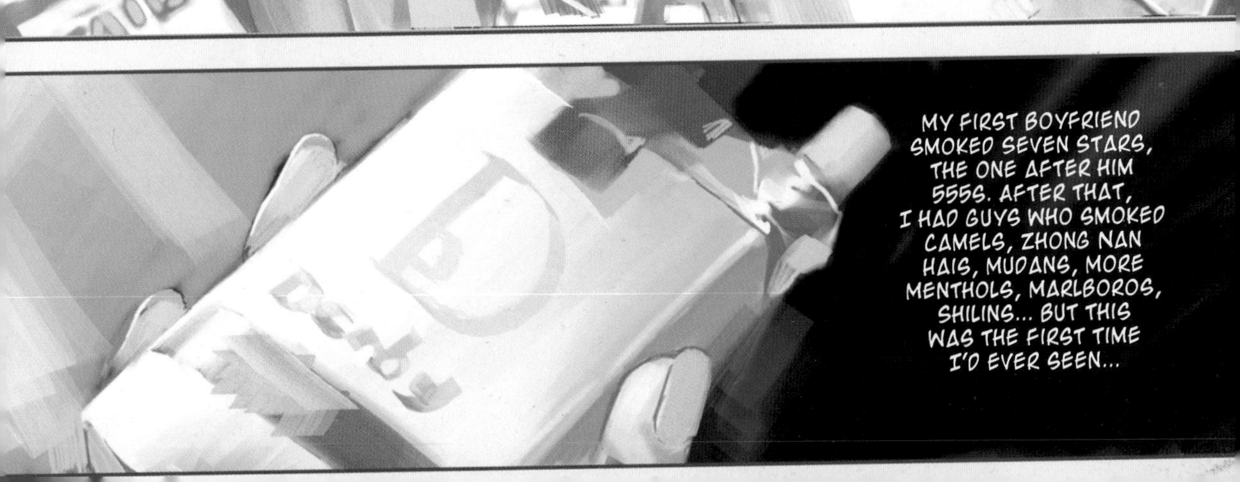
MY FIRST BOYFRIEND SMOKED SEVEN STARS, THE ONE AFTER HIM 555S. AFTER THAT, I HAD GUYS WHO SMOKED CAMELS, ZHONG NAN HAIS, MUDANS, MORE MENTHOLS, MARLBOROS, SHILINS... BUT THIS WAS THE FIRST TIME I'D EVER SEEN...

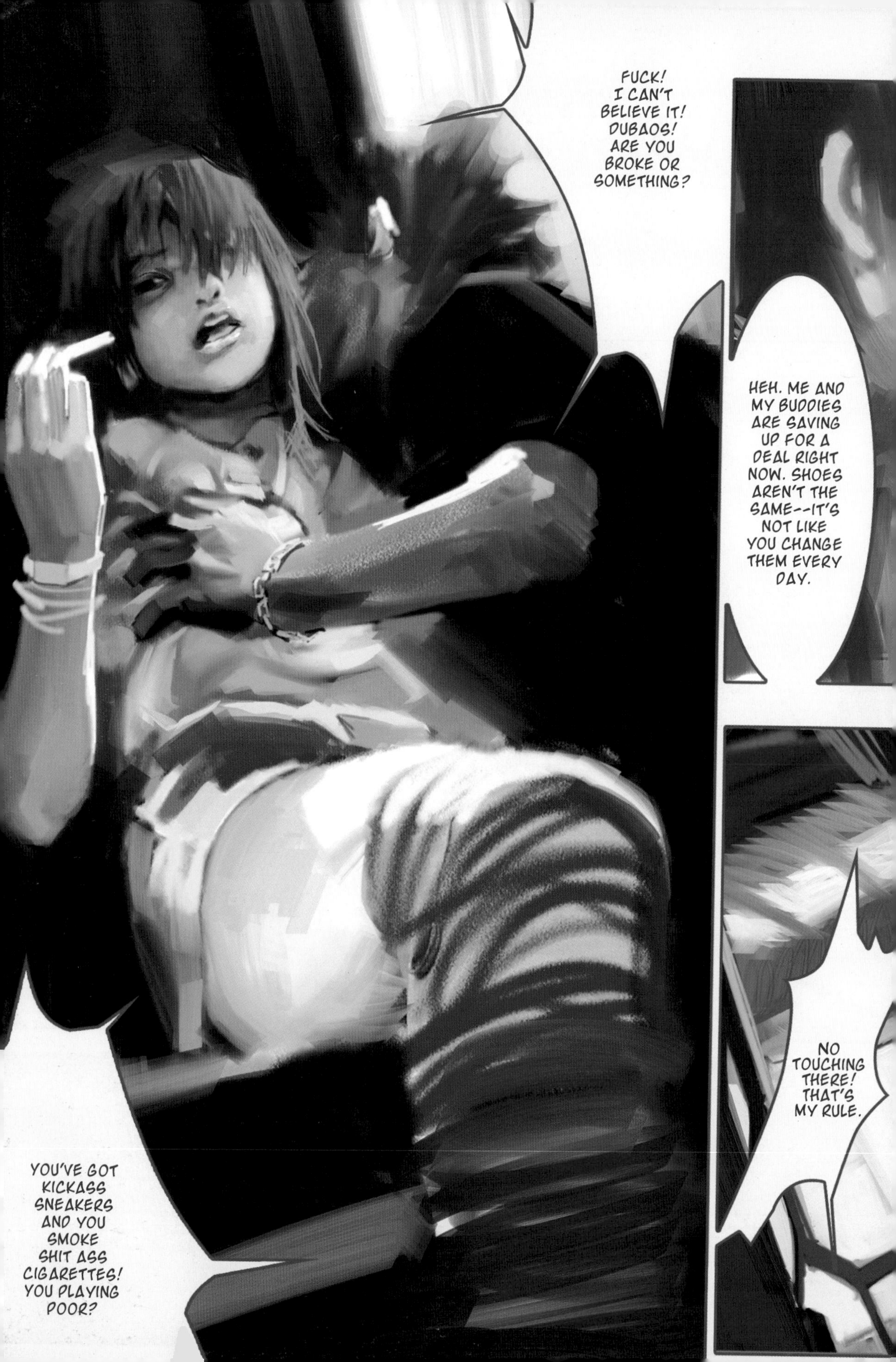
FUCK! I CAN'T BELIEVE IT! DUBAOS! ARE YOU BROKE OR SOMETHING?
YOU'VE GOT KICKASS SNEAKERS AND YOU SMOKE SHIT ASS CIGARETTES! YOU PLAYING POOR?
HEH. ME AND MY BUDDIES ARE SAVING UP FOR A DEAL RIGHT NOW. SHOES AREN'T THE SAME--IT'S NOT LIKE YOU CHANGE THEM EVERY DAY.
NO TOUCHING THERE! THAT'S MY RULE.

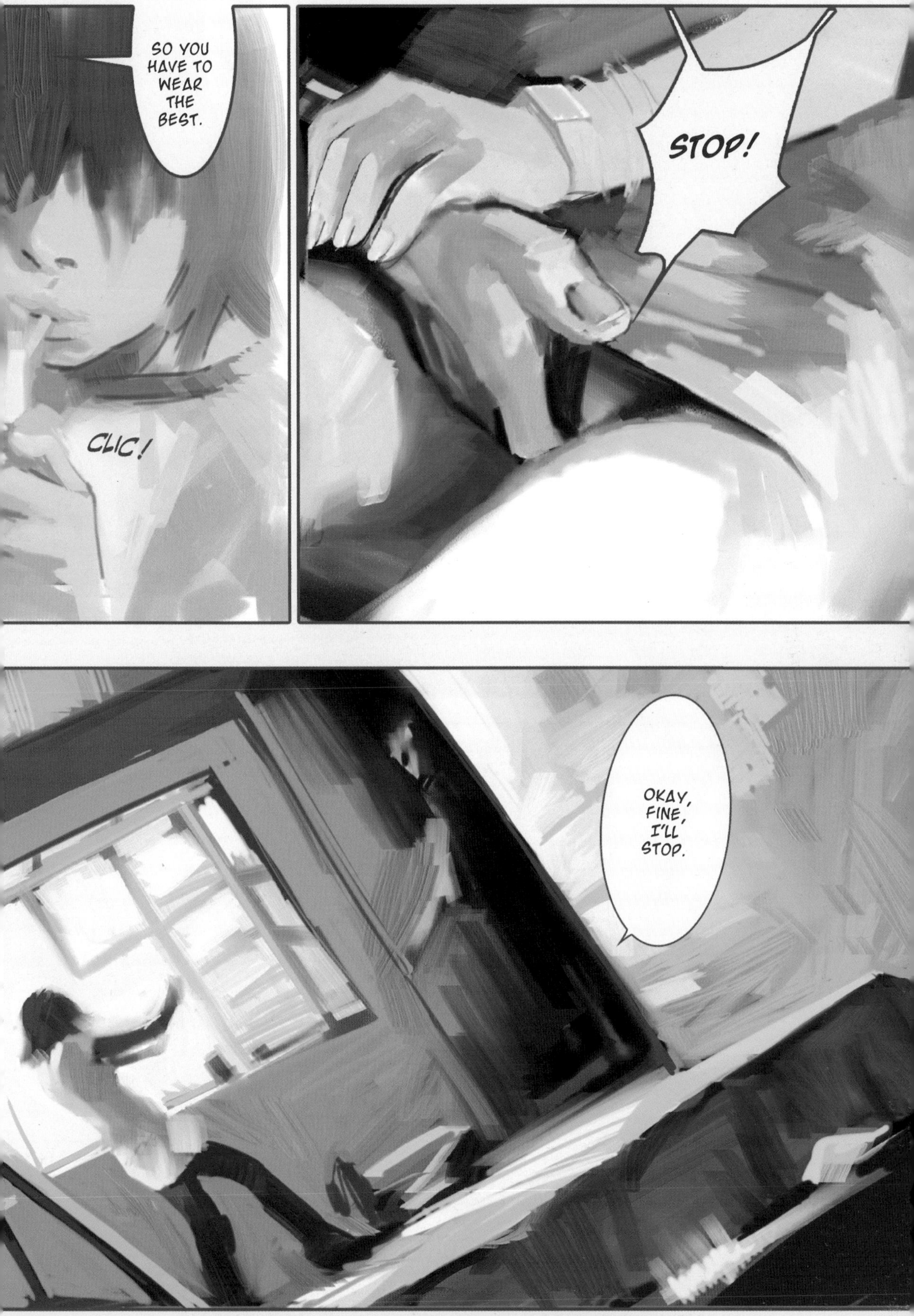
SO YOU HAVE TO WEAR THE BEST.
CLIC!
STOP!
OKAY, FINE, I'LL STOP.

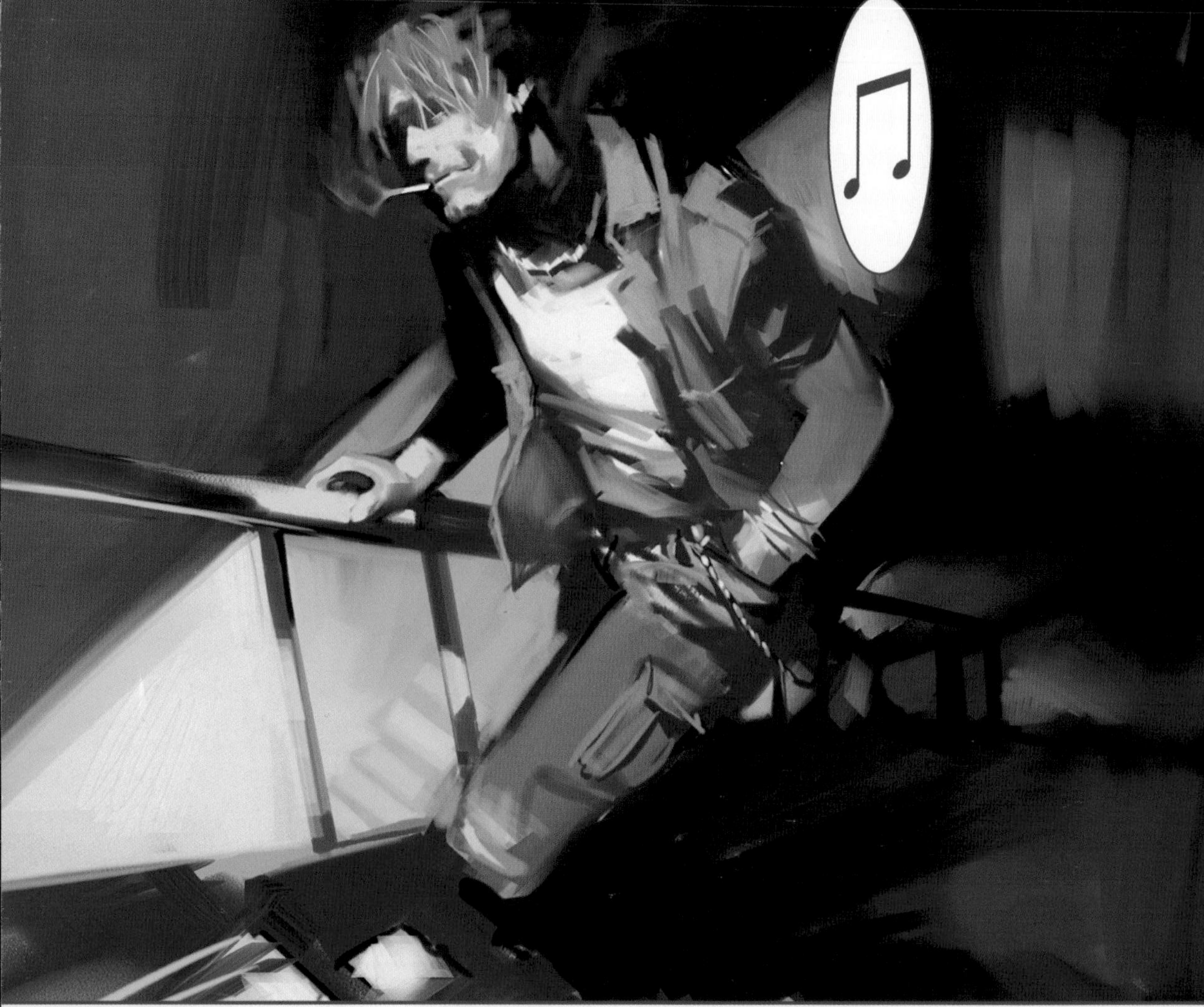

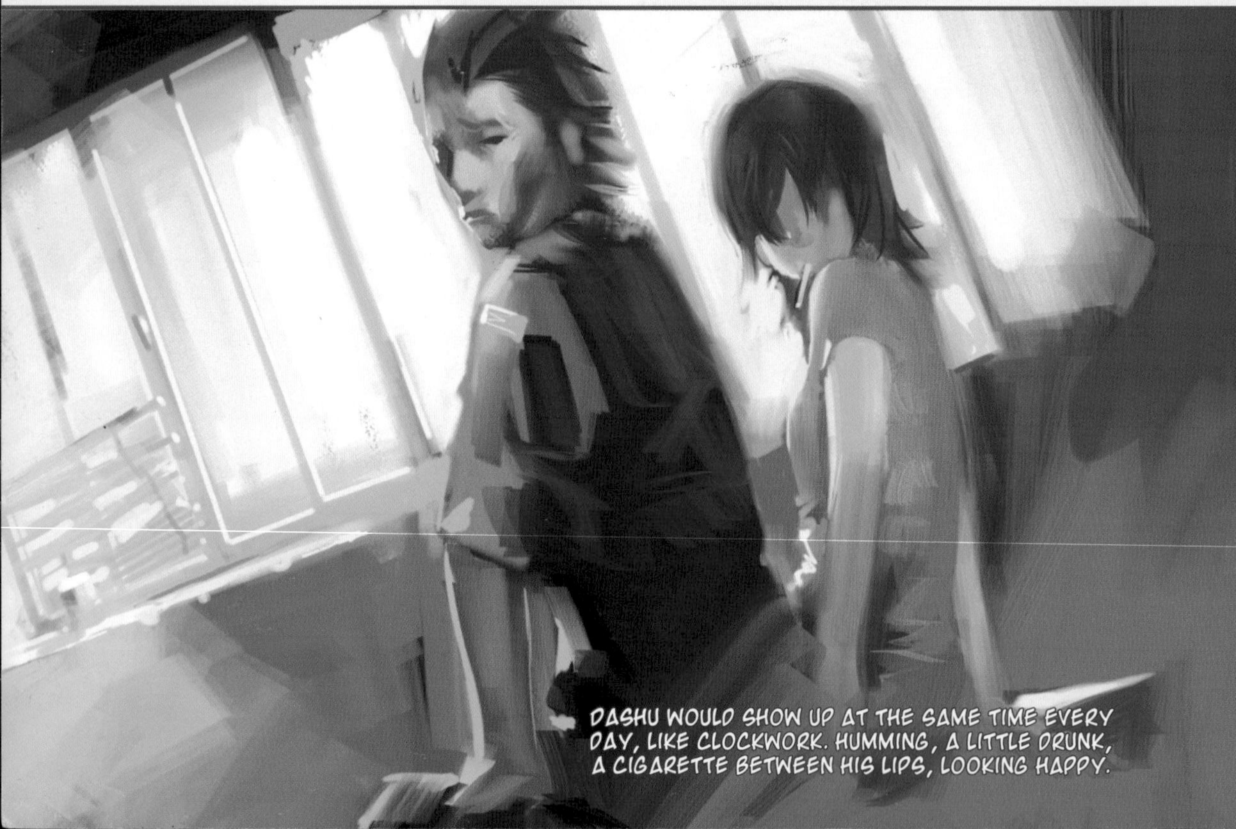
DASHU WOULD SHOW UP AT THE SAME TIME EVERY DAY, LIKE CLOCKWORK. HUMMING, A LITTLE DRUNK, A CIGARETTE BETWEEN HIS LIPS, LOOKING HAPPY.

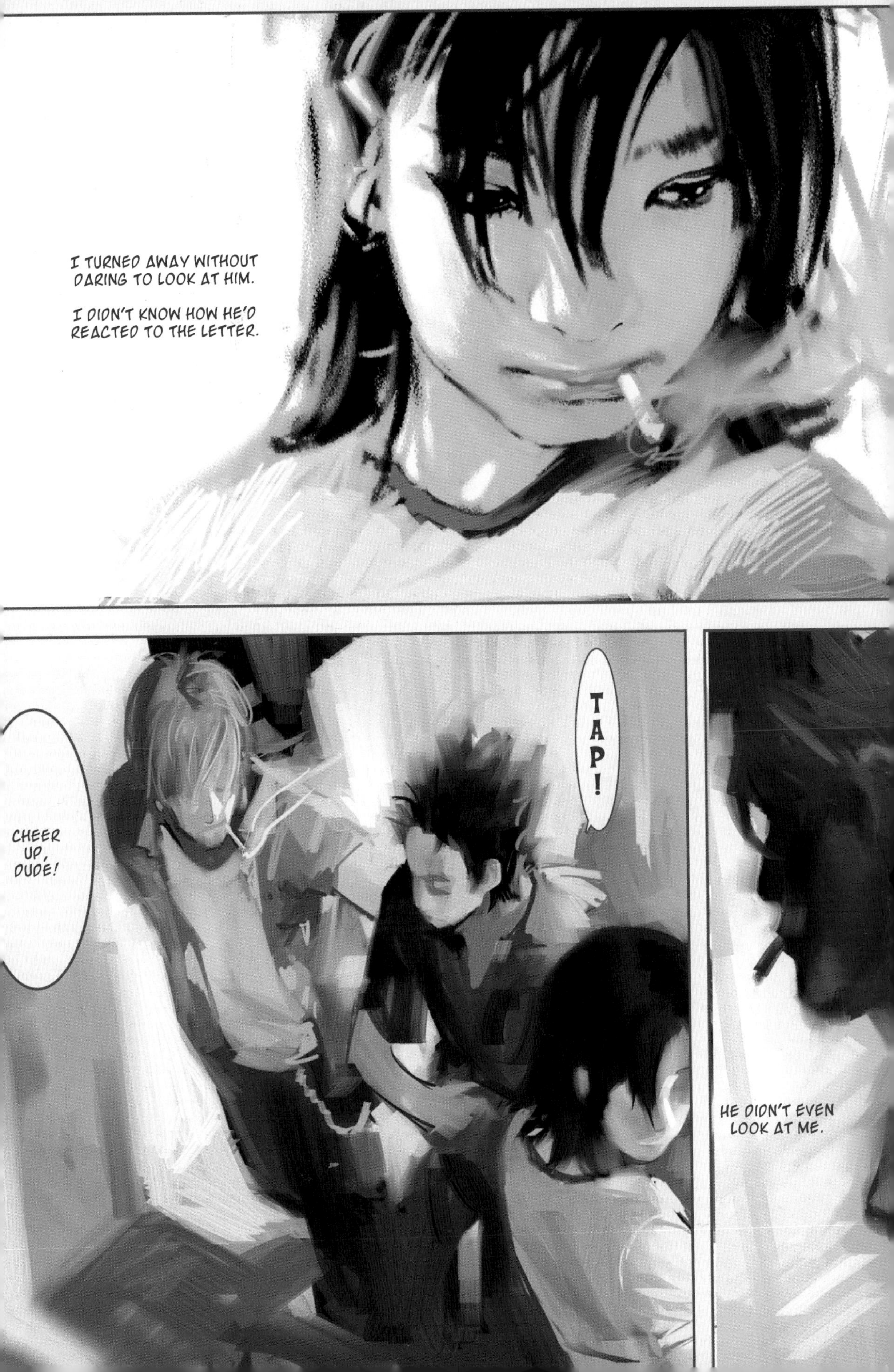
I TURNED AWAY WITHOUT DARING TO LOOK AT HIM.
I DIDN'T KNOW HOW HE'D REACTED TO THE LETTER.
TAP!
CHEER UP, DUDE!
HE DIDN'T EVEN LOOK AT ME.

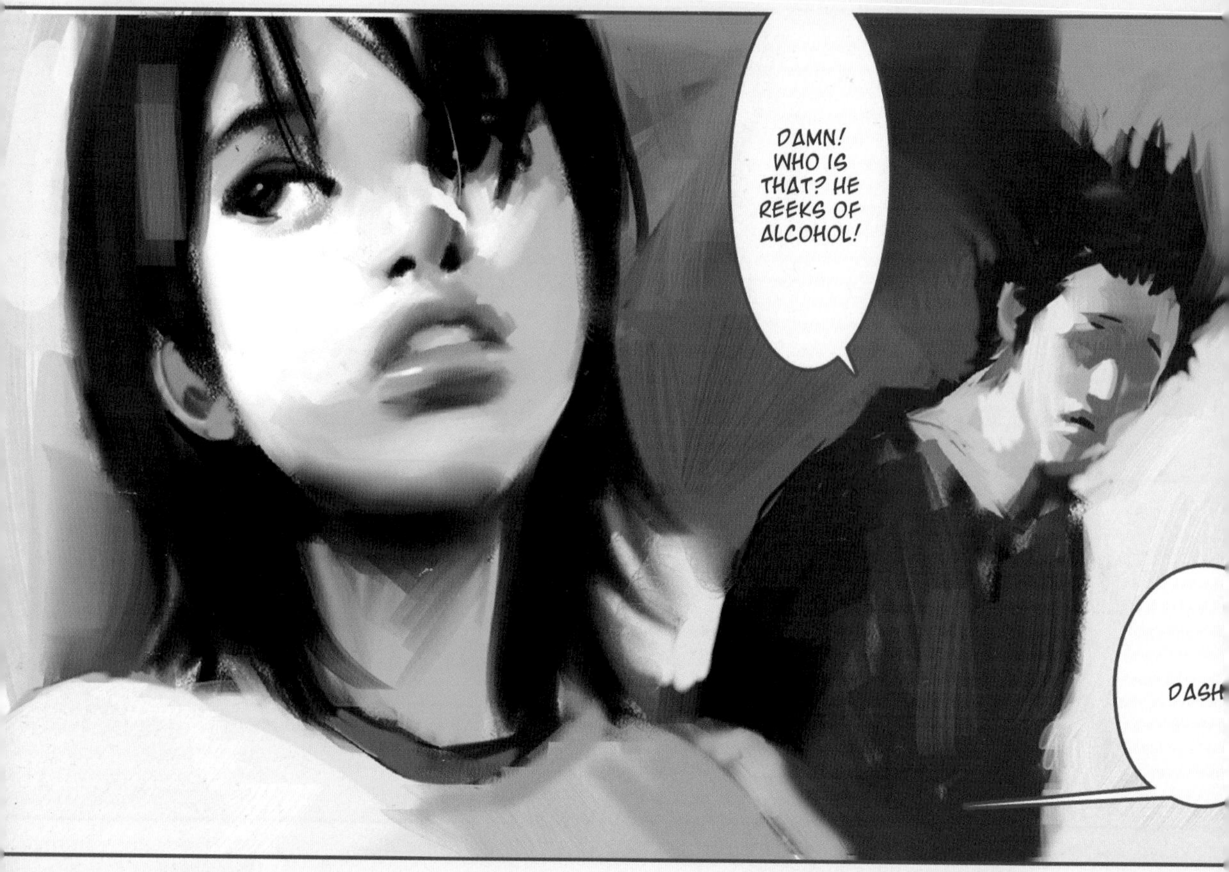
DAMN! WHO IS THAT? HE REEKS OF ALCOHOL!
DASH

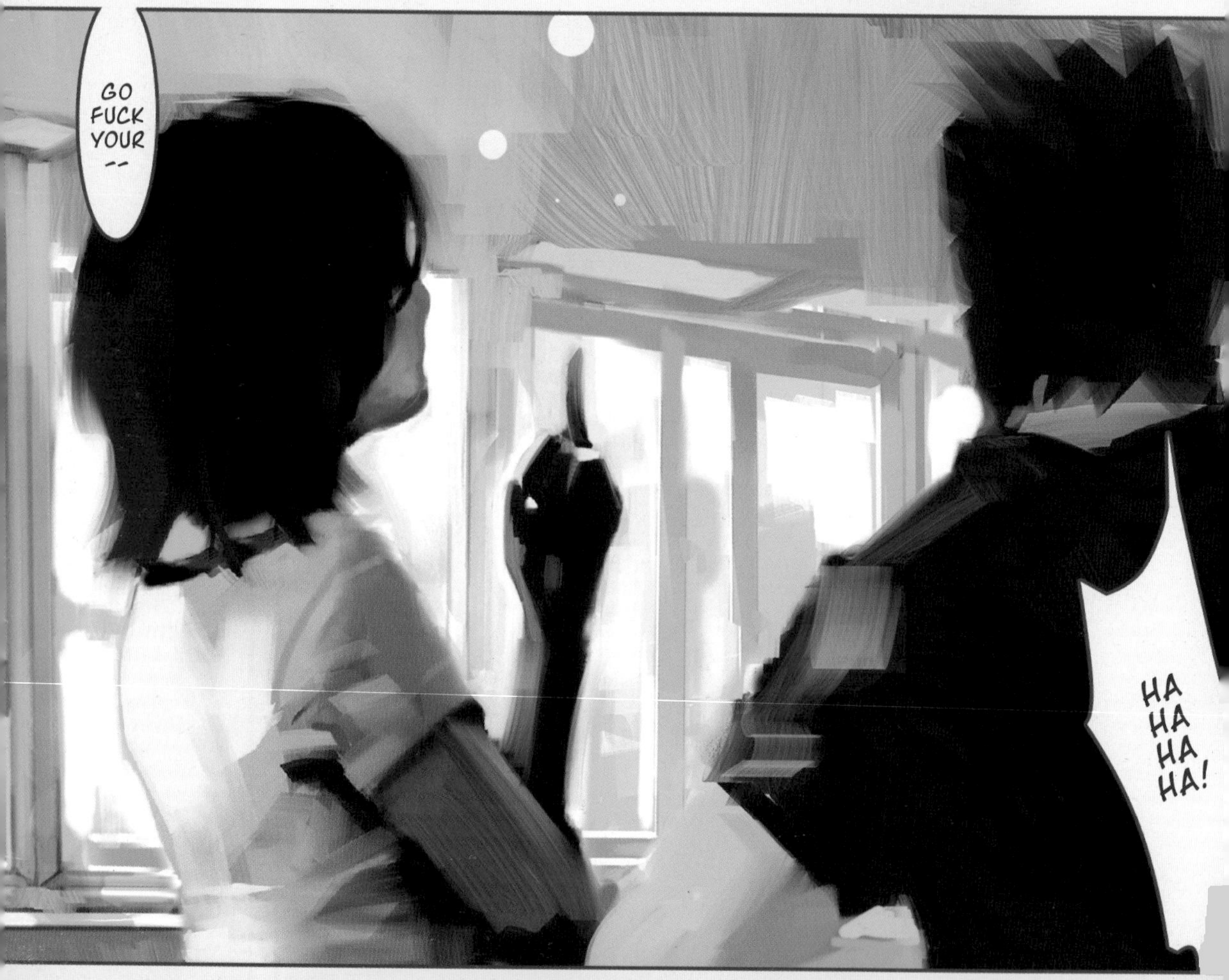
GO FUCK YOUR --
HA HA HA HA!

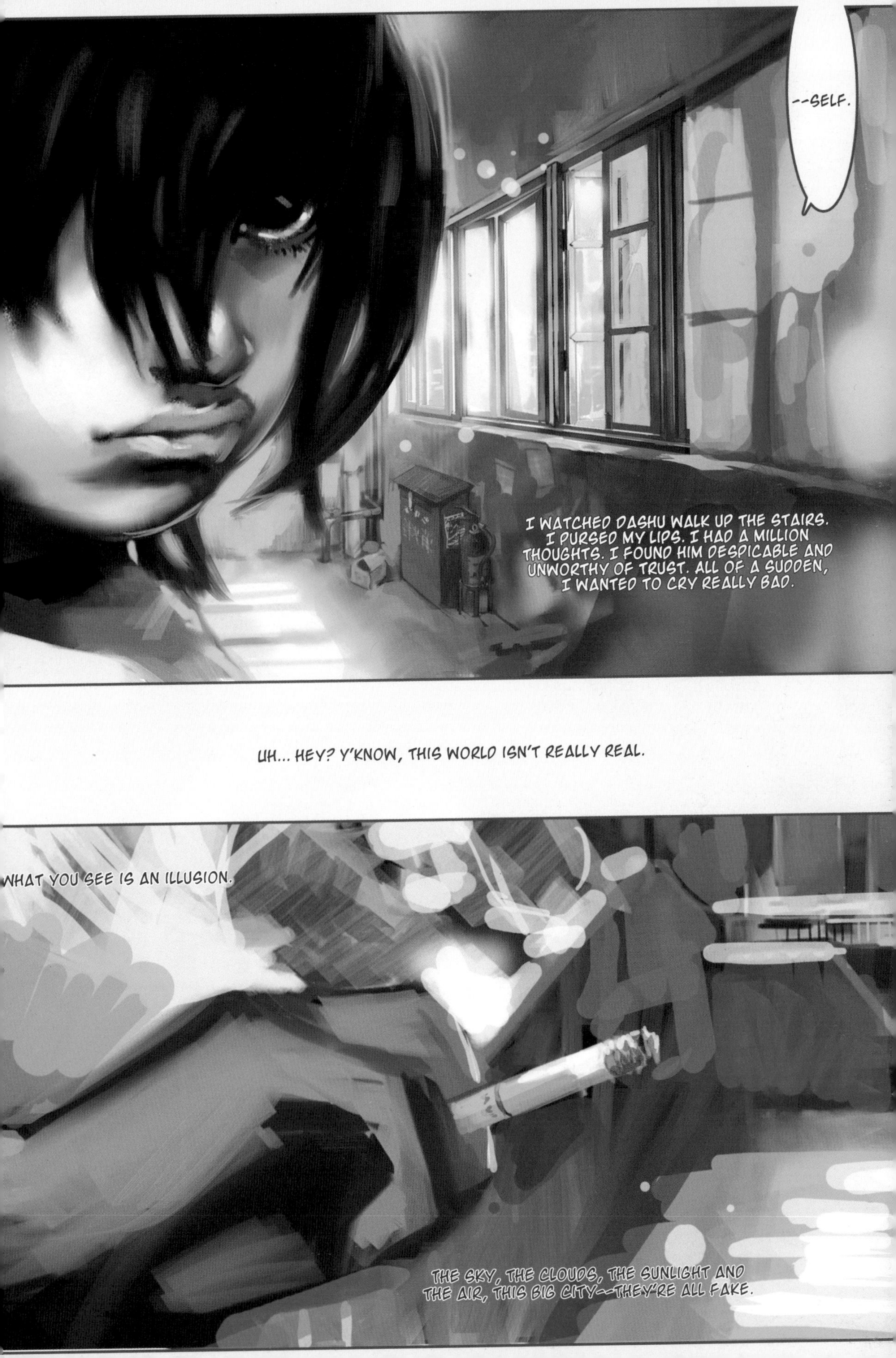
--SELF.
I WATCHED DASHU WALK UP THE STAIRS. I PURSED MY LIPS. I HAD A MILLION THOUGHTS. I FOUND HIM DESPICABLE AND UNWORTHY OF TRUST. ALL OF A SUDDEN, I WANTED TO CRY REALLY BAD.
UH... HEY? Y'KNOW, THIS WORLD ISN'T REALLY REAL.
WHAT YOU SEE IS AN ILLUSION.
THE SKY, THE CLOUDS, THE SUNLIGHT AND THE AIR, THIS BIG CITY--THEY'RE ALL FAKE.

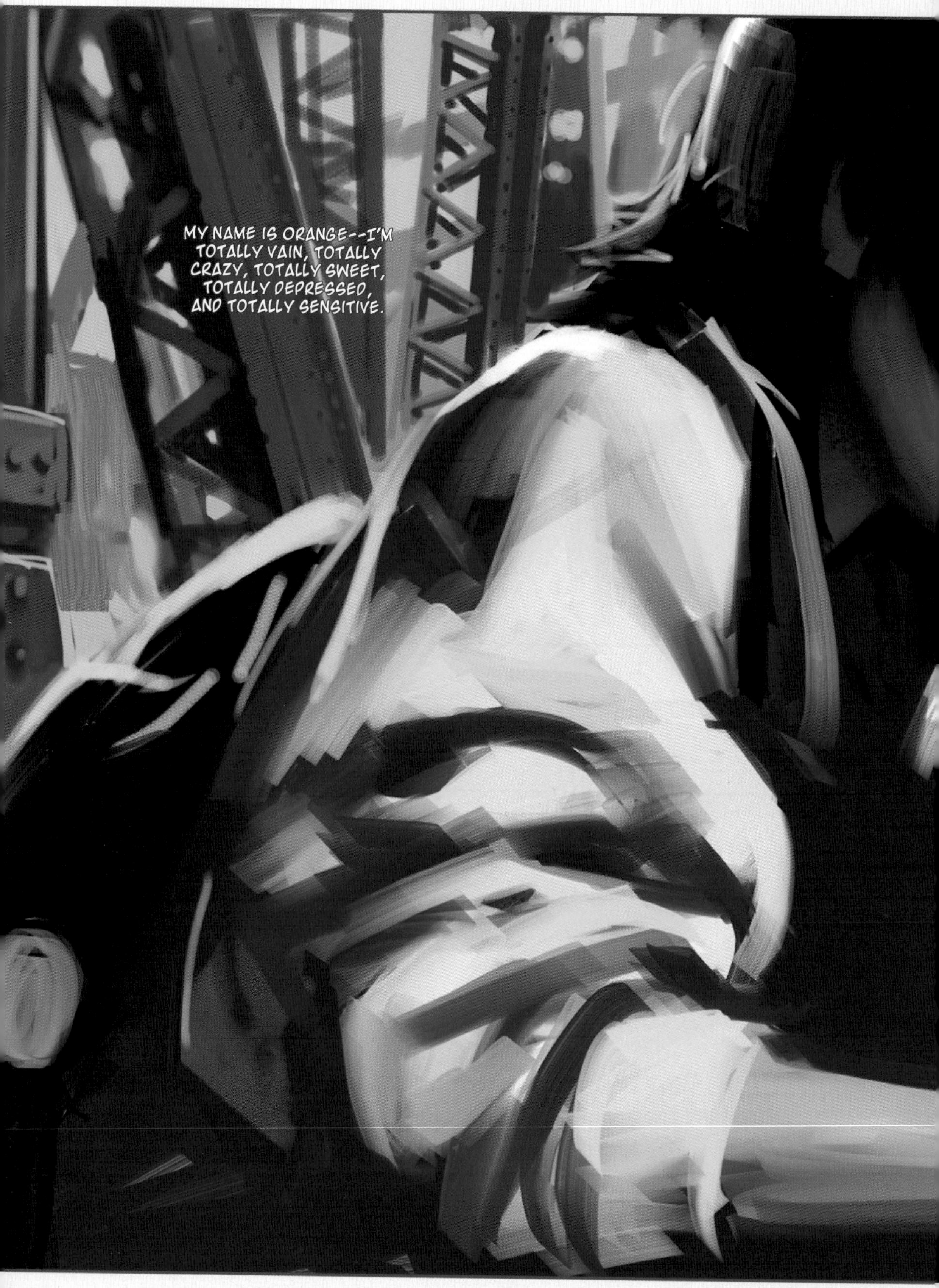
MY NAME IS ORANGE--I'M TOTALLY VAIN, TOTALLY CRAZY, TOTALLY SWEET, TOTALLY DEPRESSED, AND TOTALLY SENSITIVE.

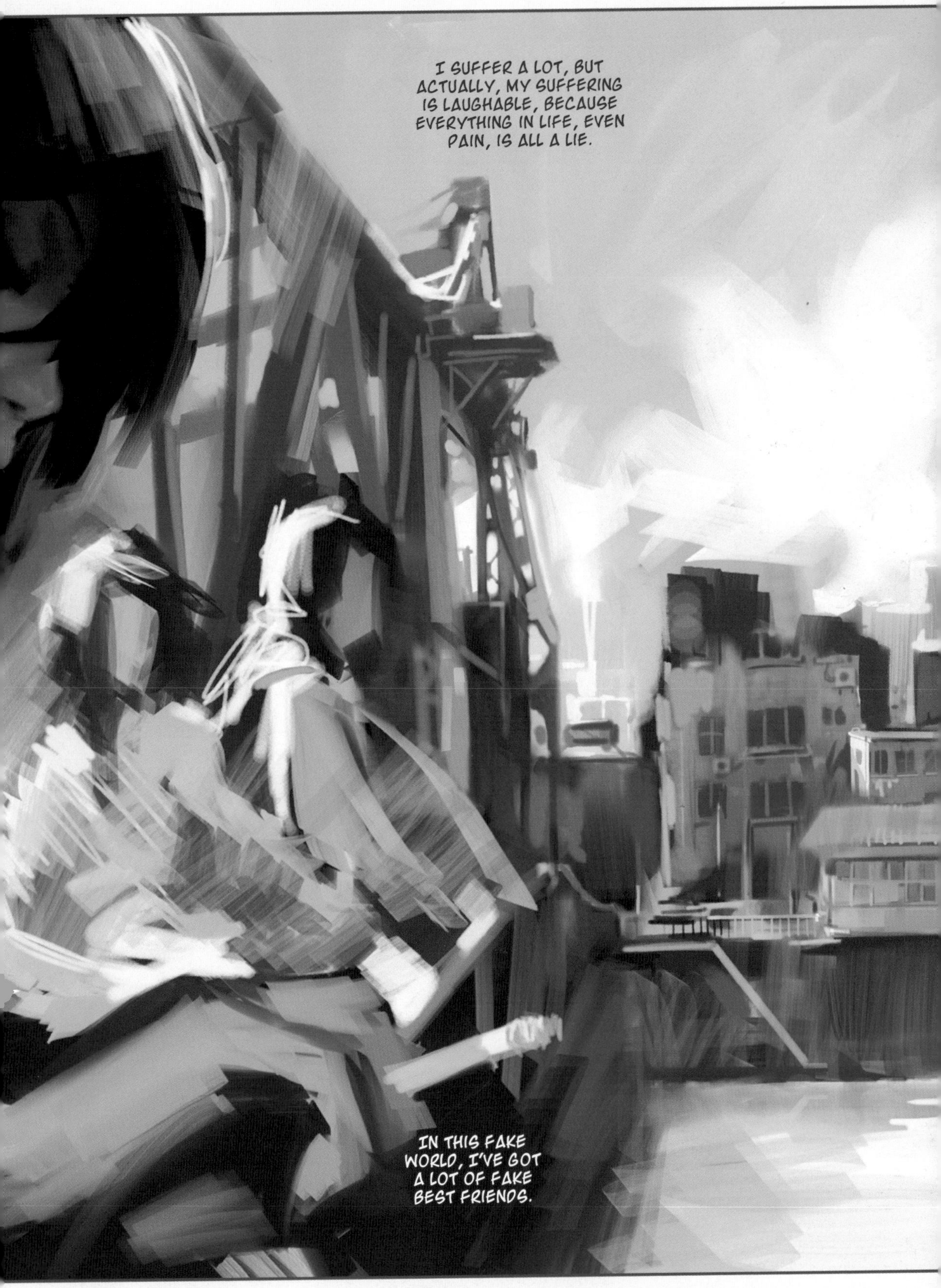
I SUFFER A LOT, BUT ACTUALLY, MY SUFFERING IS LAUGHABLE, BECAUSE EVERYTHING IN LIFE, EVEN PAIN, IS ALL A LIE.
IN THIS FAKE WORLD, I'VE GOT A LOT OF FAKE BEST FRIENDS.

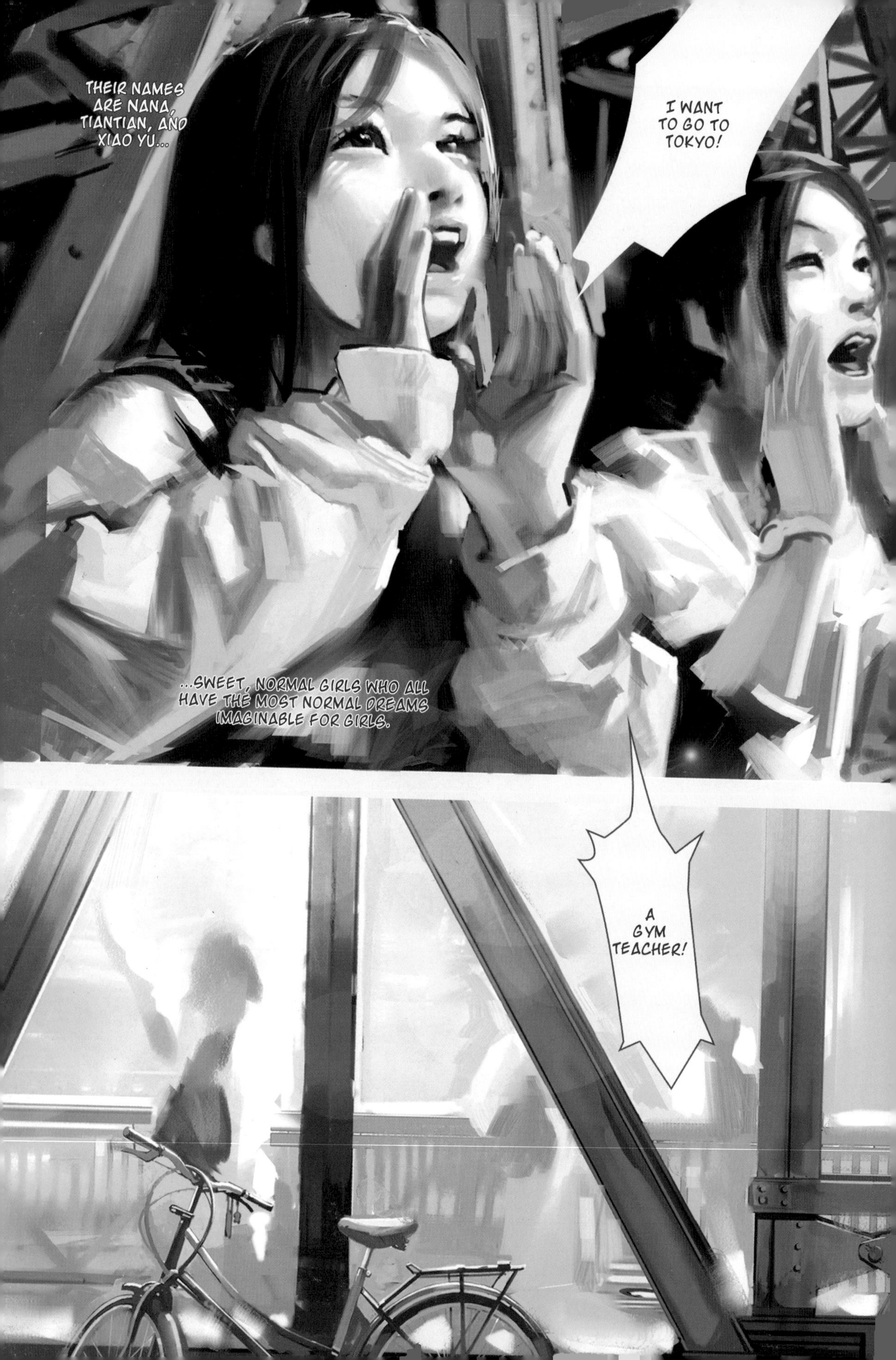
THEIR NAMES ARE NANA, TIANTIAN, AND XIAO YU...
I WANT TO GO TO TOKYO!
...SWEET, NORMAL GIRLS WHO ALL HAVE THE MOST NORMAL DREAMS IMAGINABLE FOR GIRLS.
A GYM TEACHER!

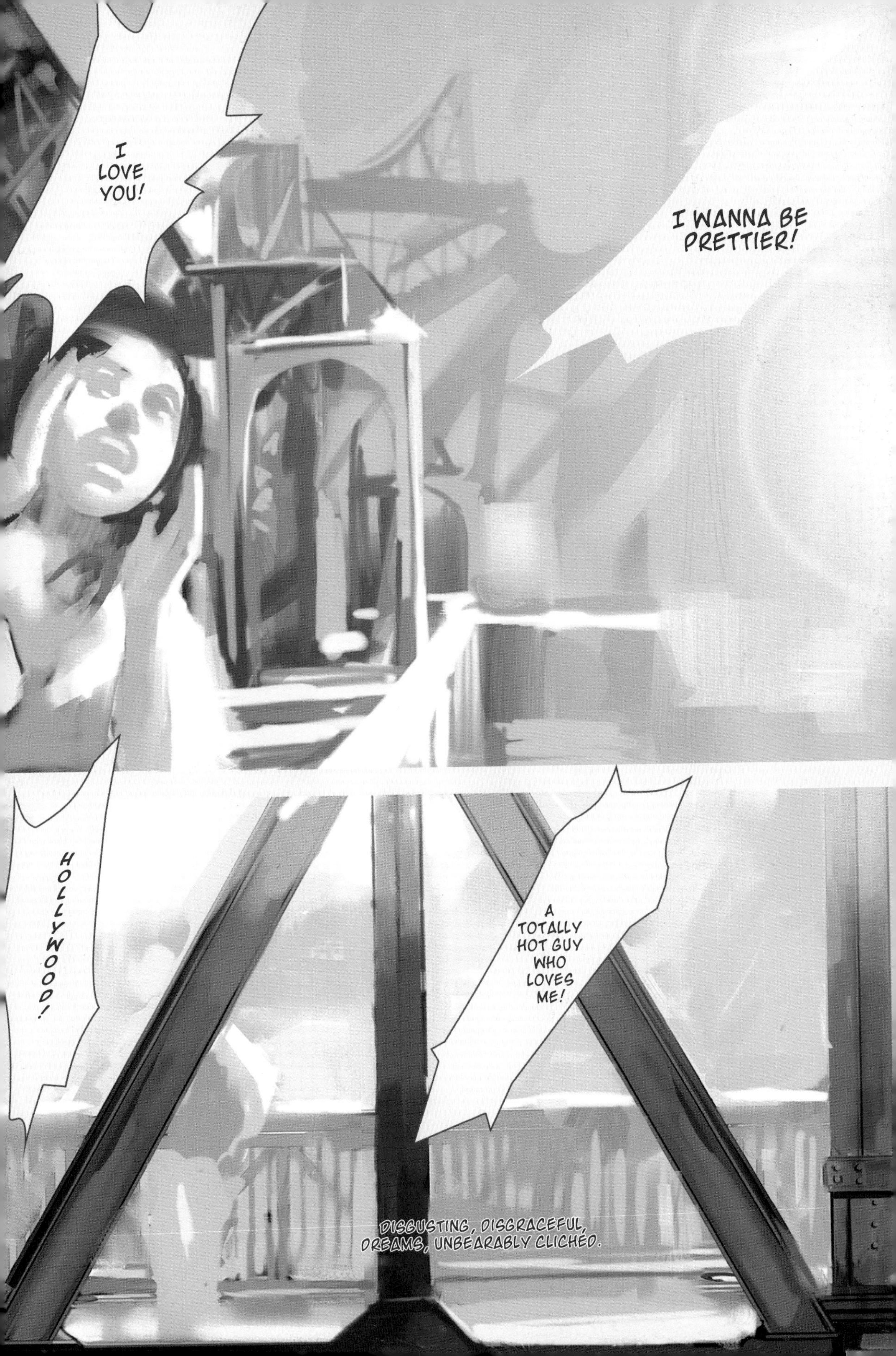
I LOVE YOU!
I WANNA BE PRETTIER!
HOLLYWOOD!
A TOTALLY HOT GUY WHO LOVES ME!
DISGUSTING, DISGRACEFUL, DREAMS, UNBEARABLY CLICHÉD.

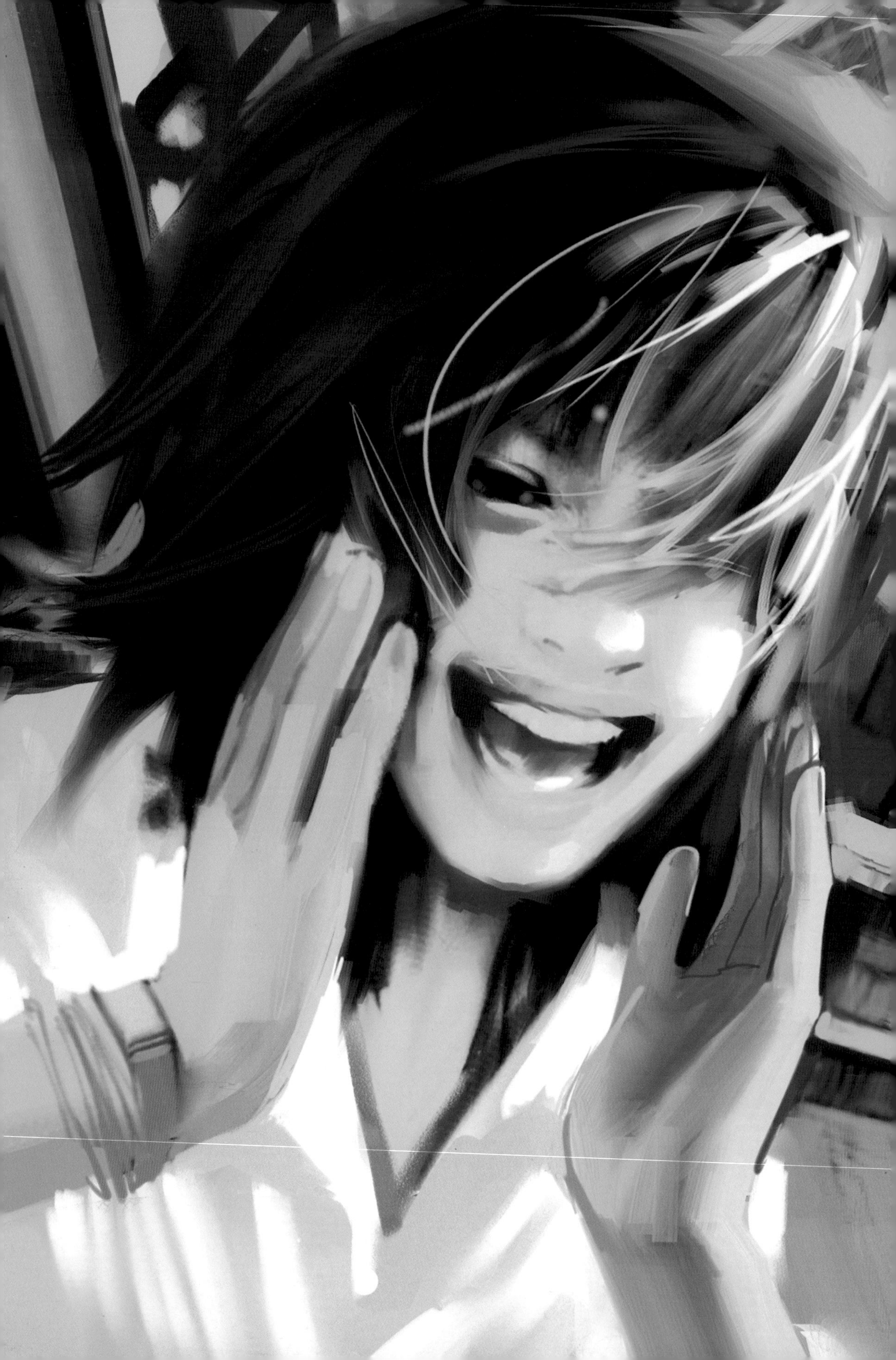

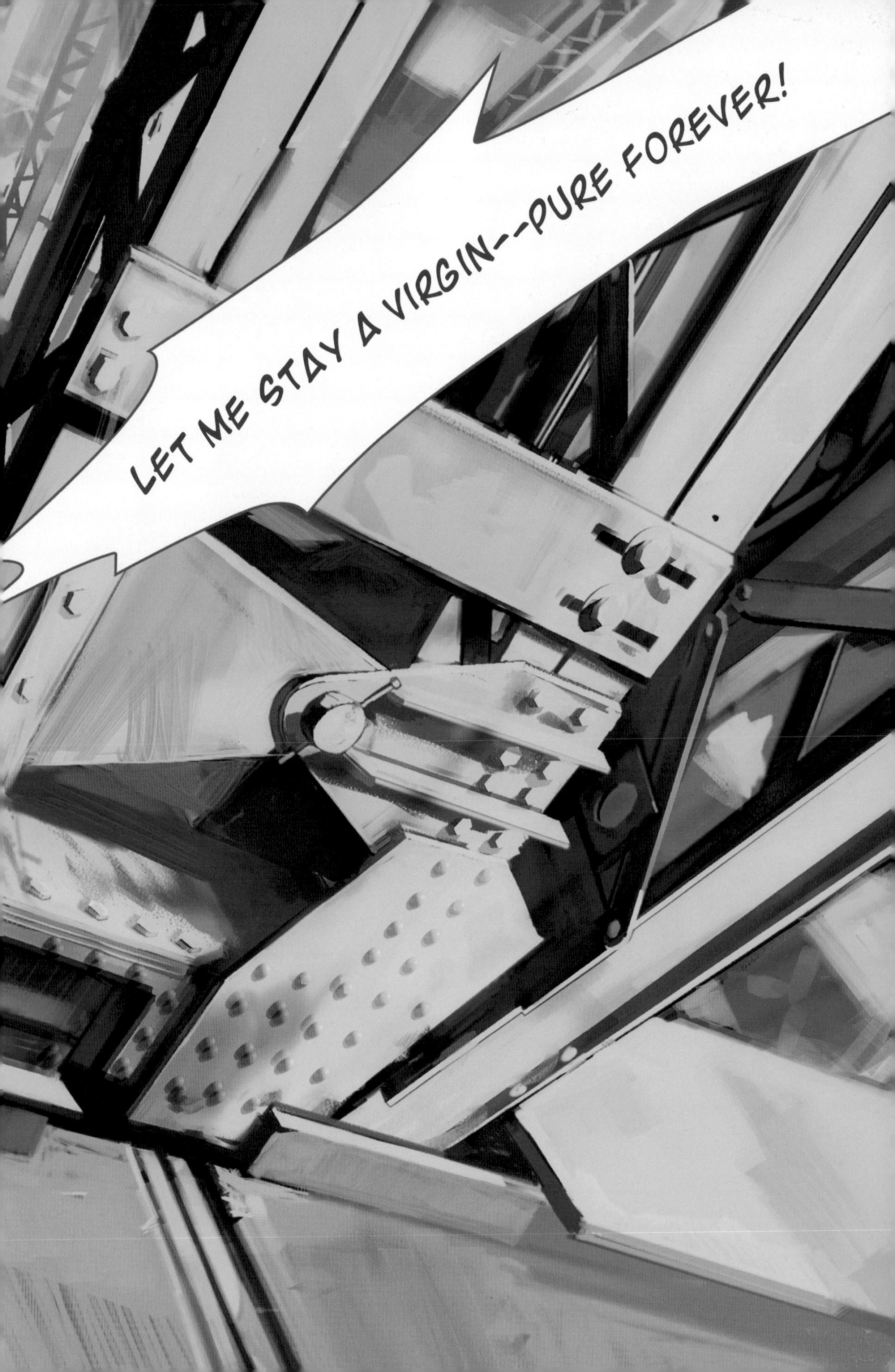
LET ME STAY A VIRGIN--PURE FOREVER!

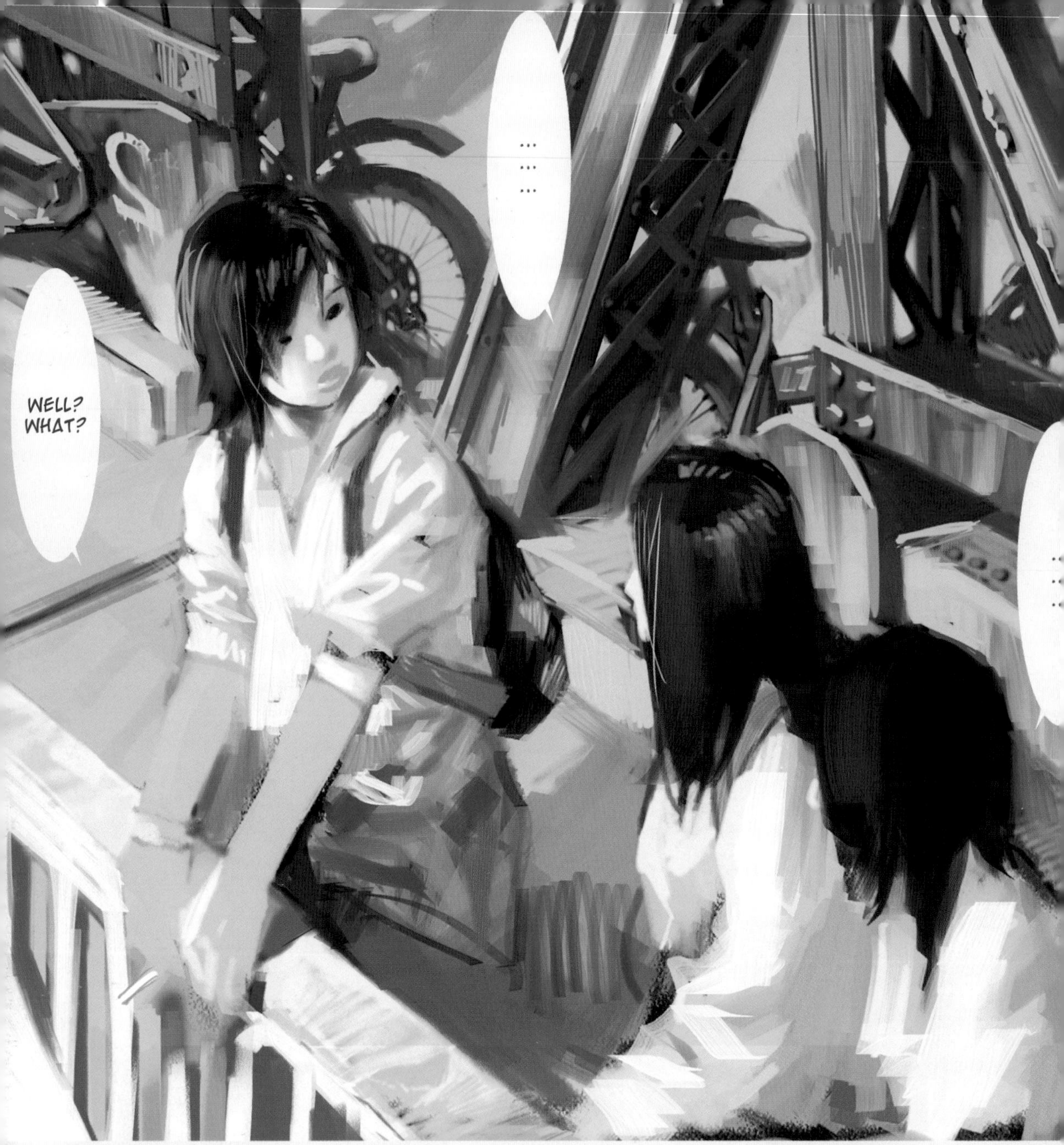
WELL? WHAT?
...
...
...

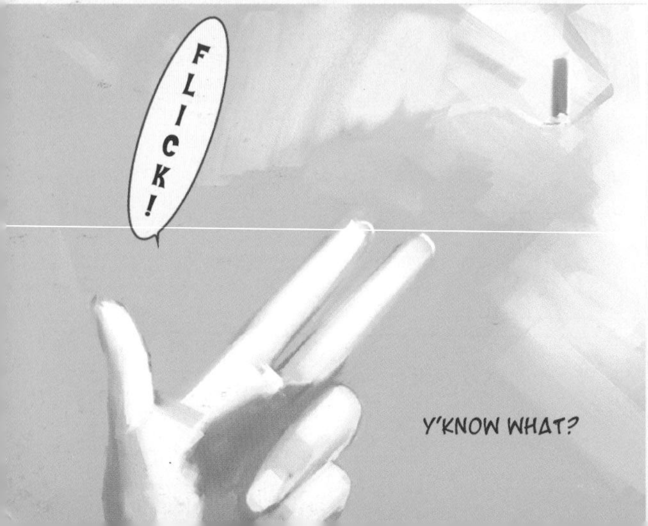
FLICK!
Y'KNOW WHAT?

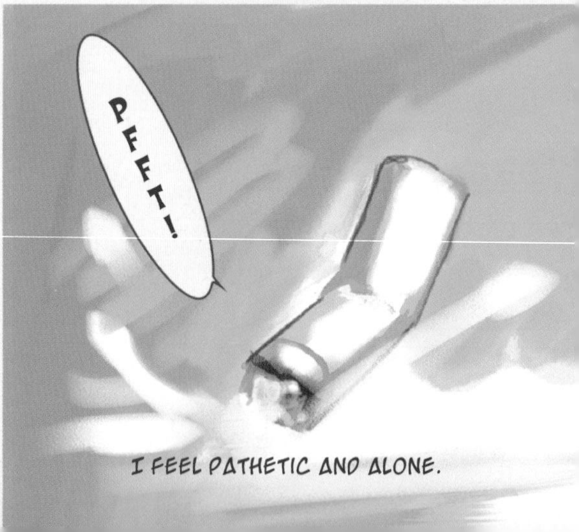
PFFT!
I FEEL PATHETIC AND ALONE.

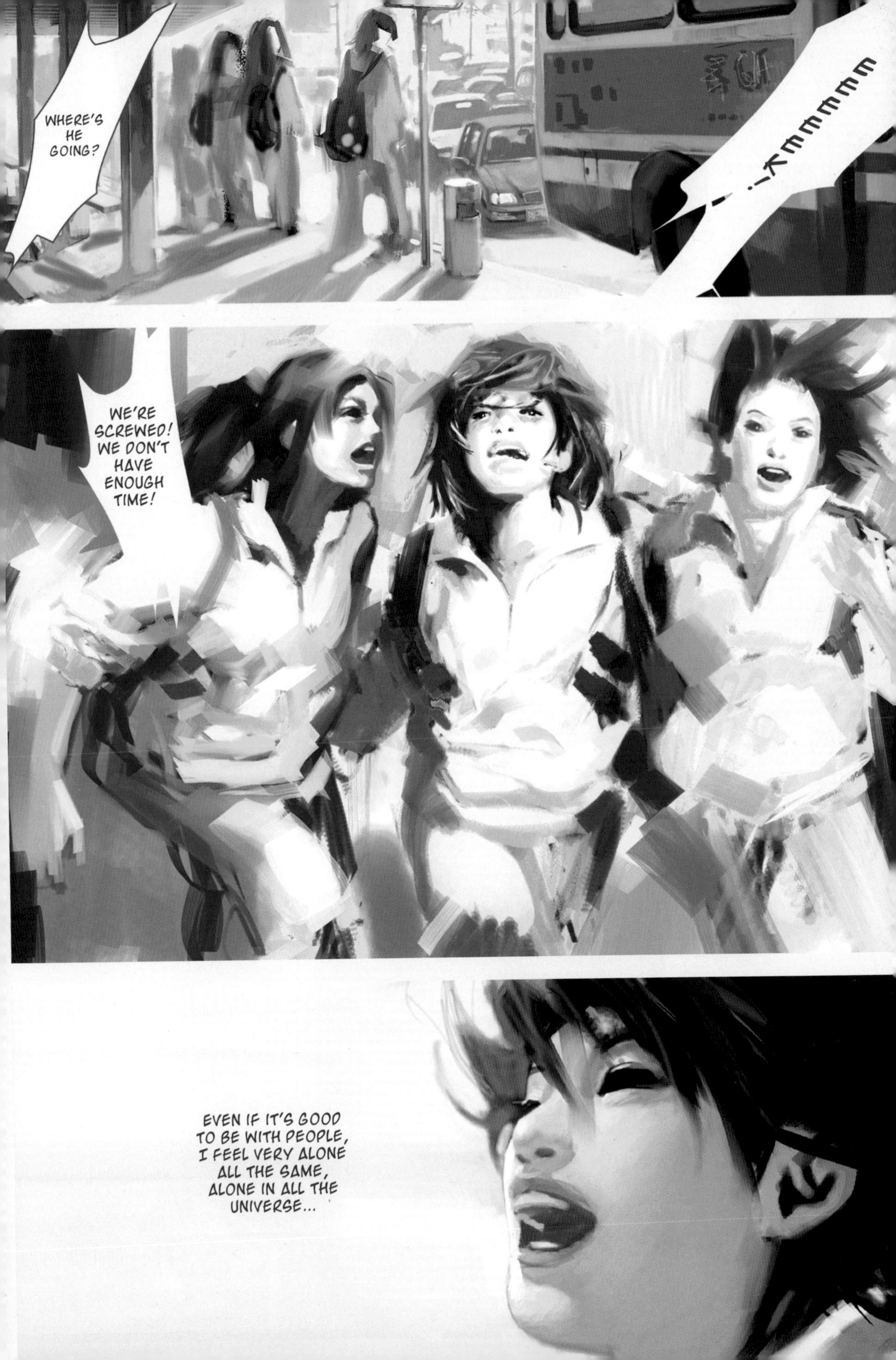
WHERE'S HE GOING?
WE'RE SCREWED! WE DON'T HAVE ENOUGH TIME!
EVEN IF IT'S GOOD TO BE WITH PEOPLE, I FEEL VERY ALONE ALL THE SAME, ALONE IN ALL THE UNIVERSE...

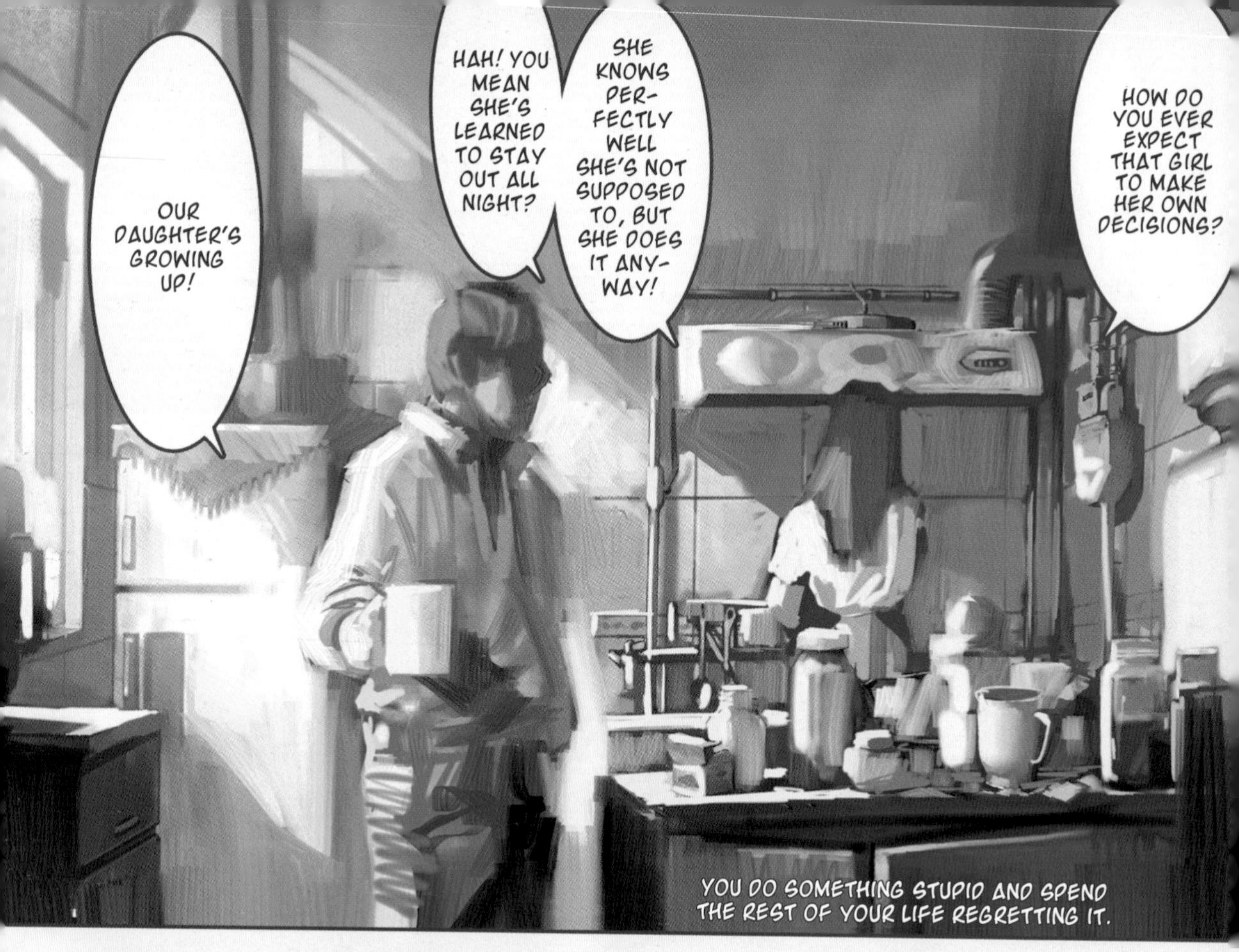
OUR DAUGHTER'S GROWING UP!
HAH! YOU MEAN SHE'S LEARNED TO STAY OUT ALL NIGHT?
SHE KNOWS PER-FECTLY WELL SHE'S NOT SUPPOSED TO, BUT SHE DOES IT ANY-WAY!
HOW DO YOU EVER EXPECT THAT GIRL TO MAKE HER OWN DECISIONS?
YOU DO SOMETHING STUPID AND SPEND THE REST OF YOUR LIFE REGRETTING IT.

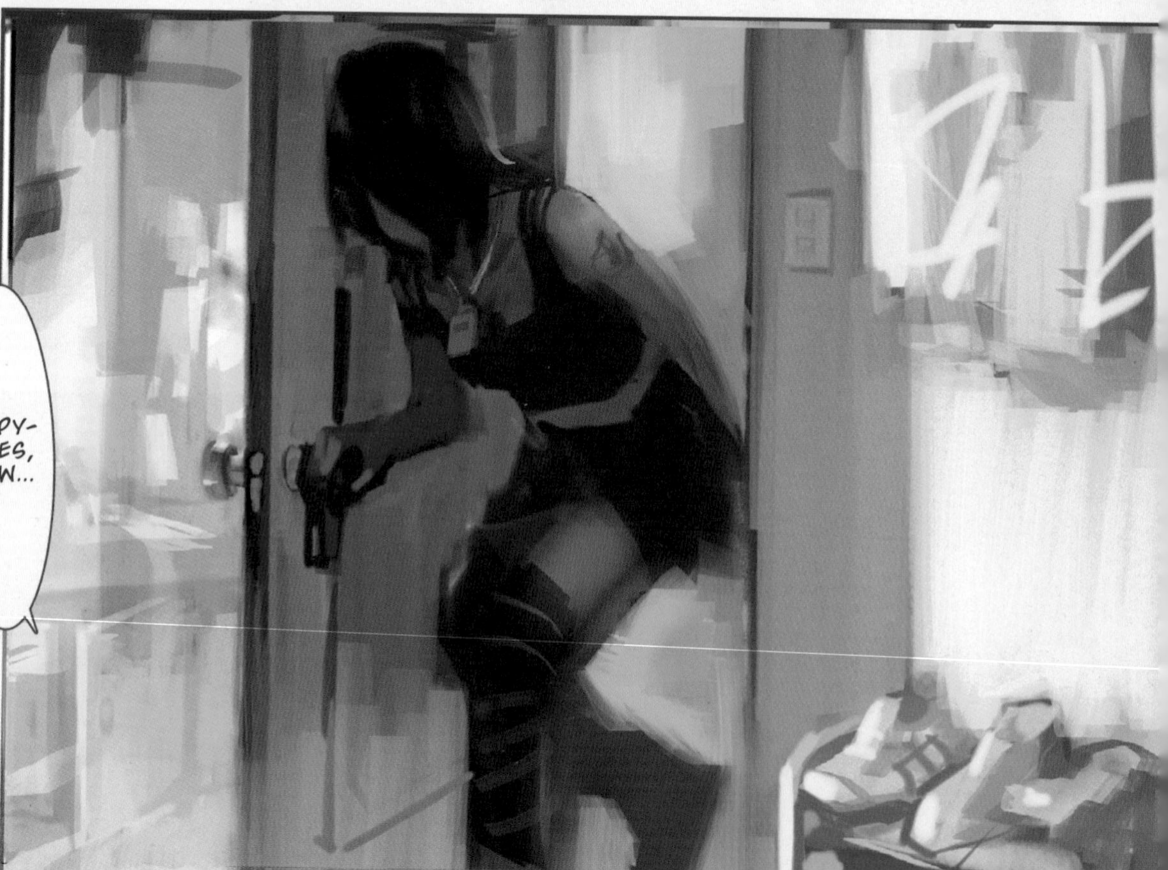
TIPPY-TOES, NOW...

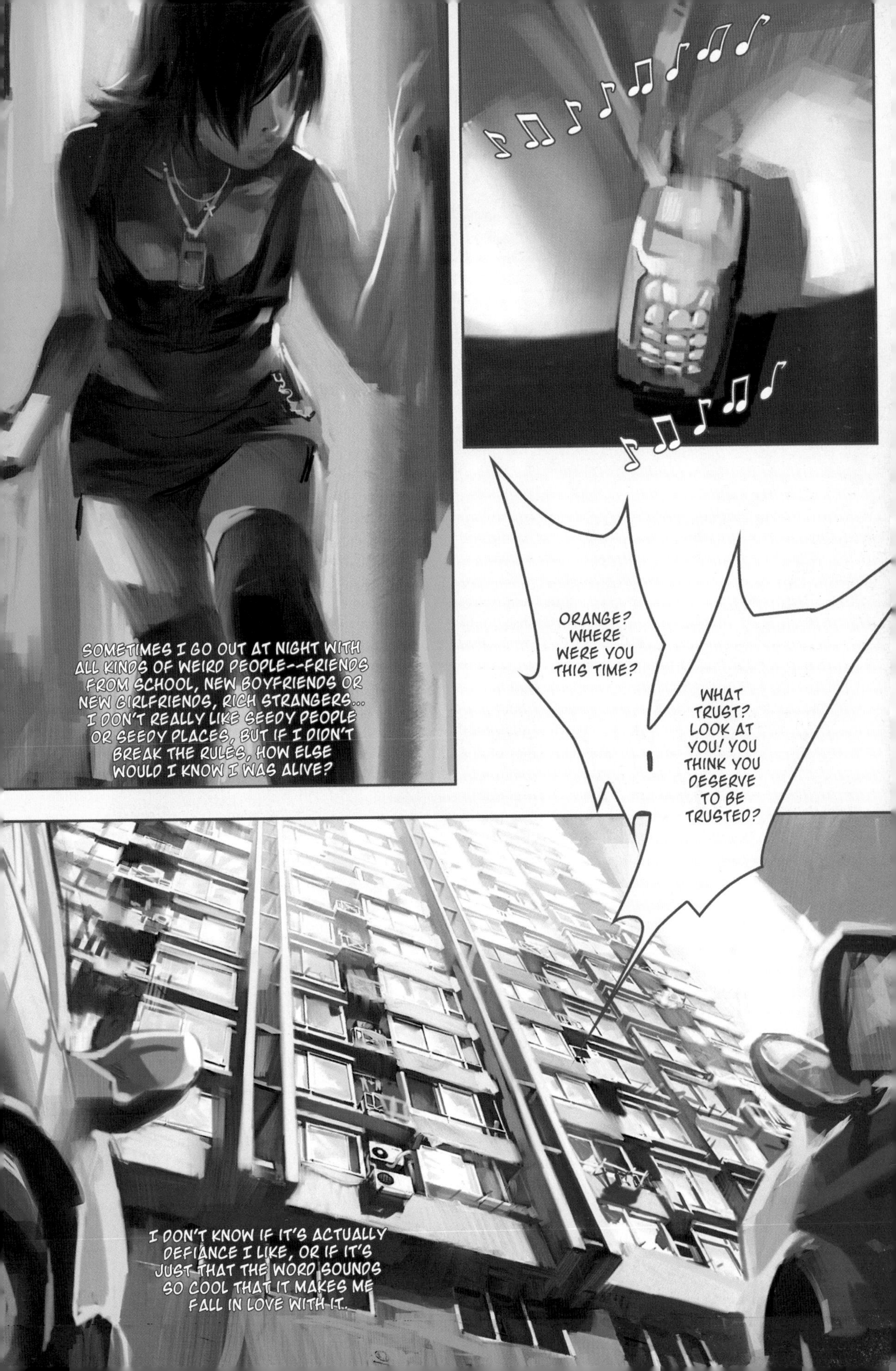
SOMETIMES I GO OUT AT NIGHT WITH ALL KINDS OF WEIRD PEOPLE--FRIENDS FROM SCHOOL, NEW BOYFRIENDS OR NEW GIRLFRIENDS, RICH STRANGERS... I DON'T REALLY LIKE SEEDY PEOPLE OR SEEDY PLACES, BUT IF I DIDN'T BREAK THE RULES, HOW ELSE WOULD I KNOW I WAS ALIVE?
ORANGE? WHERE WERE YOU THIS TIME?
WHAT TRUST? LOOK AT YOU! YOU THINK YOU DESERVE TO BE TRUSTED?
I DON'T KNOW IF IT'S ACTUALLY DEFIANCE I LIKE, OR IF IT'S JUST THAT THE WORD SOUNDS SO COOL THAT IT MAKES ME FALL IN LOVE WITH IT.

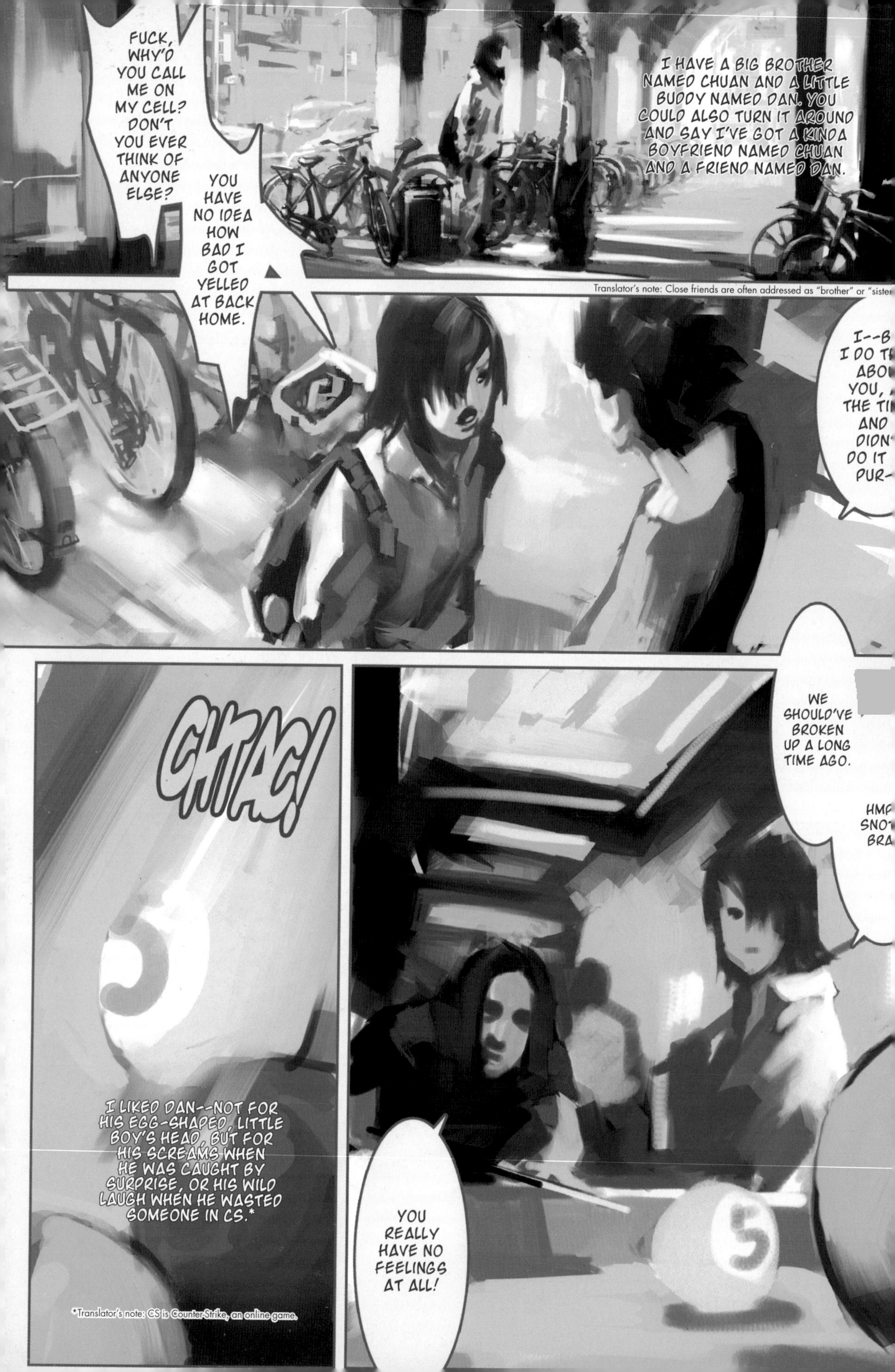
I HAVE A BIG BROTHER NAMED CHUAN AND A LITTLE BUDDY NAMED DAN. YOU COULD ALSO TURN IT AROUND AND SAY I'VE GOT A KINDA BOYFRIEND NAMED CHUAN AND A FRIEND NAMED DAN.
FUCK, WHY'D YOU CALL ME ON MY CELL? DON'T YOU EVER THINK OF ANYONE ELSE?
YOU HAVE NO IDEA HOW BAD I GOT YELLED AT BACK HOME.
I--B I DO T ABO YOU, THE TI AND DIDN DO IT PUR-
CHTAC!
I LIKED DAN--NOT FOR HIS EGG-SHAPED, LITTLE BOY'S HEAD, BUT FOR HIS SCREAMS WHEN HE WAS CAUGHT BY SURPRISE, OR HIS WILD LAUGH WHEN HE WASTED SOMEONE IN CS.*
WE SHOULD'VE BROKEN UP A LONG TIME AGO.
HMP SNO BRA
YOU REALLY HAVE NO FEELINGS AT ALL!
Translator's note: Close friends are often addressed as "brother" or "sister

*Translator's note: CS is Counter-Strike, an online game.

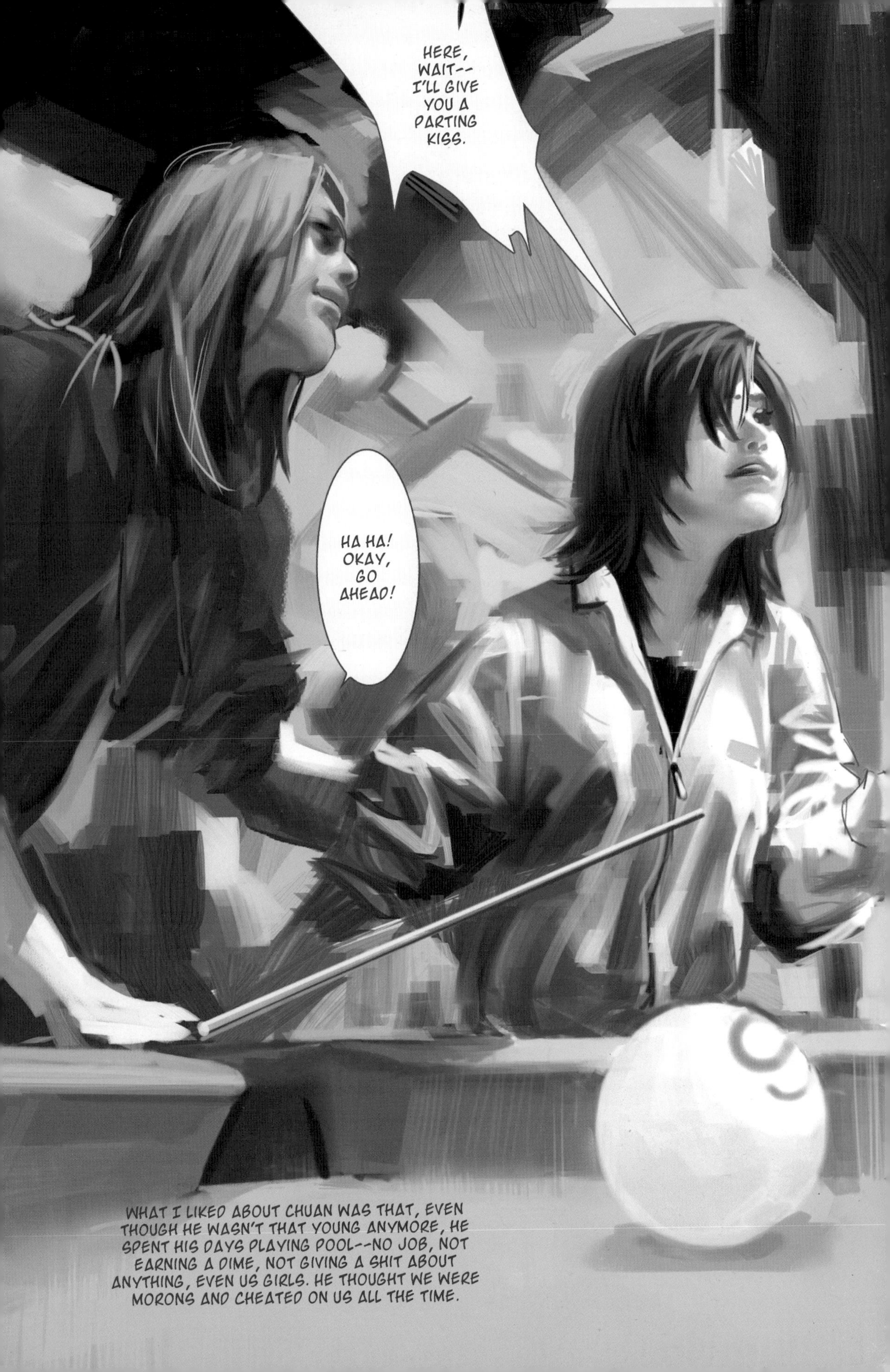
HERE, WAIT-- I'LL GIVE YOU A PARTING KISS.
HA HA! OKAY, GO AHEAD!
WHAT I LIKED ABOUT CHUAN WAS THAT, EVEN THOUGH HE WASN'T THAT YOUNG ANYMORE, HE SPENT HIS DAYS PLAYING POOL--NO JOB, NOT EARNING A DIME, NOT GIVING A SHIT ABOUT ANYTHING, EVEN US GIRLS. HE THOUGHT WE WERE MORONS AND CHEATED ON US ALL THE TIME.

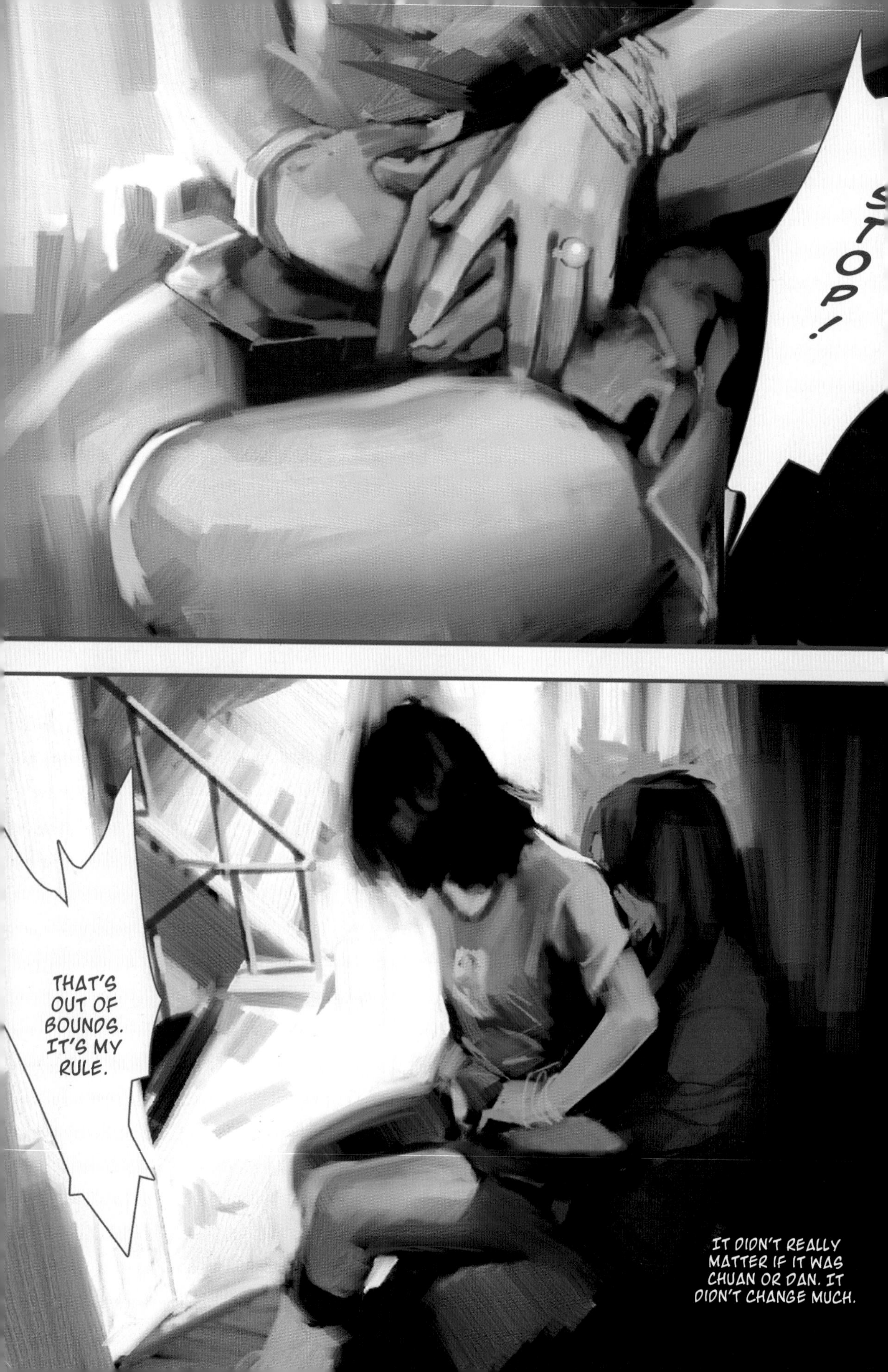
STOP!
THAT'S OUT OF BOUNDS. IT'S MY RULE.
IT DIDN'T REALLY MATTER IF IT WAS CHUAN OR DAN. IT DIDN'T CHANGE MUCH.

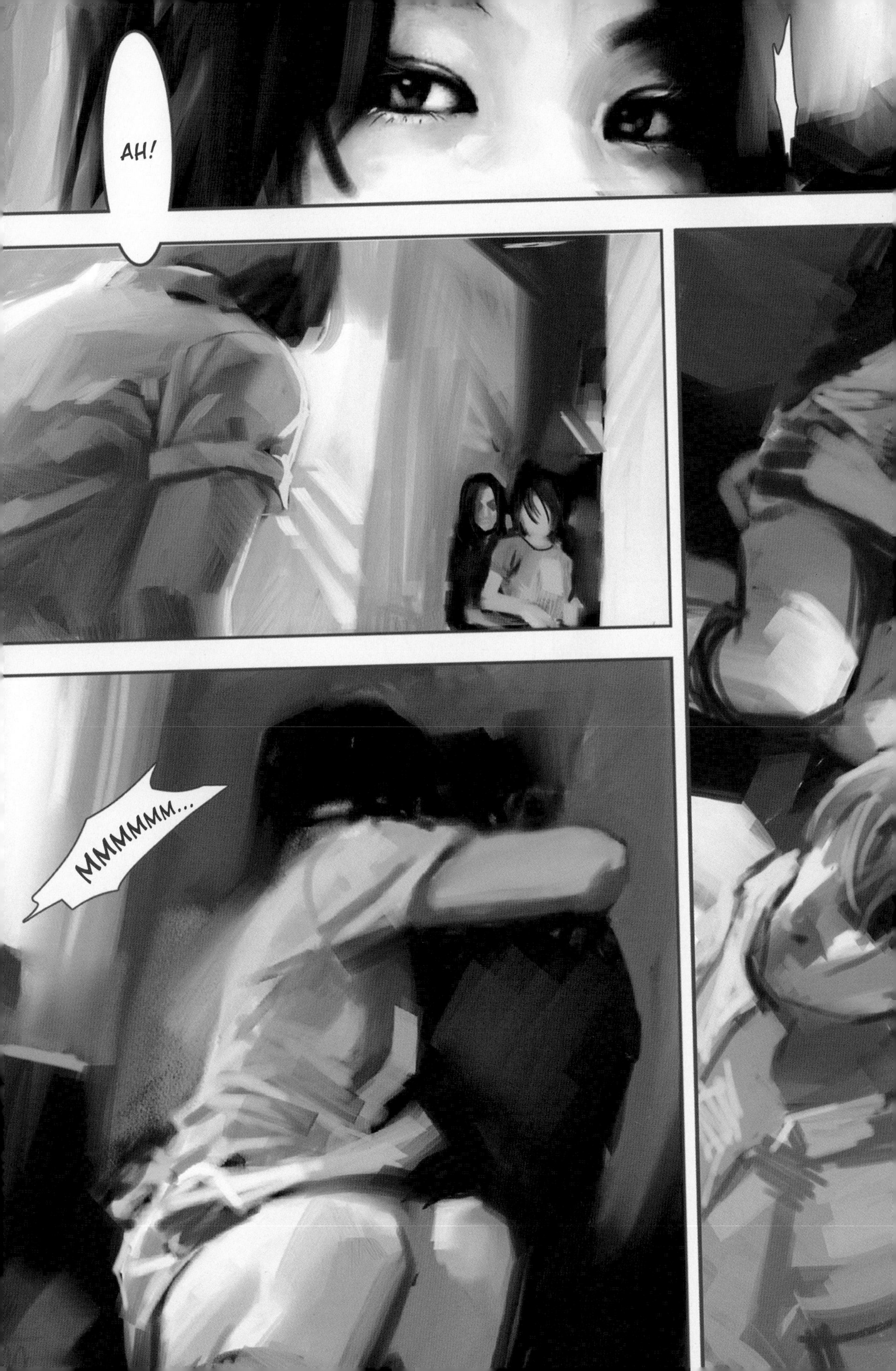
AH!
MMMMMM...

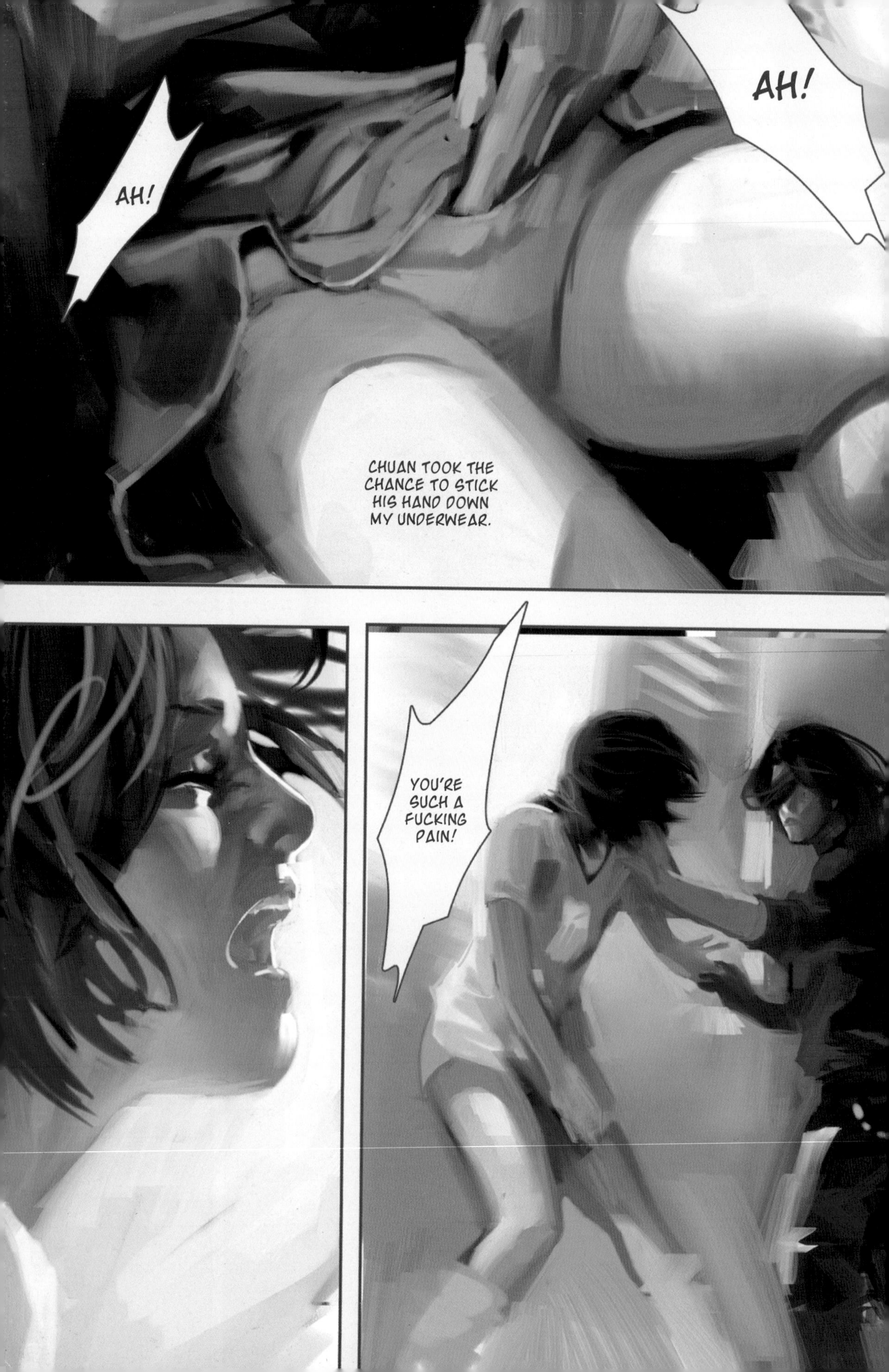

AH!
AH!
CHUAN TOOK THE CHANCE TO STICK HIS HAND DOWN MY UNDERWEAR.
YOU'RE SUCH A FUCKING PAIN!

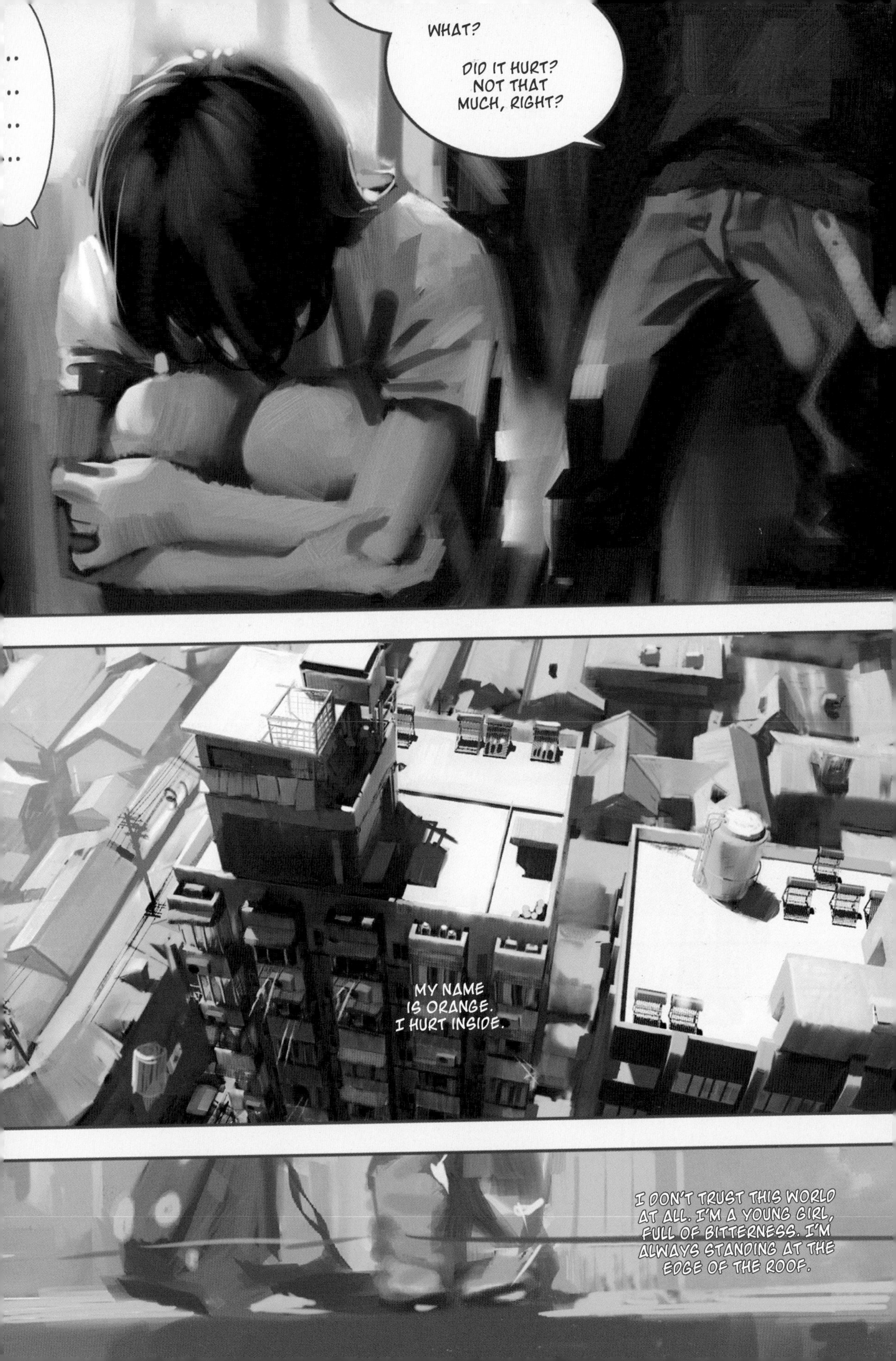

....
WHAT?
DID IT HURT? NOT THAT MUCH, RIGHT?
MY NAME IS ORANGE. I HURT INSIDE.
I DON'T TRUST THIS WORLD AT ALL. I'M A YOUNG GIRL, FULL OF BITTERNESS. I'M ALWAYS STANDING AT THE EDGE OF THE ROOF.

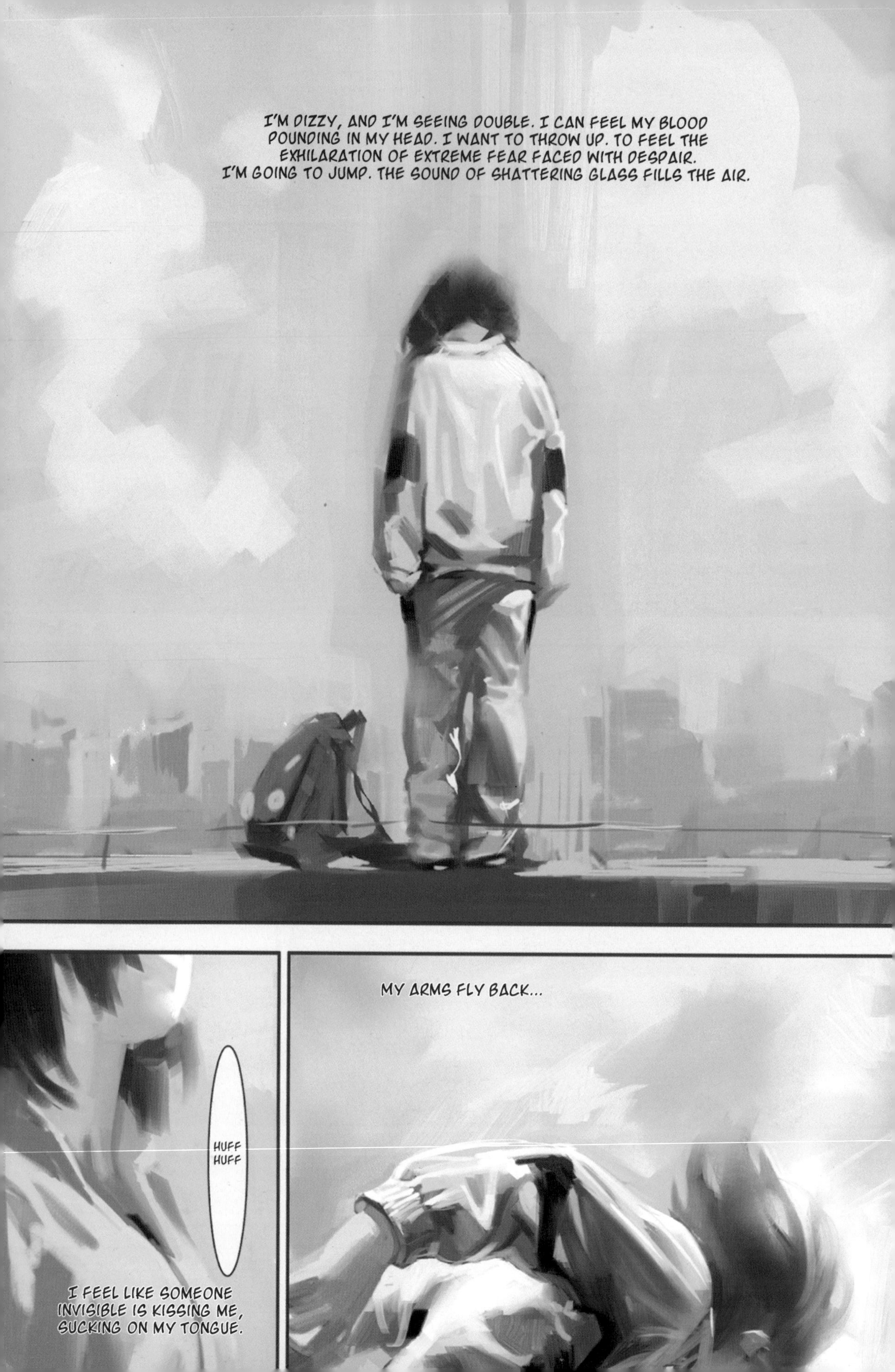
I'M DIZZY, AND I'M SEEING DOUBLE. I CAN FEEL MY BLOOD POUNDING IN MY HEAD. I WANT TO THROW UP. TO FEEL THE EXHILARATION OF EXTREME FEAR FACED WITH DESPAIR. I'M GOING TO JUMP. THE SOUND OF SHATTERING GLASS FILLS THE AIR.
HUFF HUFF
I FEEL LIKE SOMEONE INVISIBLE IS KISSING ME, SUCKING ON MY TONGUE.
MY ARMS FLY BACK...

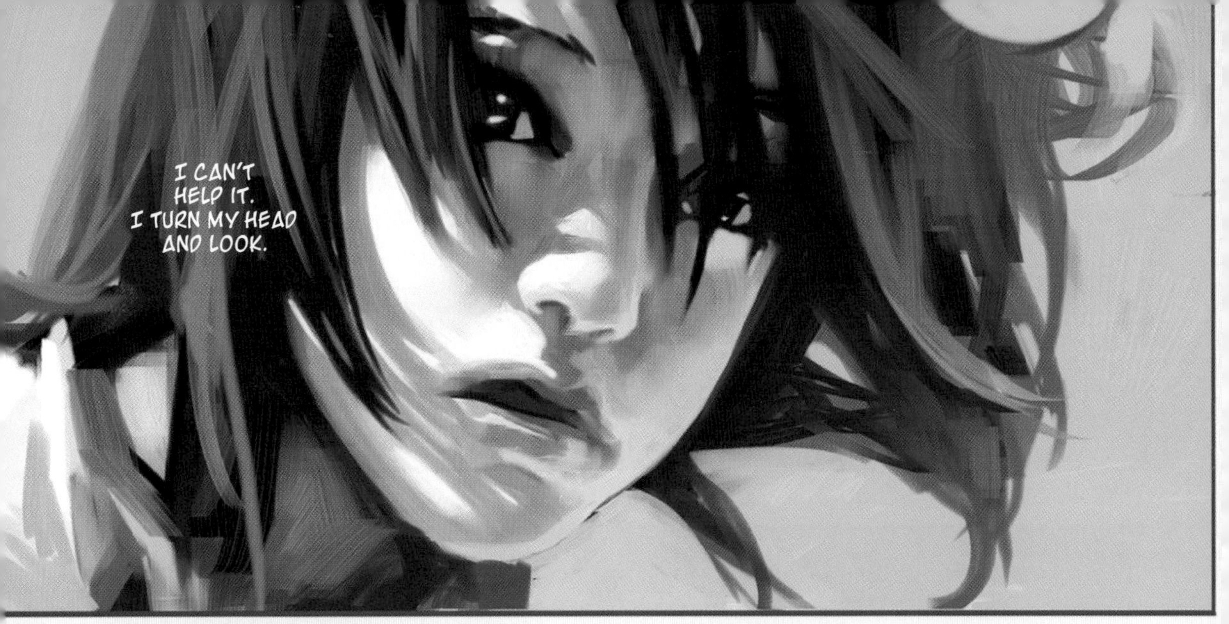
I CAN'T HELP IT. I TURN MY HEAD AND LOOK.

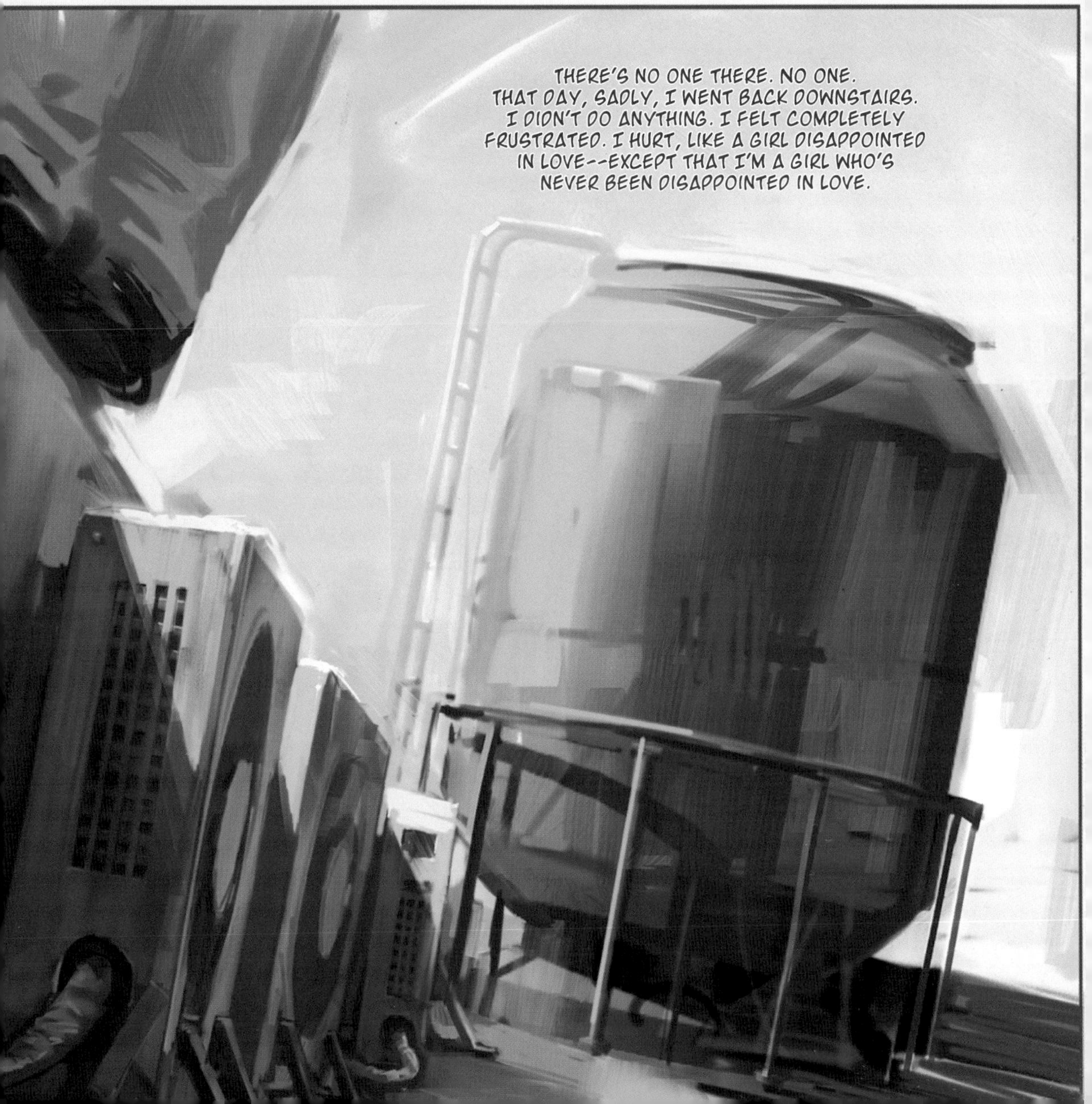
THERE'S NO ONE THERE. NO ONE. THAT DAY, SADLY, I WENT BACK DOWNSTAIRS. I DIDN'T DO ANYTHING. I FELT COMPLETELY FRUSTRATED. I HURT, LIKE A GIRL DISAPPOINTED IN LOVE--EXCEPT THAT I'M A GIRL WHO'S NEVER BEEN DISAPPOINTED IN LOVE.

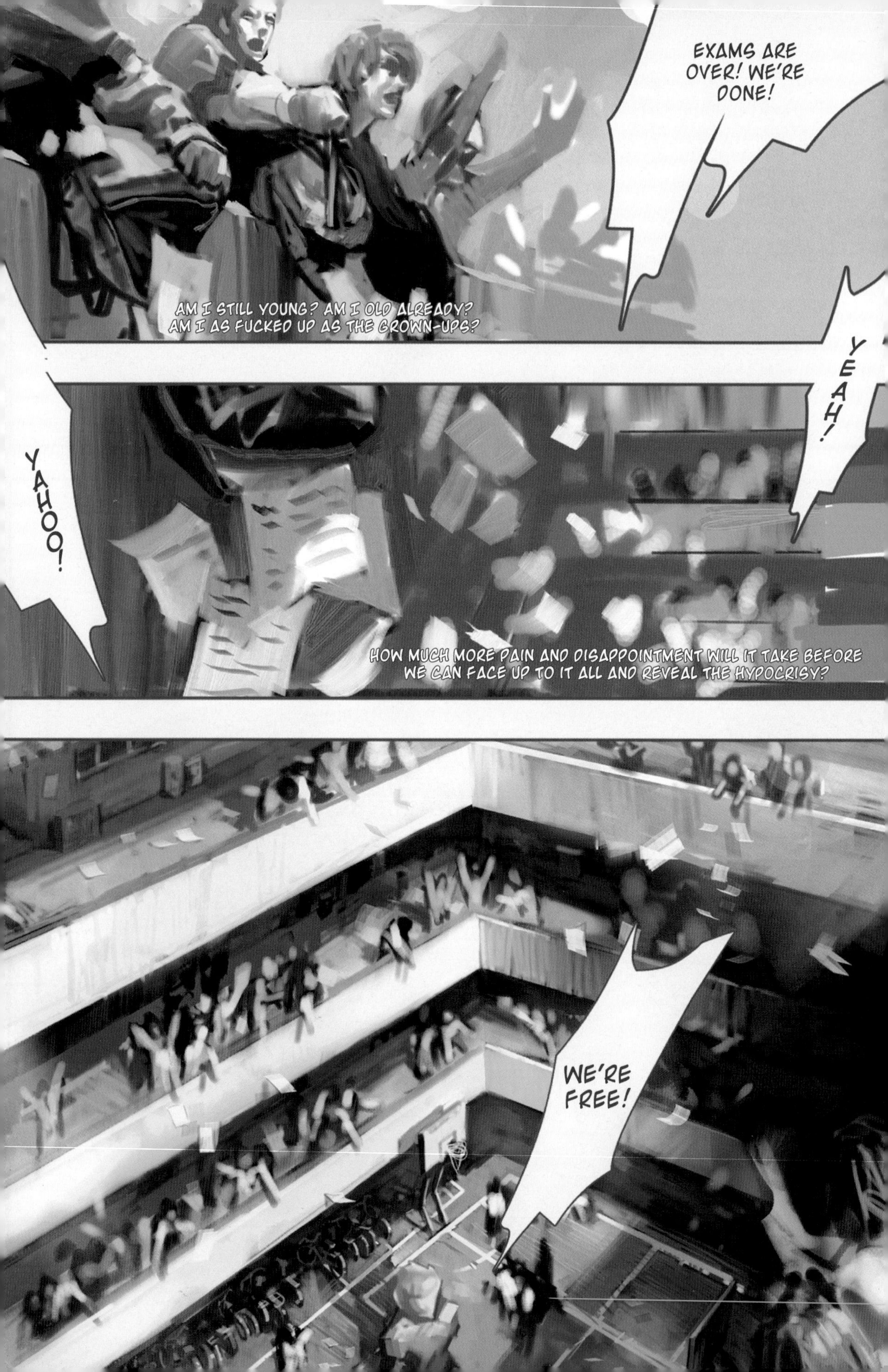
EXAMS ARE OVER! WE'RE DONE!
AM I STILL YOUNG? AM I OLD ALREADY? AM I AS FUCKED UP AS THE GROWN-UPS?
YEAH!
YAHOO!
HOW MUCH MORE PAIN AND DISAPPOINTMENT WILL IT TAKE BEFORE WE CAN FACE UP TO IT ALL AND REVEAL THE HYPOCRISY?
WE'RE FREE!

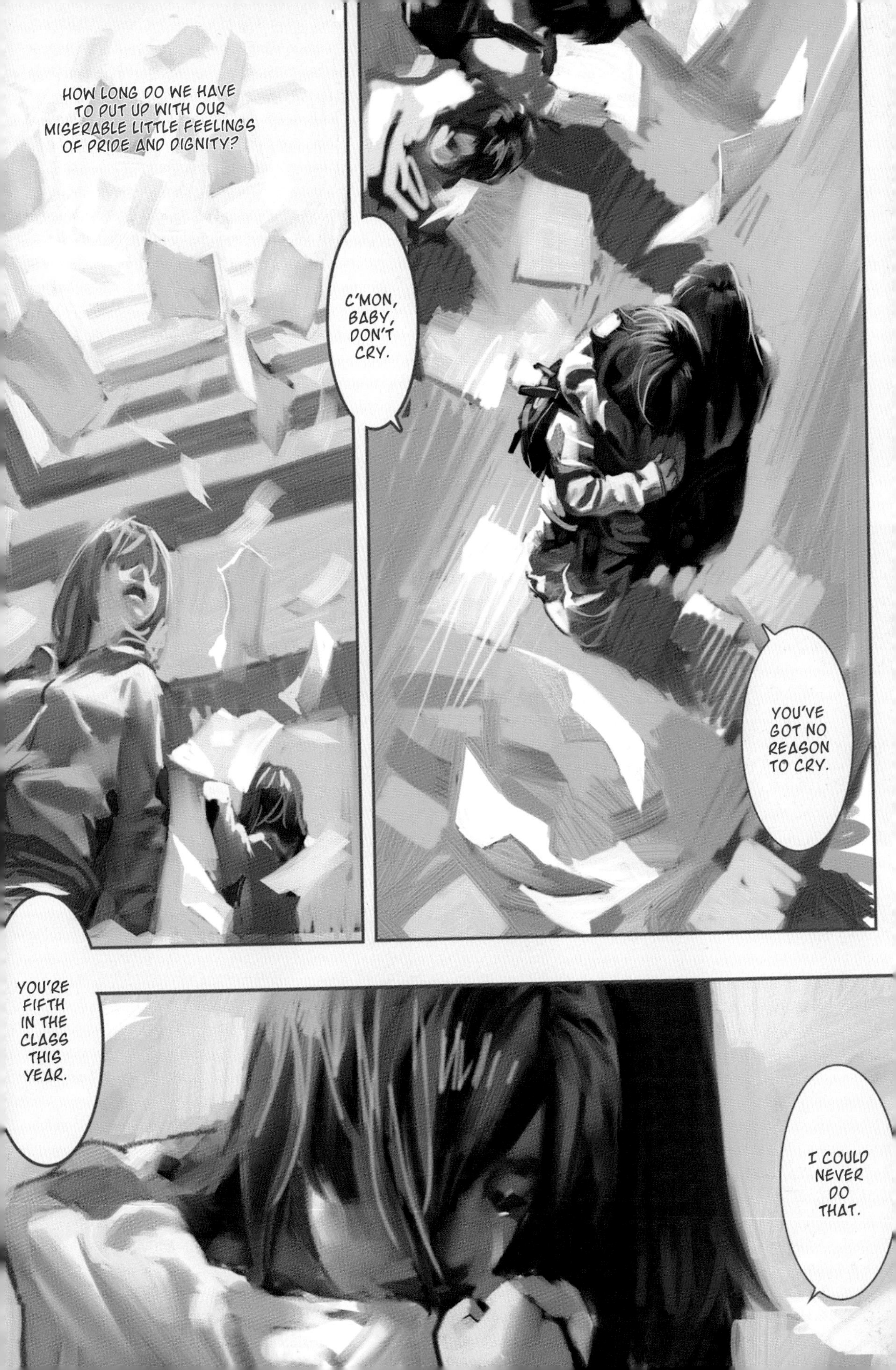
HOW LONG DO WE HAVE TO PUT UP WITH OUR MISERABLE LITTLE FEELINGS OF PRIDE AND DIGNITY?
C'MON, BABY, DON'T CRY.
YOU'VE GOT NO REASON TO CRY.
YOU'RE FIFTH IN THE CLASS THIS YEAR.
I COULD NEVER DO THAT.

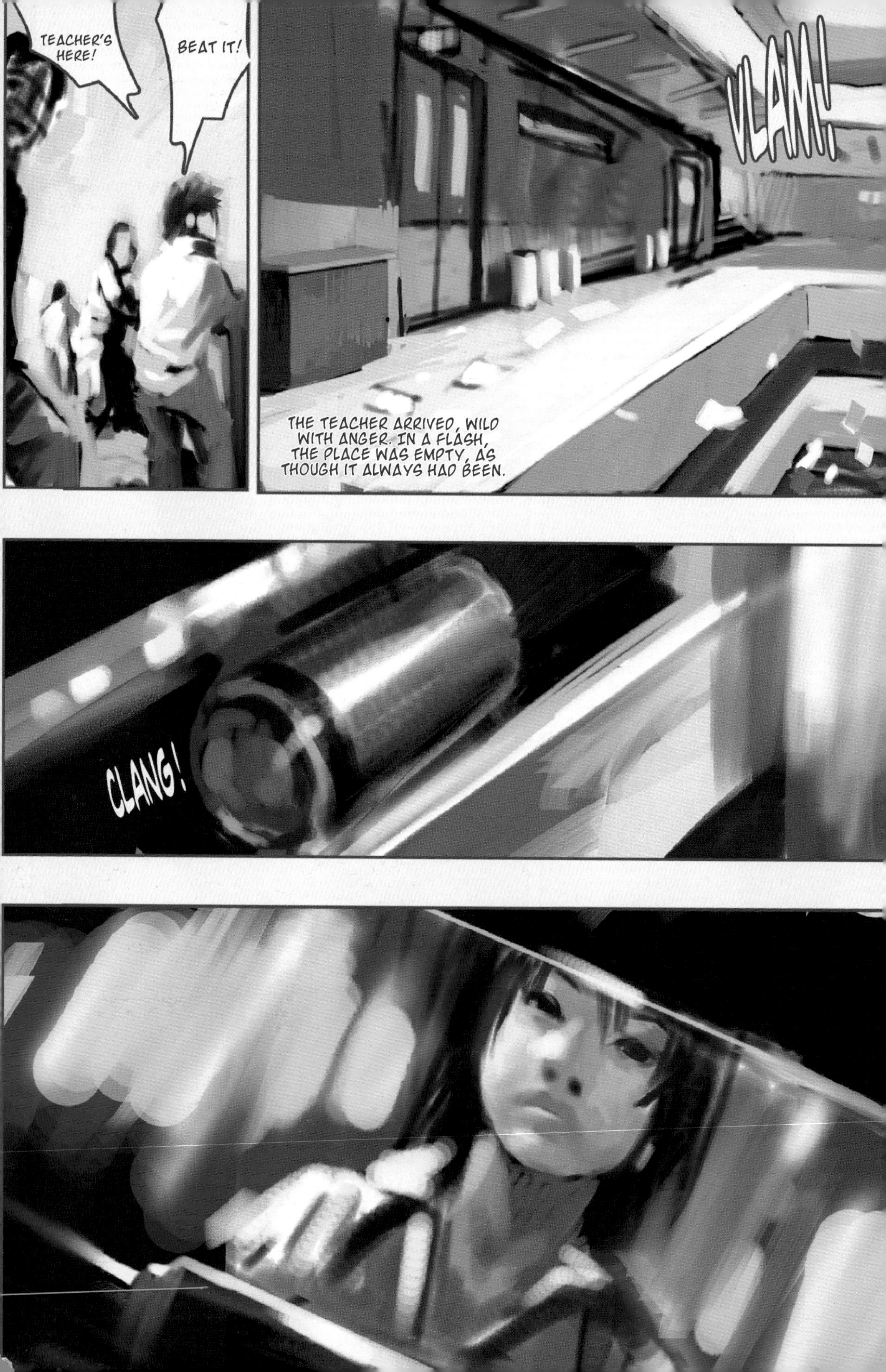
TEACHER'S HERE!
BEAT IT!
VLAM!
THE TEACHER ARRIVED, WILD WITH ANGER. IN A FLASH, THE PLACE WAS EMPTY, AS THOUGH IT ALWAYS HAD BEEN.
CLANG!

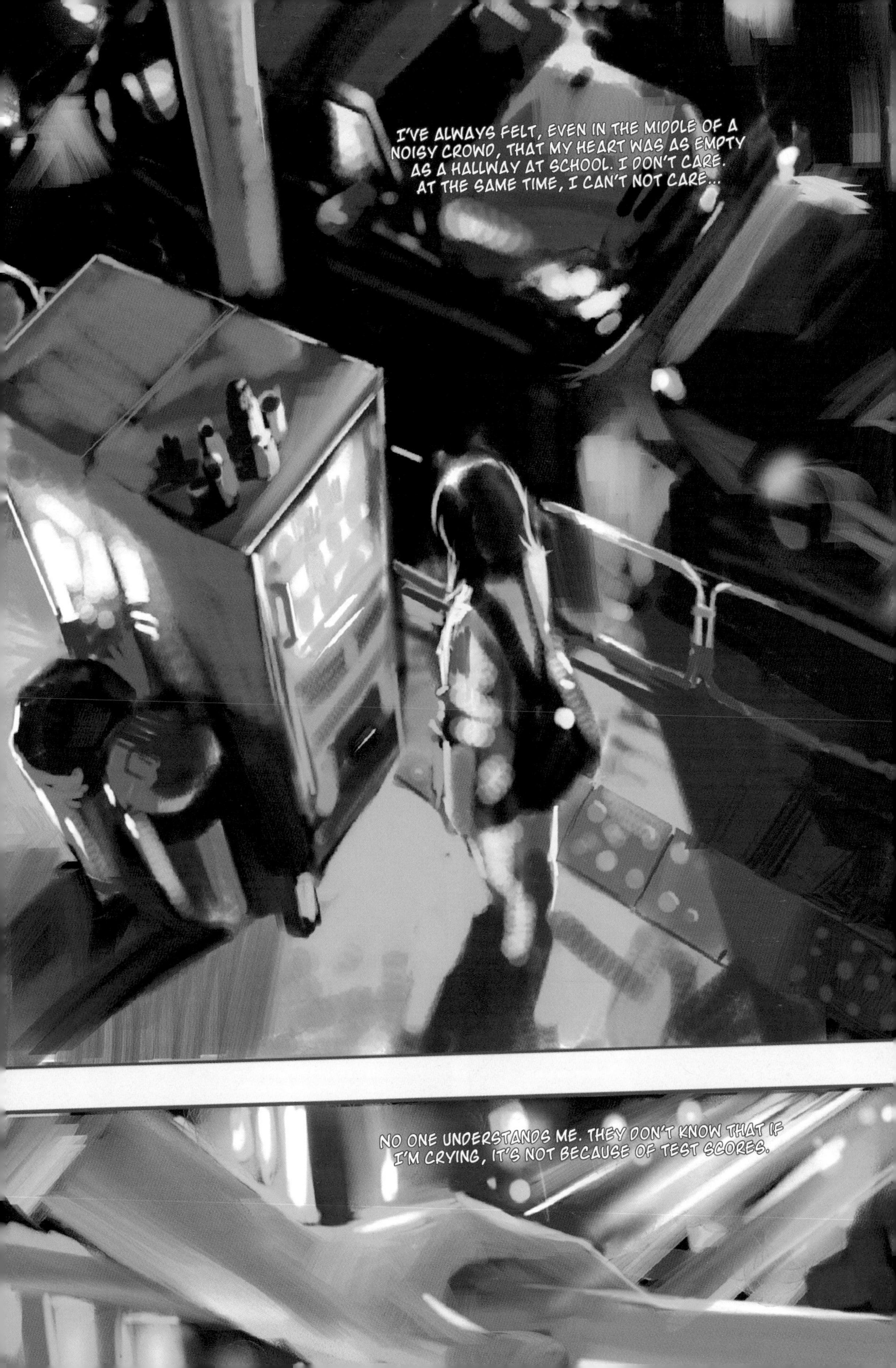
I'VE ALWAYS FELT, EVEN IN THE MIDDLE OF A NOISY CROWD, THAT MY HEART WAS AS EMPTY AS A HALLWAY AT SCHOOL. I DON'T CARE. AT THE SAME TIME, I CAN'T NOT CARE...
NO ONE UNDERSTANDS ME. THEY DON'T KNOW THAT IF I'M CRYING, IT'S NOT BECAUSE OF TEST SCORES.

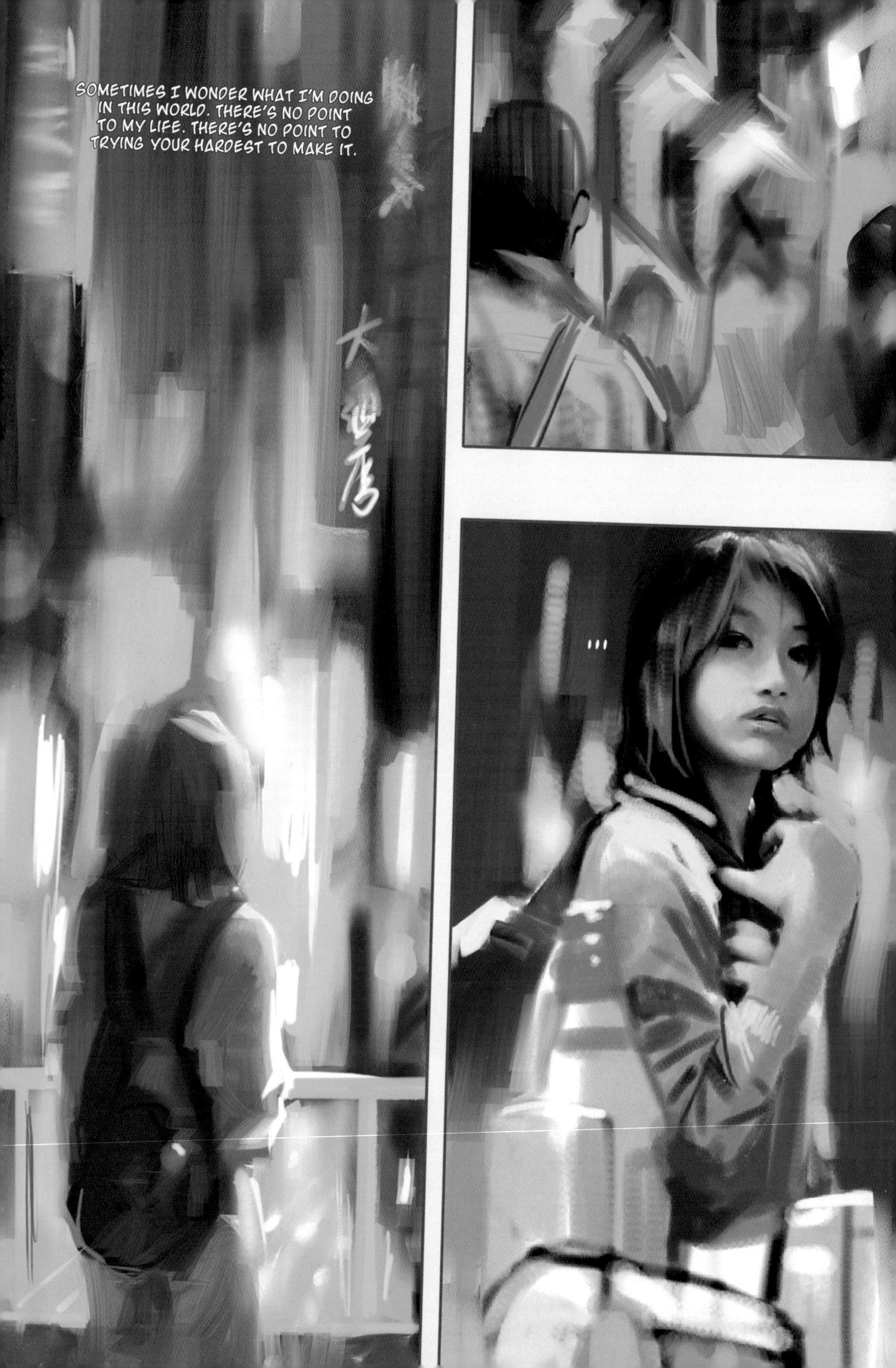
SOMETIMES I WONDER WHAT I'M DOING IN THIS WORLD. THERE'S NO POINT TO MY LIFE. THERE'S NO POINT TO TRYING YOUR HARDEST TO MAKE IT.
...

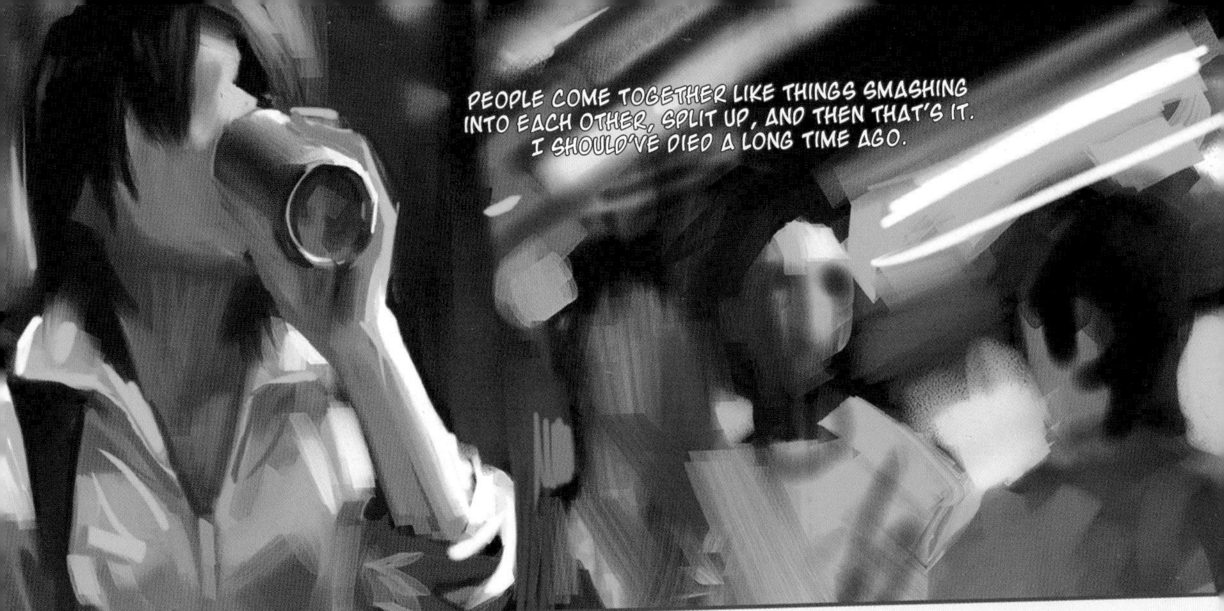
PEOPLE COME TOGETHER LIKE THINGS SMASHING INTO EACH OTHER, SPLIT UP, AND THEN THAT'S IT. I SHOULD'VE DIED A LONG TIME AGO.

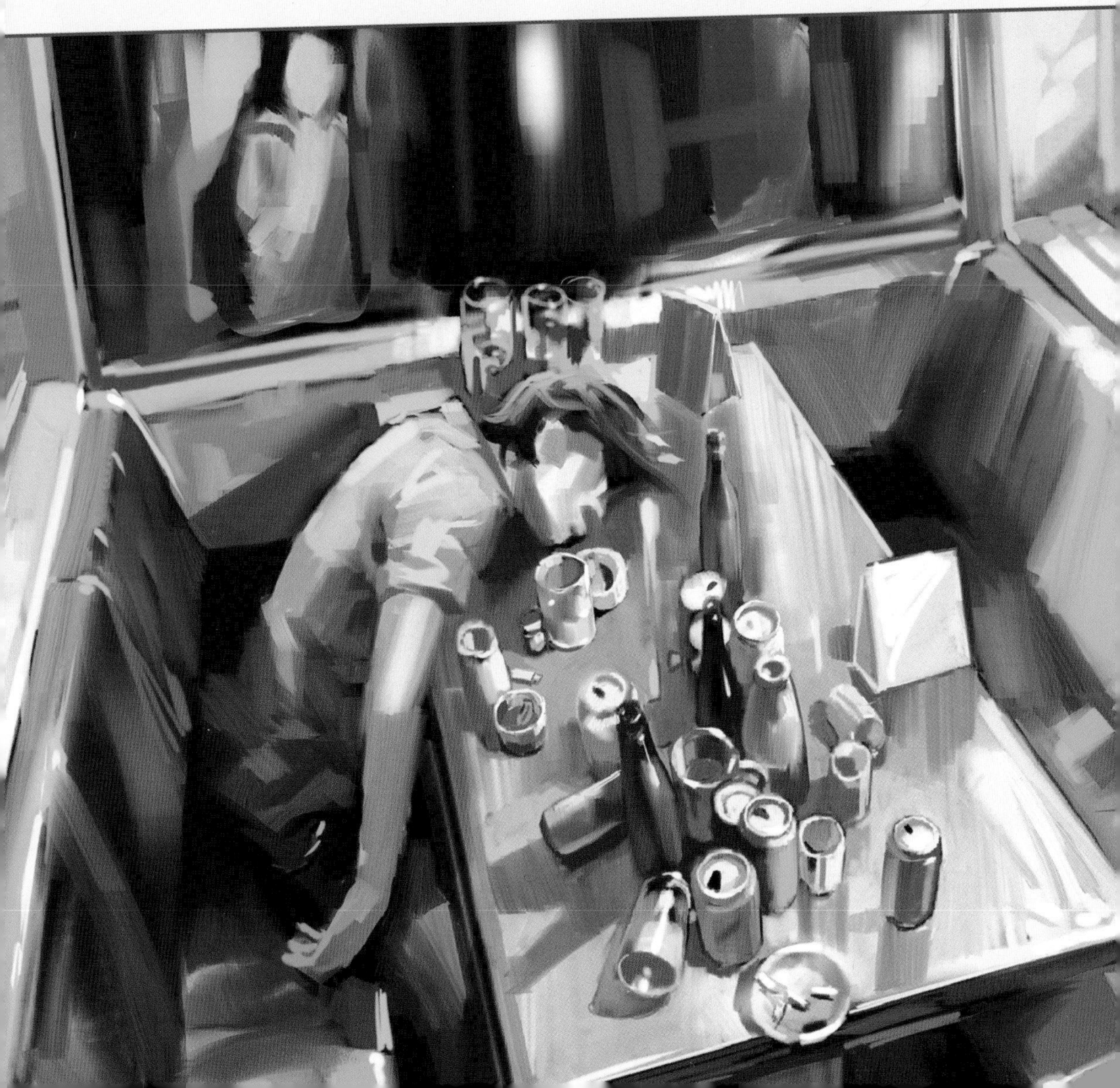

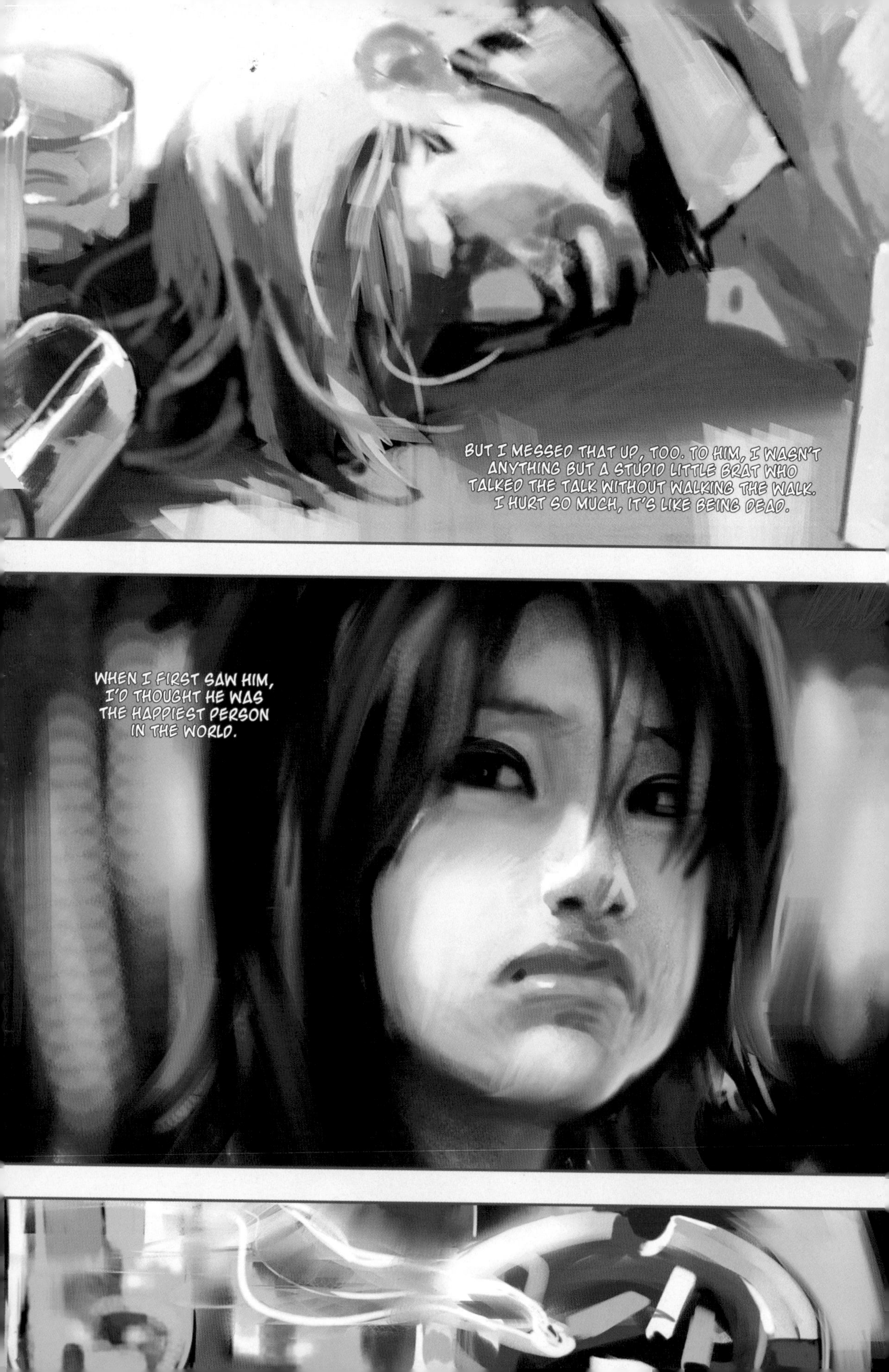
BUT I MESSED THAT UP, TOO. TO HIM, I WASN'T ANYTHING BUT A STUPID LITTLE BRAT WHO TALKED THE TALK WITHOUT WALKING THE WALK. I HURT SO MUCH, IT'S LIKE BEING DEAD.
WHEN I FIRST SAW HIM, I'D THOUGHT HE WAS THE HAPPIEST PERSON IN THE WORLD.

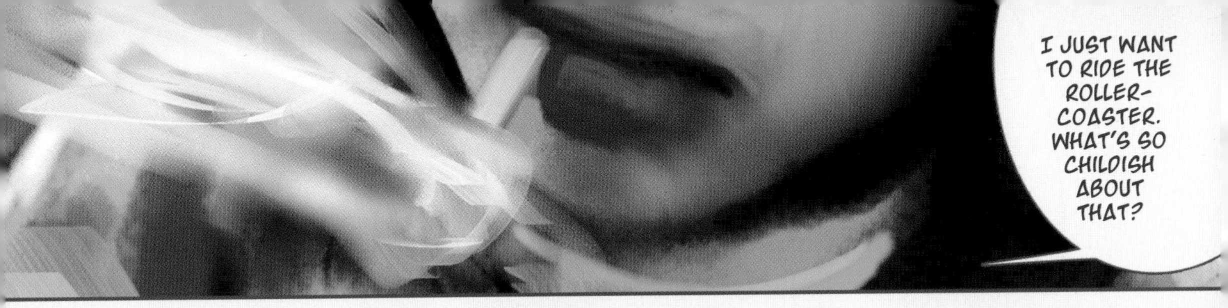
I JUST WANT TO RIDE THE ROLLER-COASTER. WHAT'S SO CHILDISH ABOUT THAT?

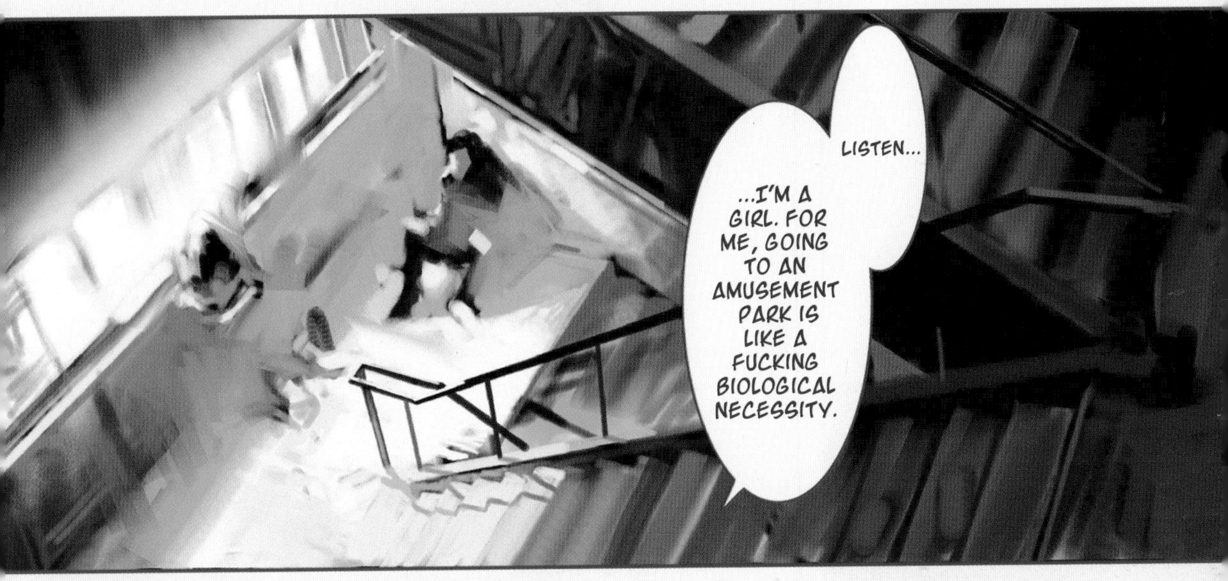
LISTEN...
...I'M A GIRL. FOR ME, GOING TO AN AMUSEMENT PARK IS LIKE A FUCKING BIOLOGICAL NECESSITY.

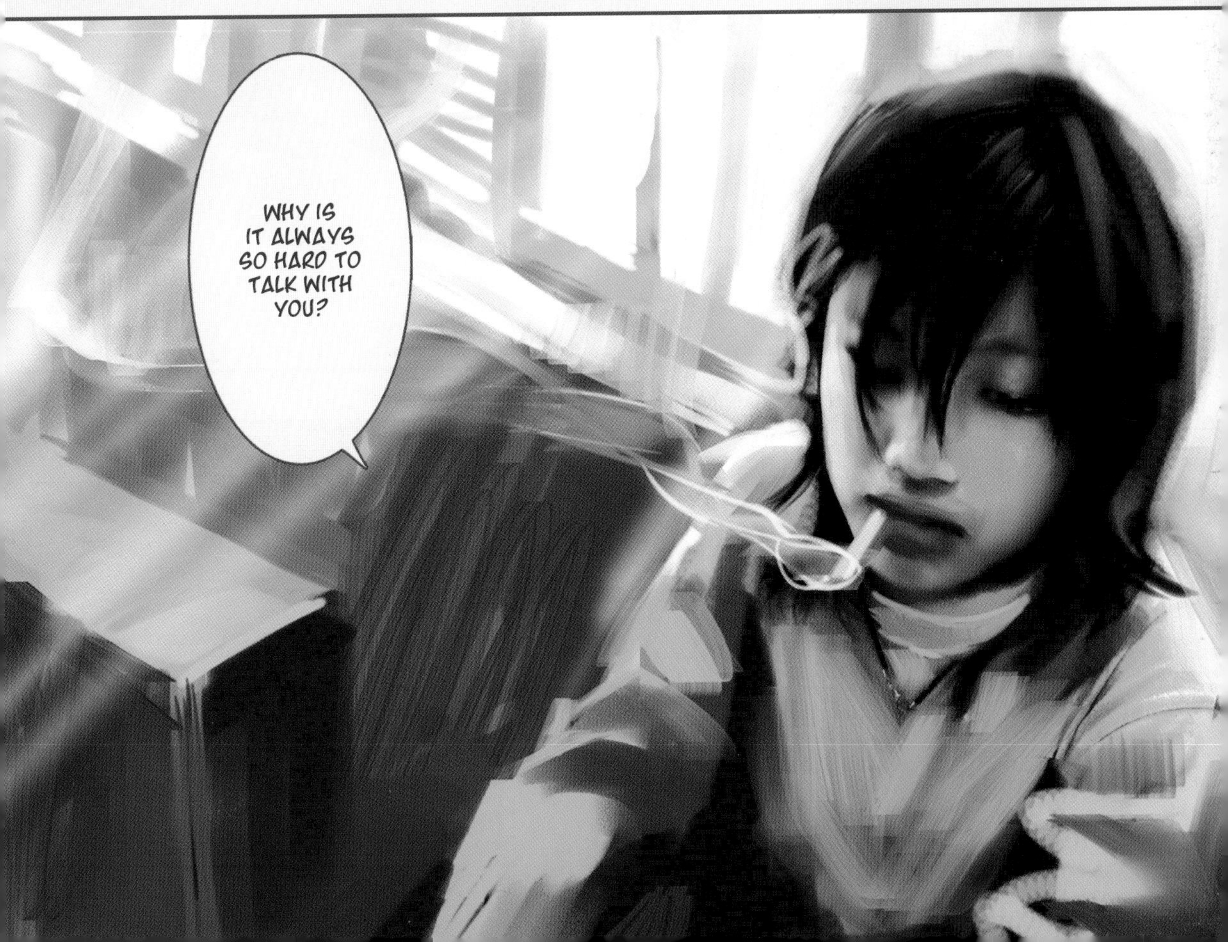
WHY IS IT ALWAYS SO HARD TO TALK WITH YOU?

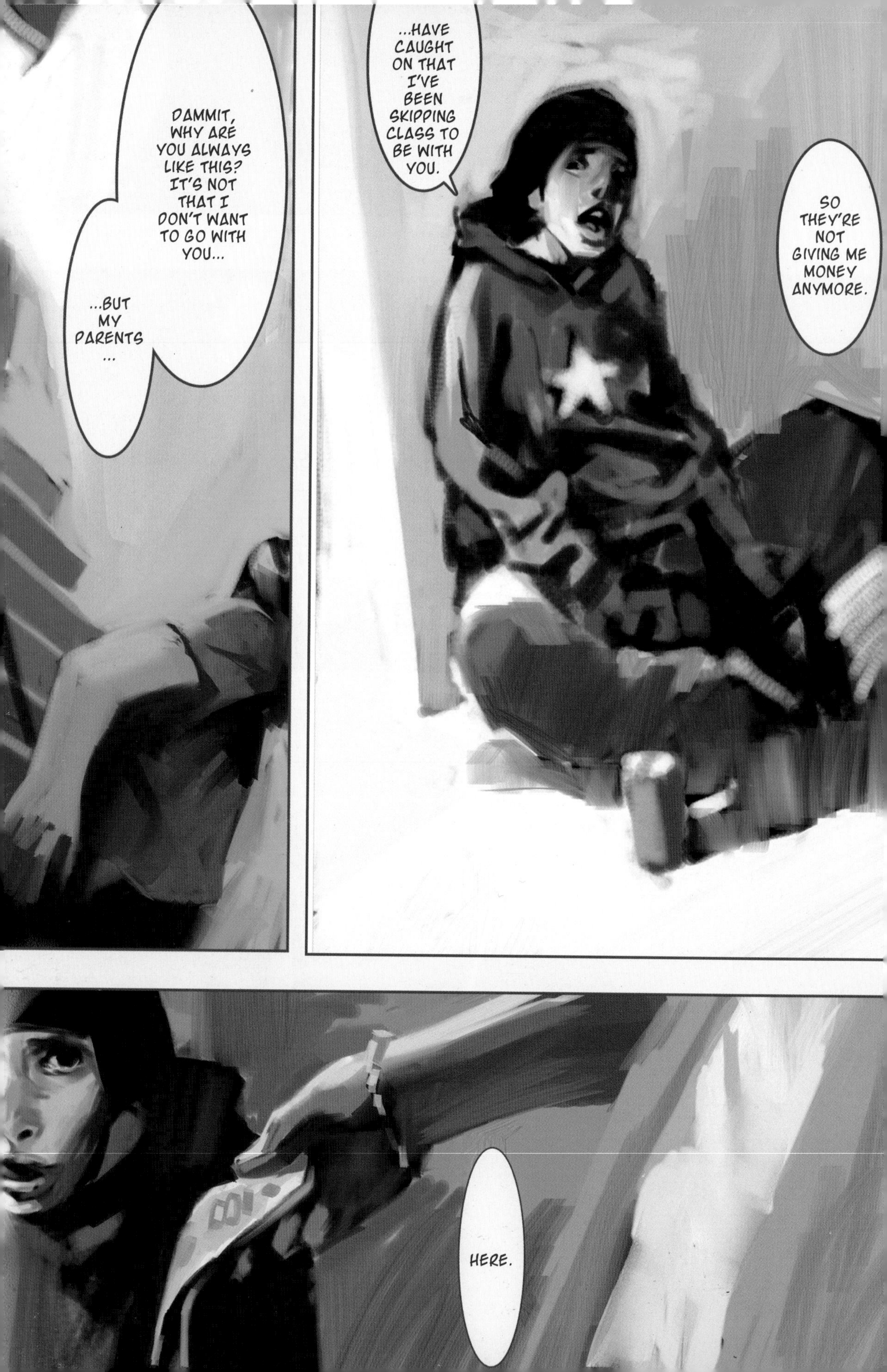
DAMMIT, WHY ARE YOU ALWAYS LIKE THIS? IT'S NOT THAT I DON'T WANT TO GO WITH YOU...
...BUT MY PARENTS ...
...HAVE CAUGHT ON THAT I'VE BEEN SKIPPING CLASS TO BE WITH YOU.
SO THEY'RE NOT GIVING ME MONEY ANYMORE.
HERE.

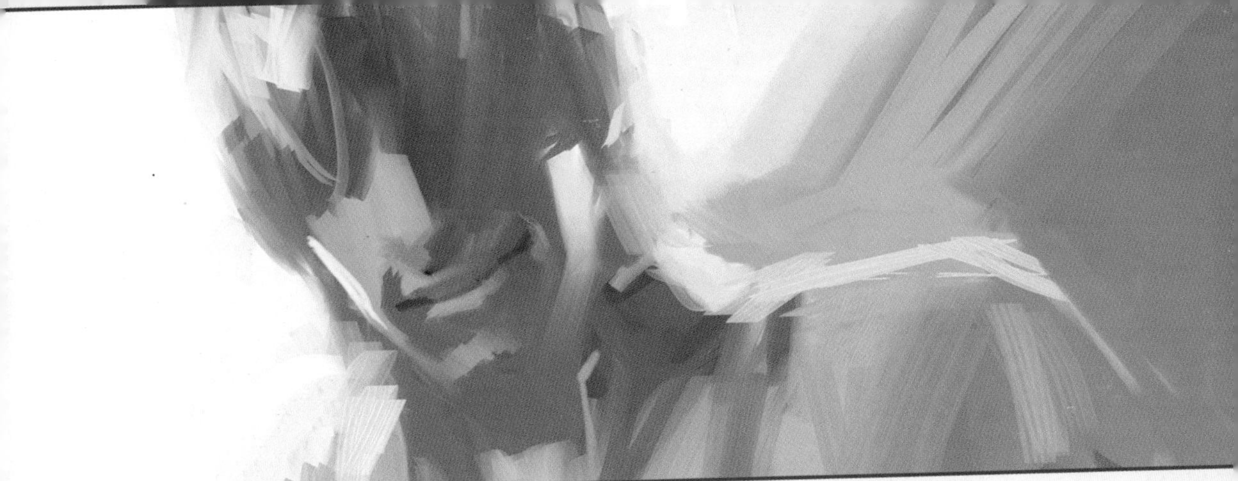

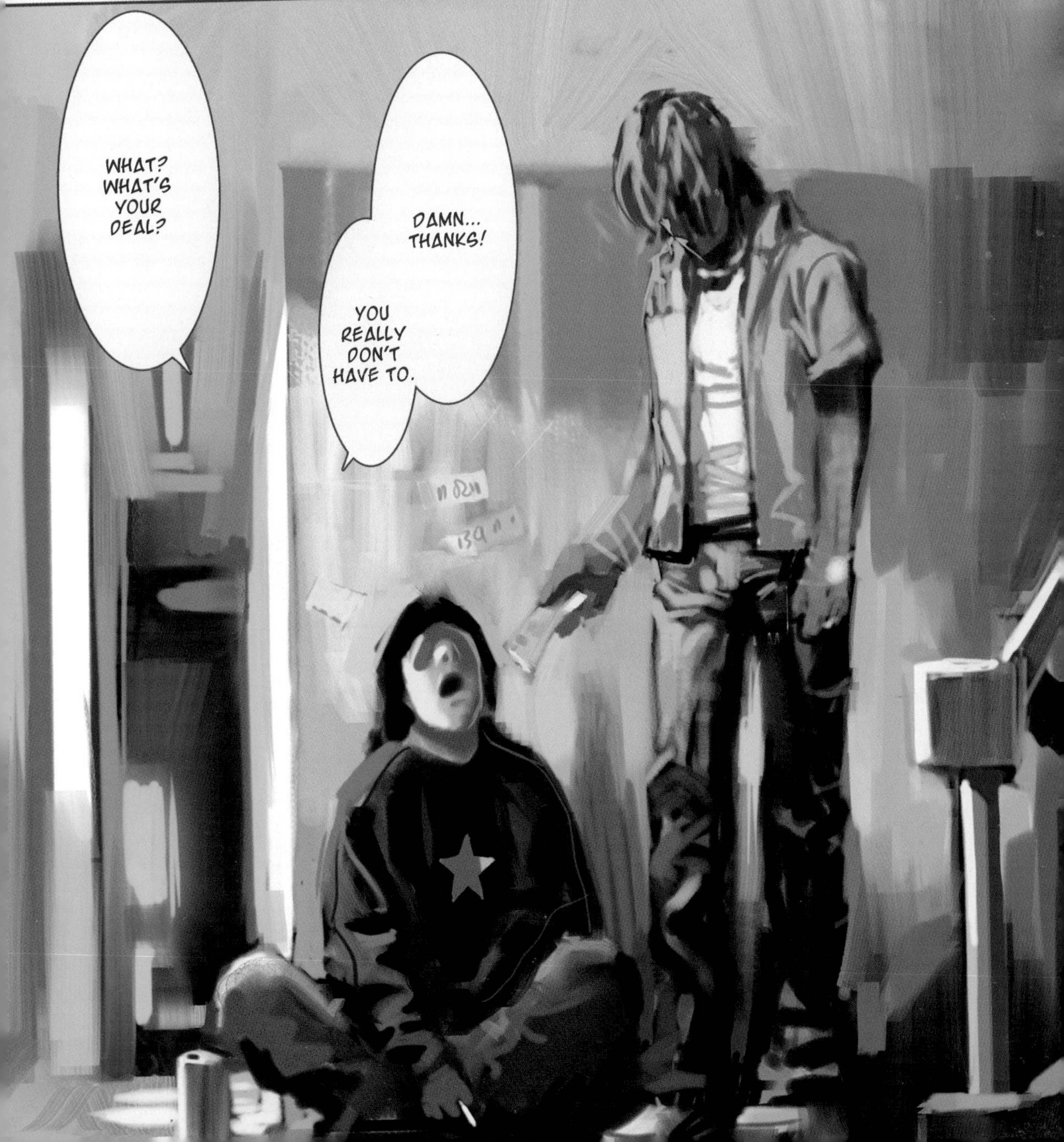
WHAT? WHAT'S YOUR DEAL?
DAMN... THANKS!
YOU REALLY DON'T HAVE TO.

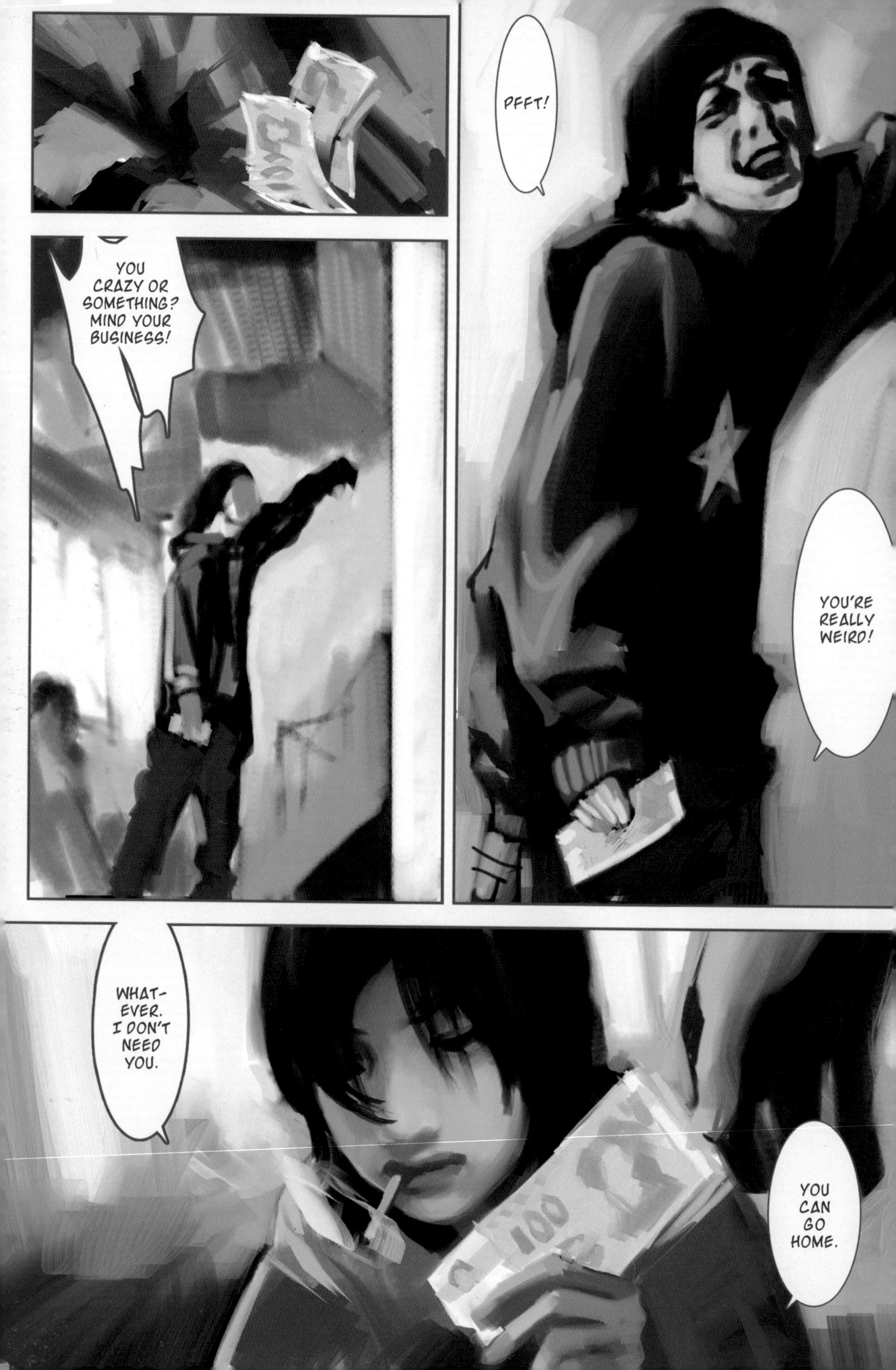
YOU CRAZY OR SOMETHING? MIND YOUR BUSINESS!
PFFT!
YOU'RE REALLY WEIRD!
WHAT-EVER. I DON'T NEED YOU.
YOU CAN GO HOME.

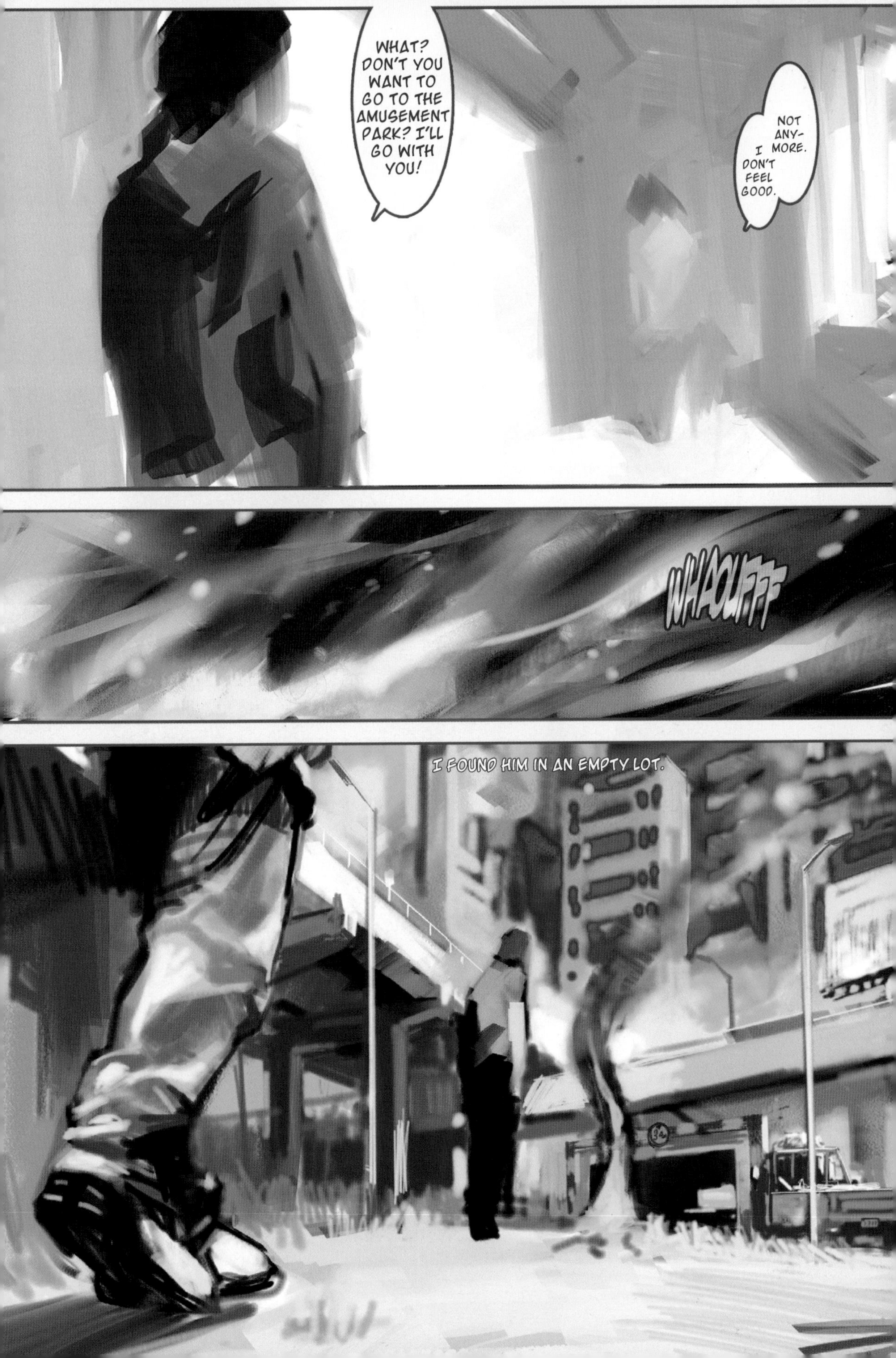
WHAT? DON'T YOU WANT TO GO TO THE AMUSEMENT PARK? I'LL GO WITH YOU!
NOT ANYMORE. I DON'T FEEL GOOD.
WHAOUFFF
I FOUND HIM IN AN EMPTY LOT.

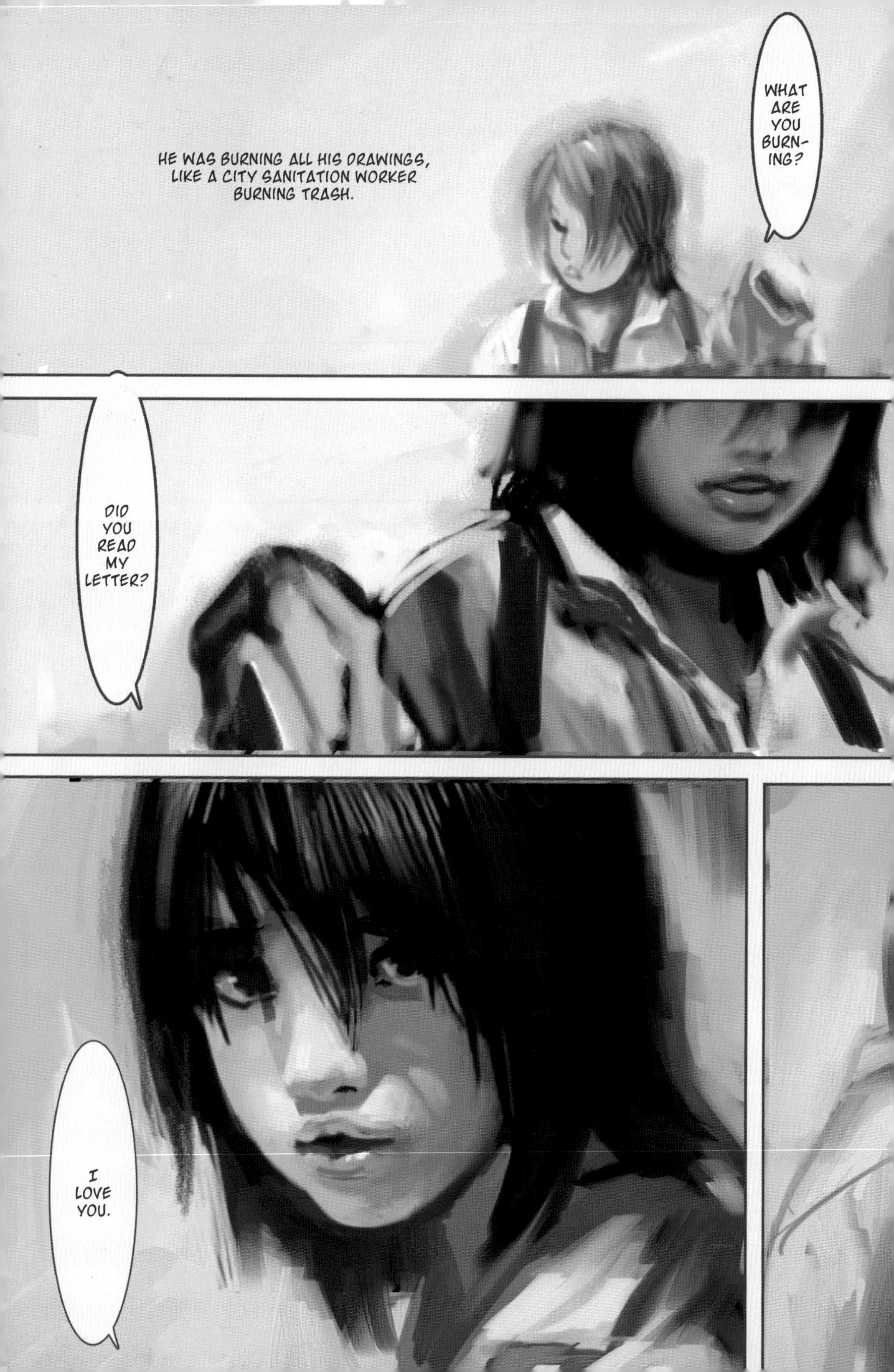
WHAT ARE YOU BURN-ING?
HE WAS BURNING ALL HIS DRAWINGS, LIKE A CITY SANITATION WORKER BURNING TRASH.
DID YOU READ MY LETTER?
I LOVE YOU.

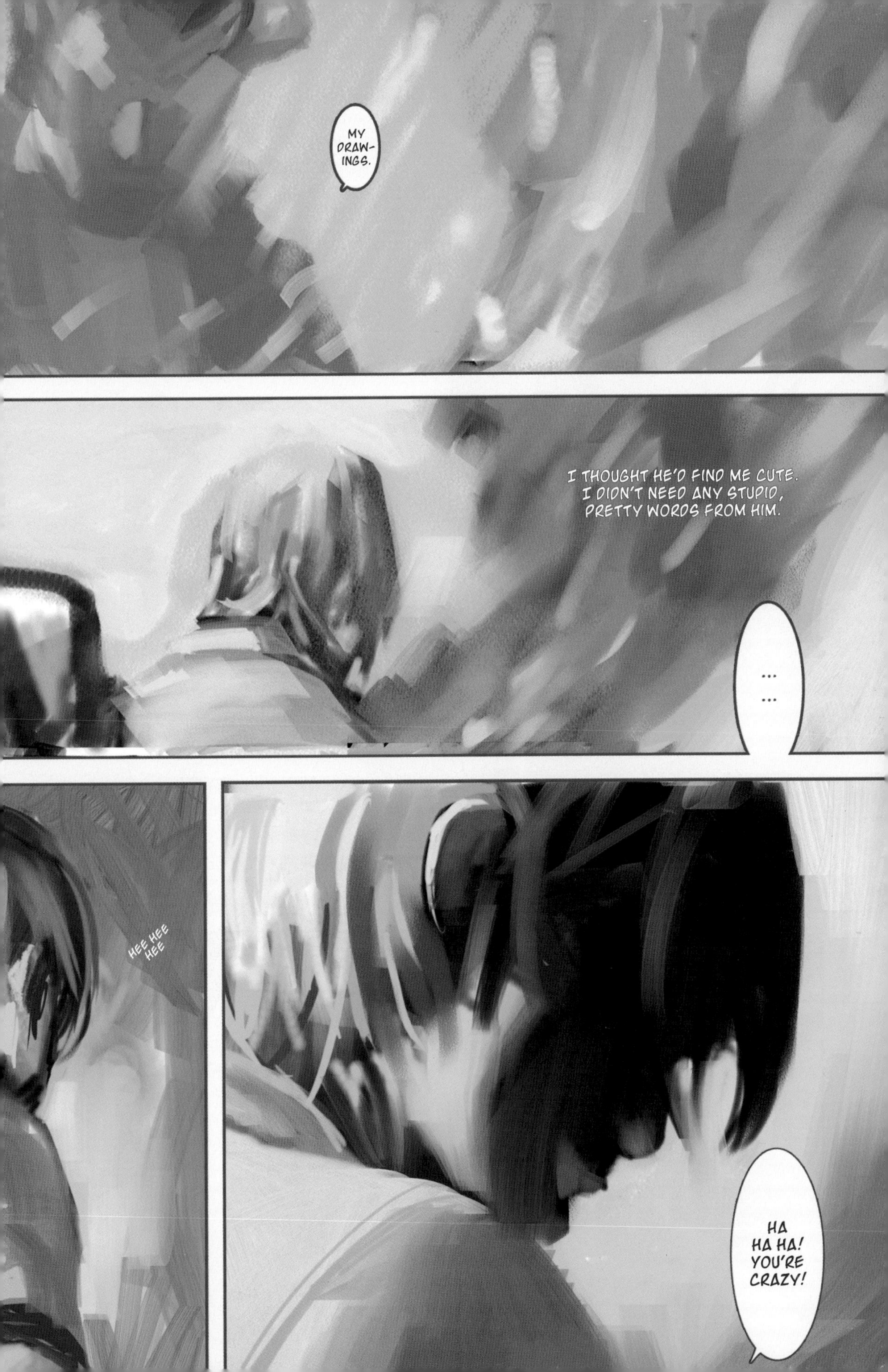
MY DRAWINGS.
I THOUGHT HE'D FIND ME CUTE. I DIDN'T NEED ANY STUPID, PRETTY WORDS FROM HIM.
......
HA HA HA! YOU'RE CRAZY!
HEE HEE HEE

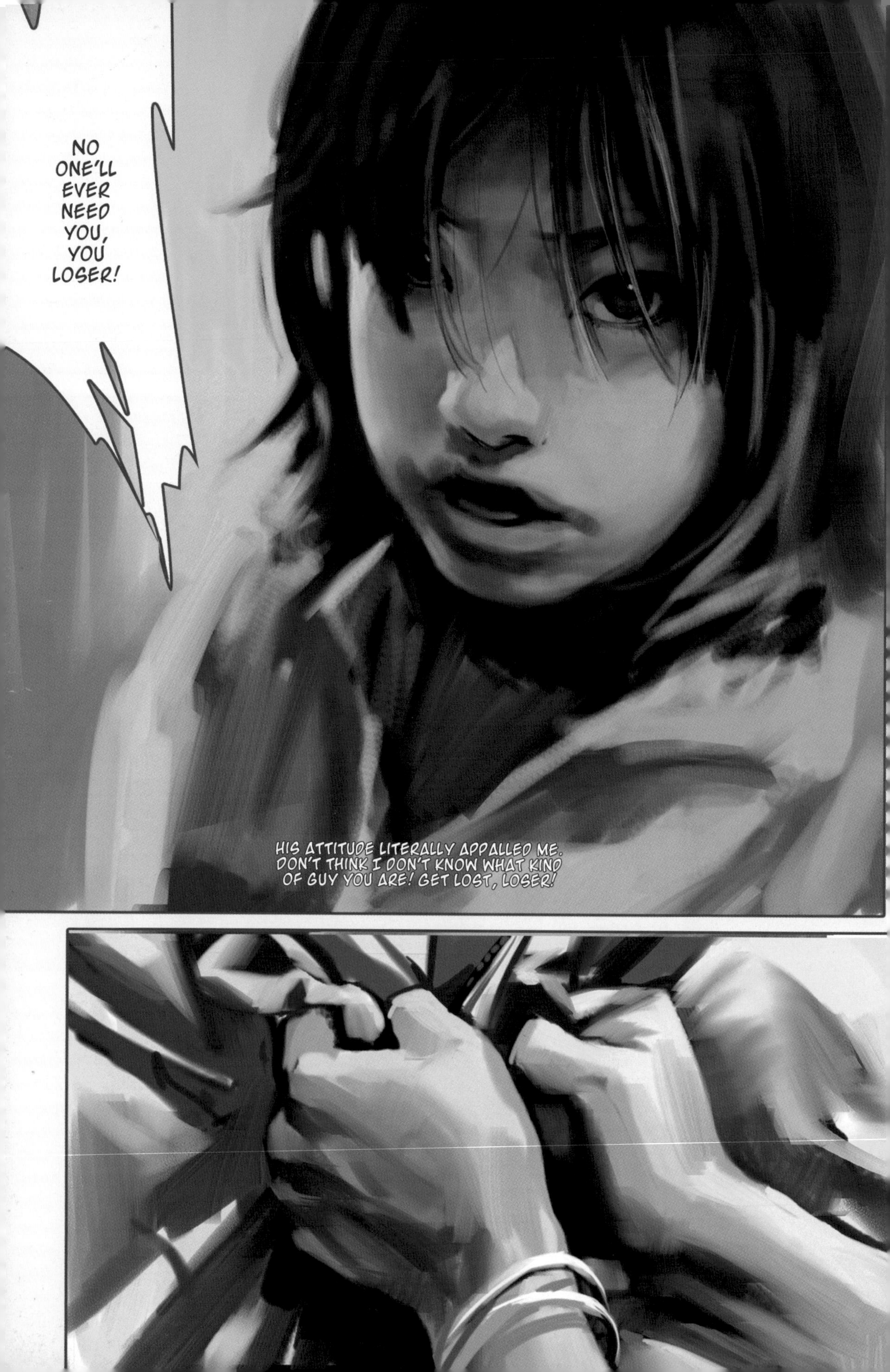
NO ONE'LL EVER NEED YOU, YOU LOSER!
HIS ATTITUDE LITERALLY APPALLED ME. DON'T THINK I DON'T KNOW WHAT KIND OF GUY YOU ARE! GET LOST, LOSER!

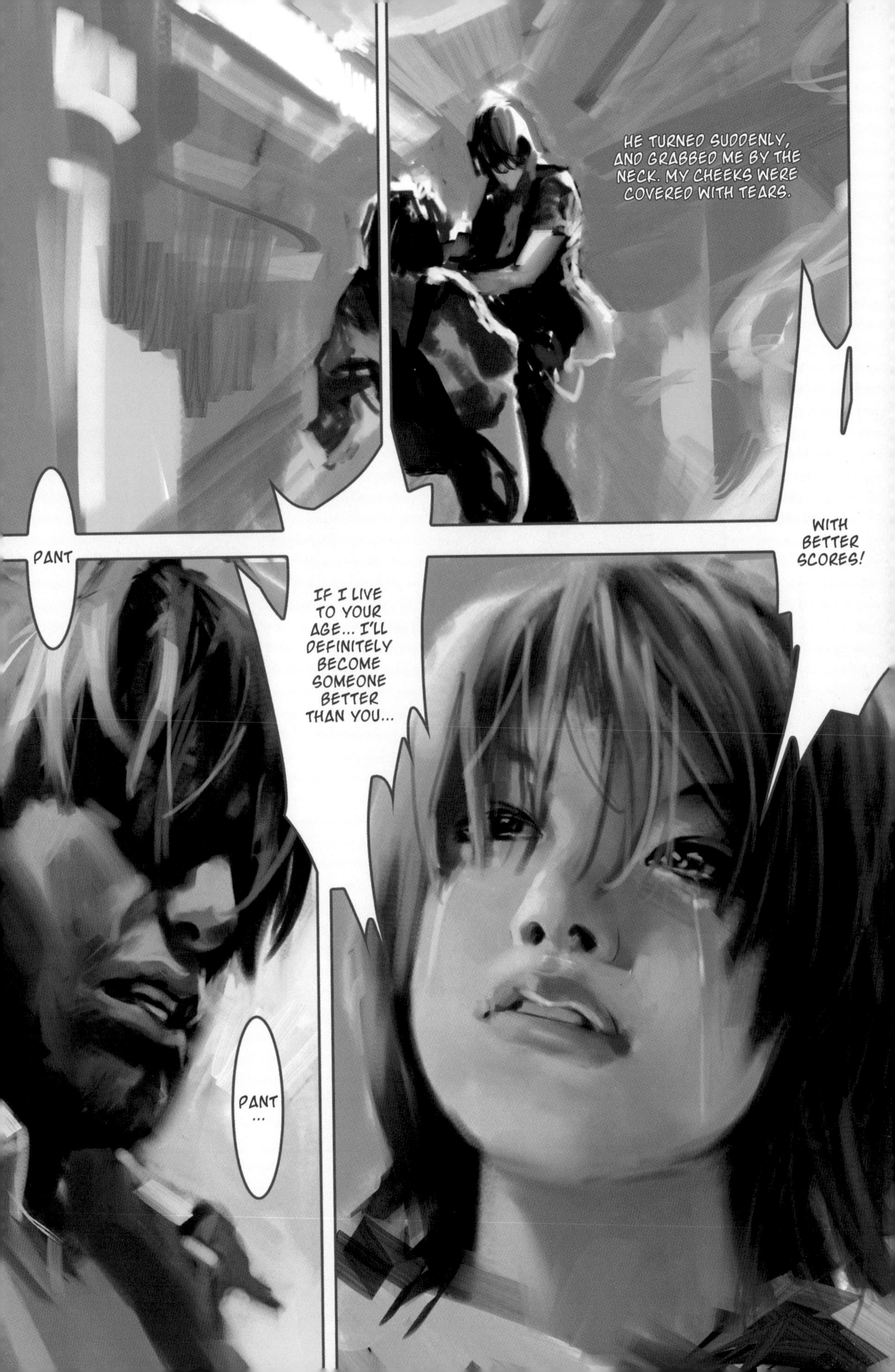
HE TURNED SUDDENLY, AND GRABBED ME BY THE NECK. MY CHEEKS WERE COVERED WITH TEARS.
PANT
IF I LIVE TO YOUR AGE... I'LL DEFINITELY BECOME SOMEONE BETTER THAN YOU...
WITH BETTER SCORES!
PANT ...

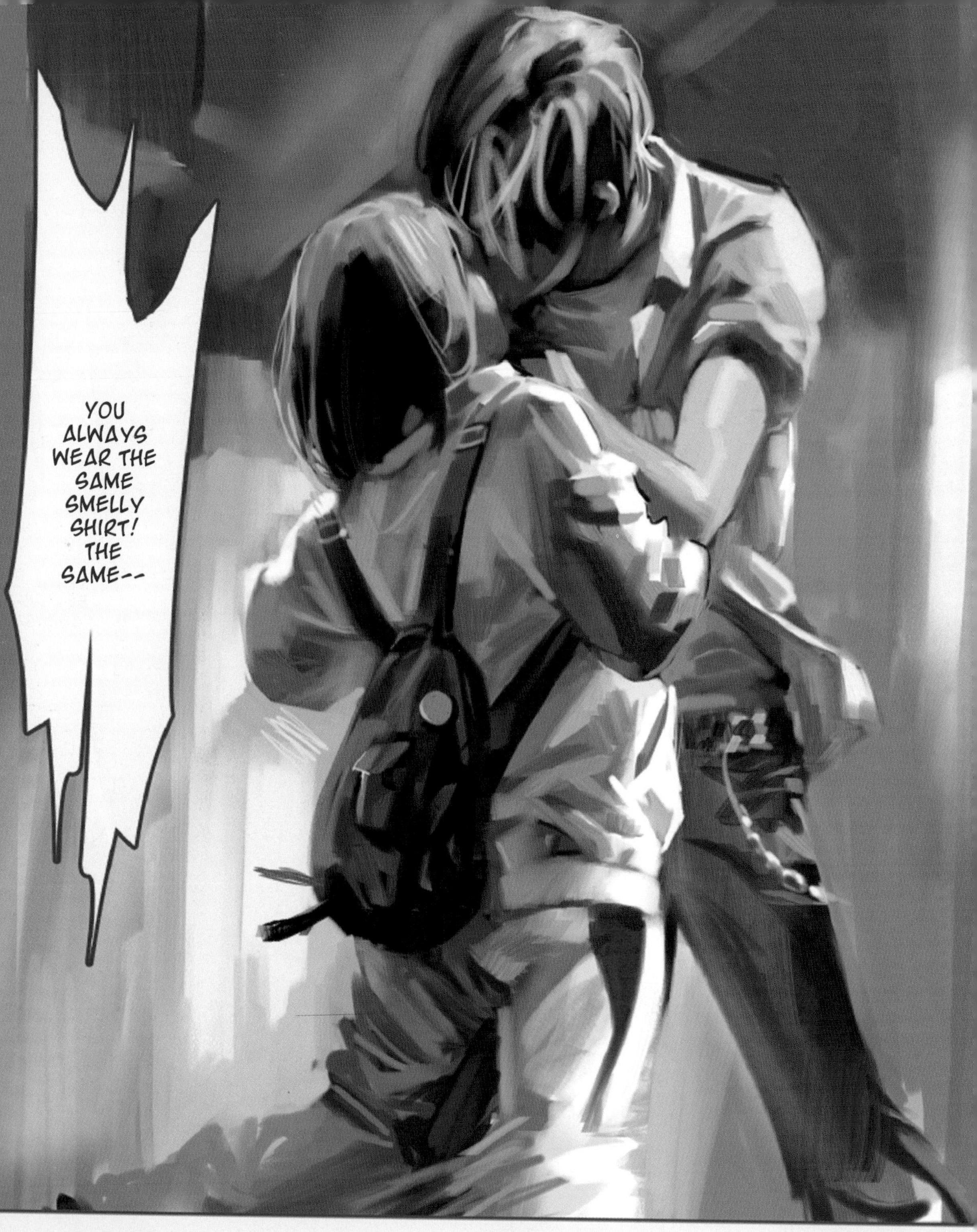
YOU ALWAYS WEAR THE SAME SMELLY SHIRT! THE SAME--

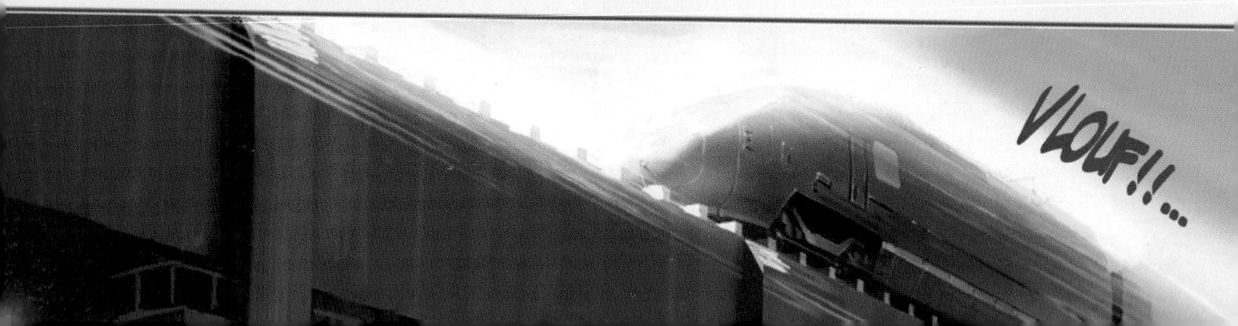
VLOUF!!...

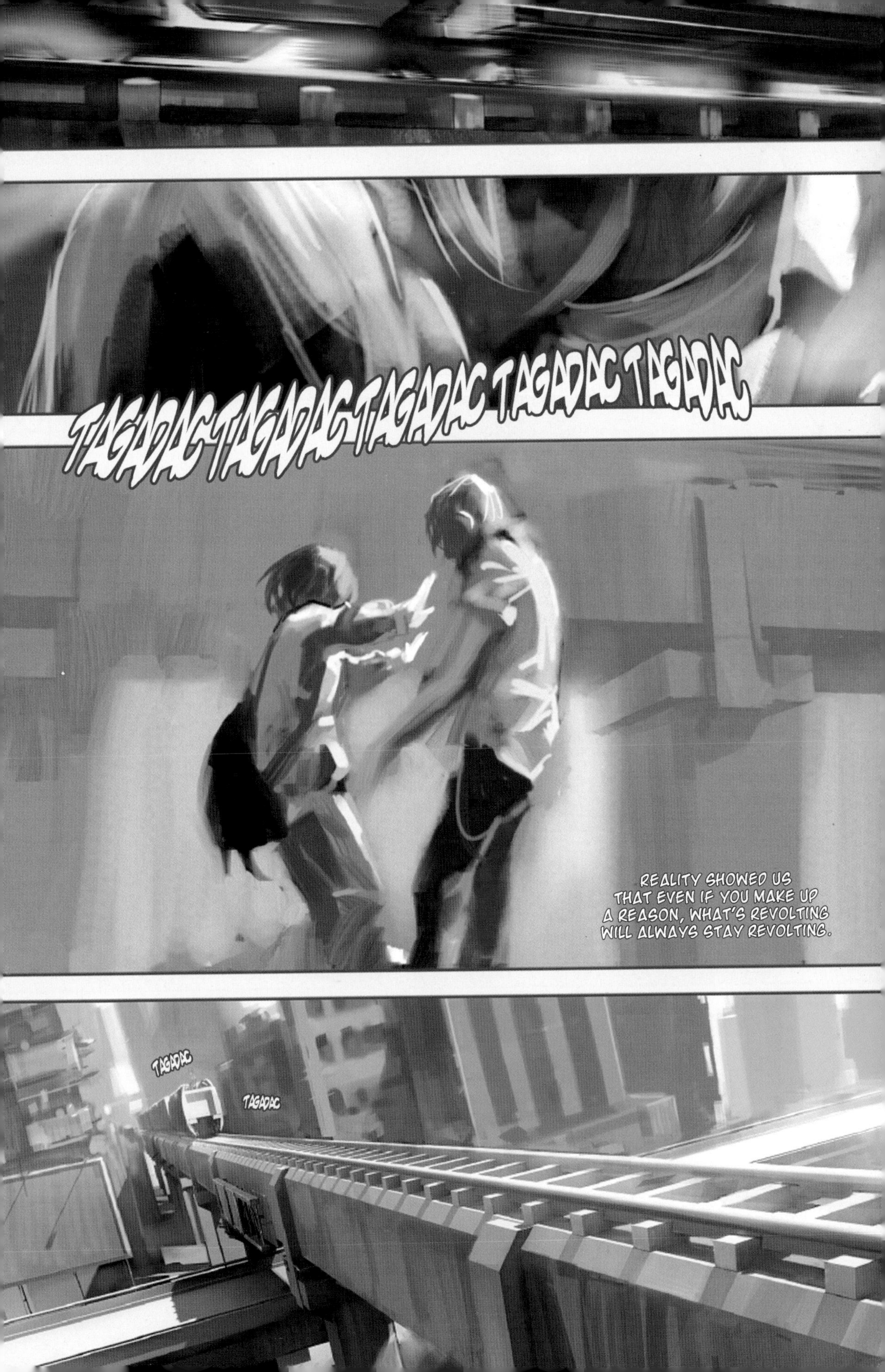
TAGADAC TAGADAC TAGADAC TAGADAC TAGADAC
REALITY SHOWED US THAT EVEN IF YOU MAKE UP A REASON, WHAT'S REVOLTING WILL ALWAYS STAY REVOLTING.
TAGADAC
TAGADAC

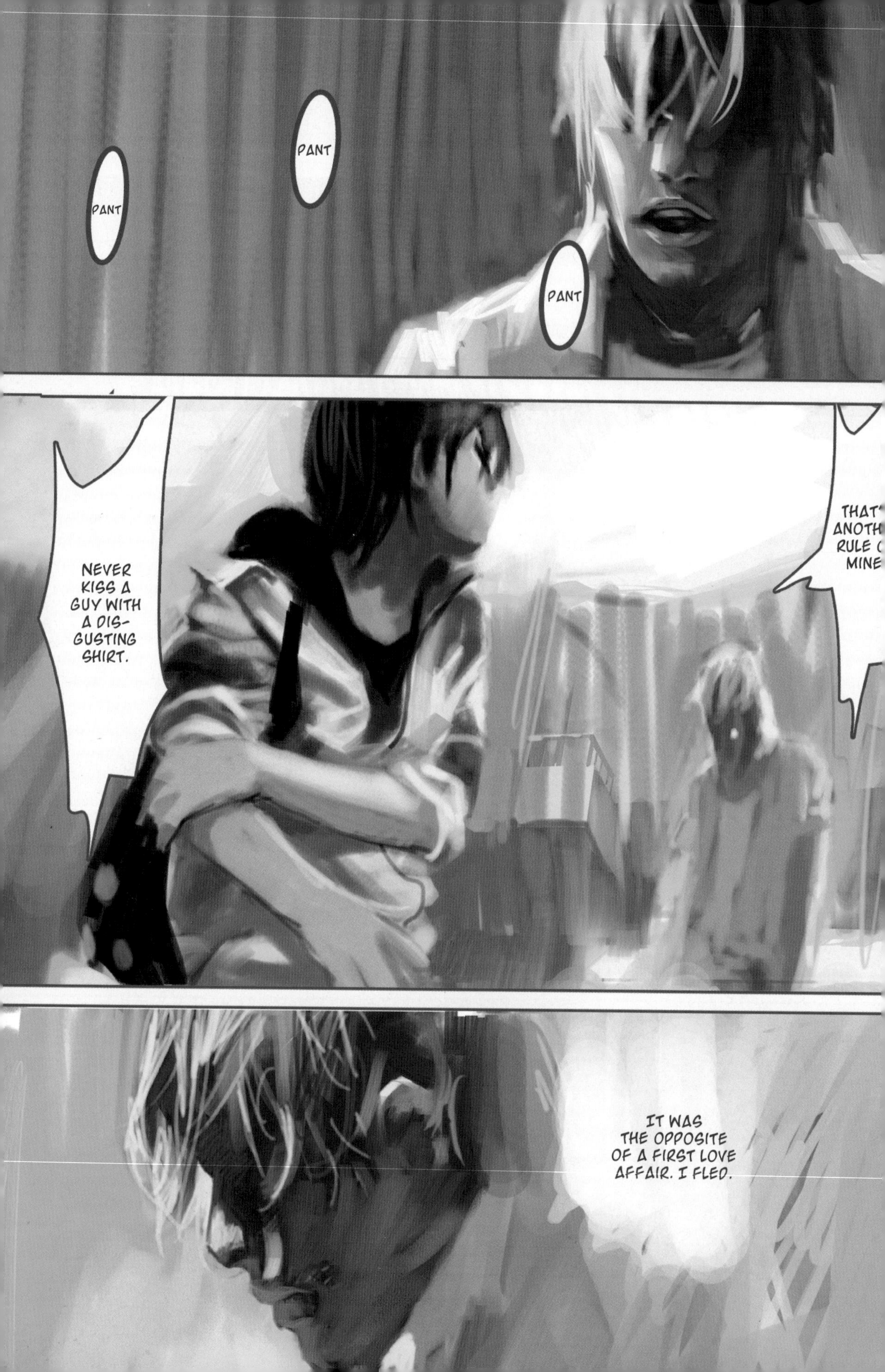
PANT
PANT
PANT
NEVER KISS A GUY WITH A DIS-GUSTING SHIRT.
IT WAS THE OPPOSITE OF A FIRST LOVE AFFAIR. I FLED.

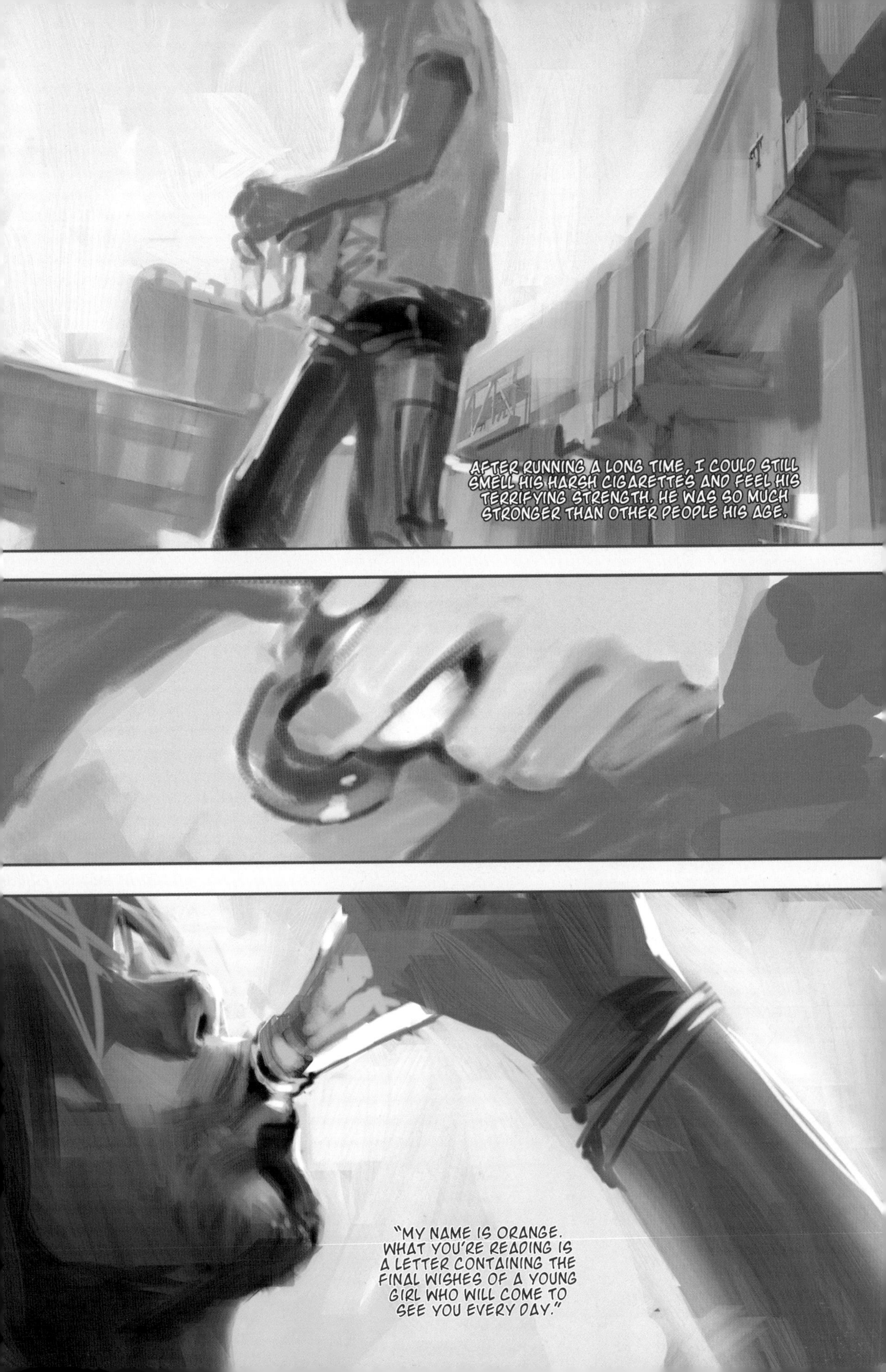
AFTER RUNNING A LONG TIME, I COULD STILL SMELL HIS HARSH CIGARETTES AND FEEL HIS TERRIFYING STRENGTH. HE WAS SO MUCH STRONGER THAN OTHER PEOPLE HIS AGE.
"MY NAME IS ORANGE. WHAT YOU'RE READING IS A LETTER CONTAINING THE FINAL WISHES OF A YOUNG GIRL WHO WILL COME TO SEE YOU EVERY DAY."

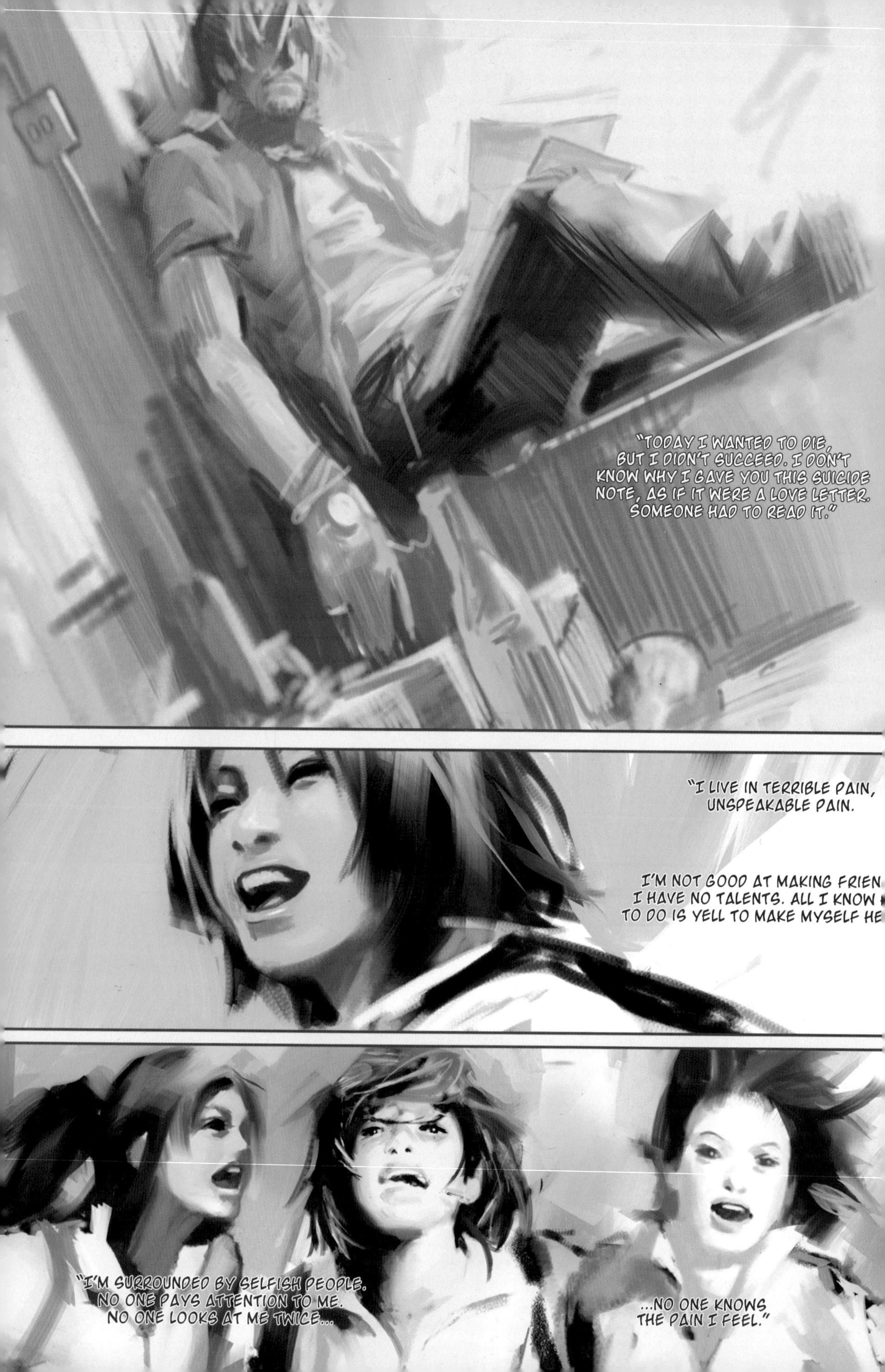
"TODAY I WANTED TO DIE, BUT I DIDN'T SUCCEED. I DON'T KNOW WHY I GAVE YOU THIS SUICIDE NOTE, AS IF IT WERE A LOVE LETTER. SOMEONE HAD TO READ IT."
"I LIVE IN TERRIBLE PAIN, UNSPEAKABLE PAIN.
I'M NOT GOOD AT MAKING FRIEN
I HAVE NO TALENTS. ALL I KNOW
TO DO IS YELL TO MAKE MYSELF HE
"I'M SURROUNDED BY SELFISH PEOPLE. NO ONE PAYS ATTENTION TO ME. NO ONE LOOKS AT ME TWICE...
...NO ONE KNOWS THE PAIN I FEEL."

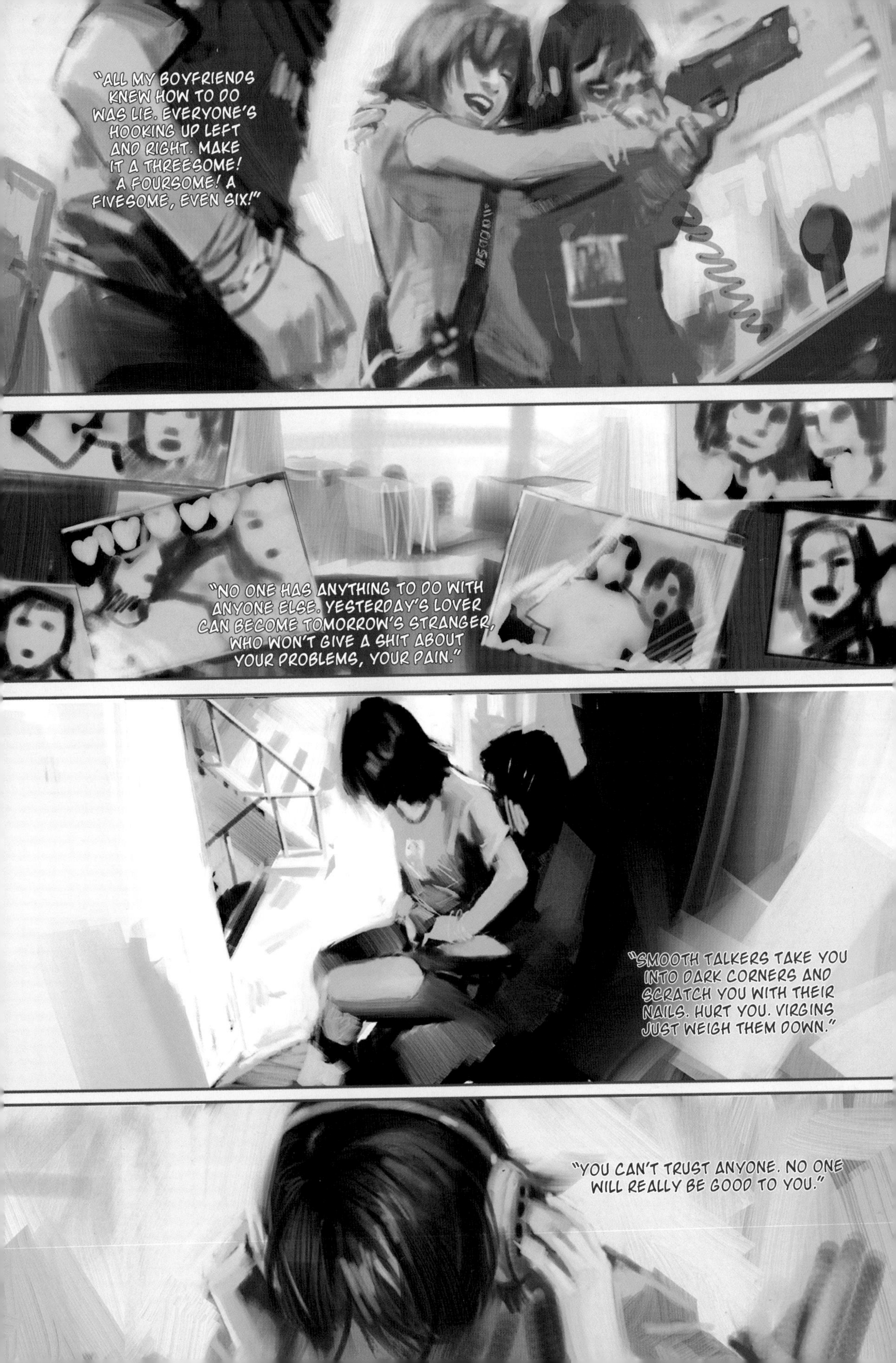
"ALL MY BOYFRIENDS KNEW HOW TO DO WAS LIE. EVERYONE'S HOOKING UP LEFT AND RIGHT. MAKE IT A THREESOME! A FOURSOME! A FIVESOME, EVEN SIX!"
"NO ONE HAS ANYTHING TO DO WITH ANYONE ELSE. YESTERDAY'S LOVER CAN BECOME TOMORROW'S STRANGER, WHO WON'T GIVE A SHIT ABOUT YOUR PROBLEMS, YOUR PAIN."
"SMOOTH TALKERS TAKE YOU INTO DARK CORNERS AND SCRATCH YOU WITH THEIR NAILS. HURT YOU. VIRGINS JUST WEIGH THEM DOWN."
"YOU CAN'T TRUST ANYONE. NO ONE WILL REALLY BE GOOD TO YOU."

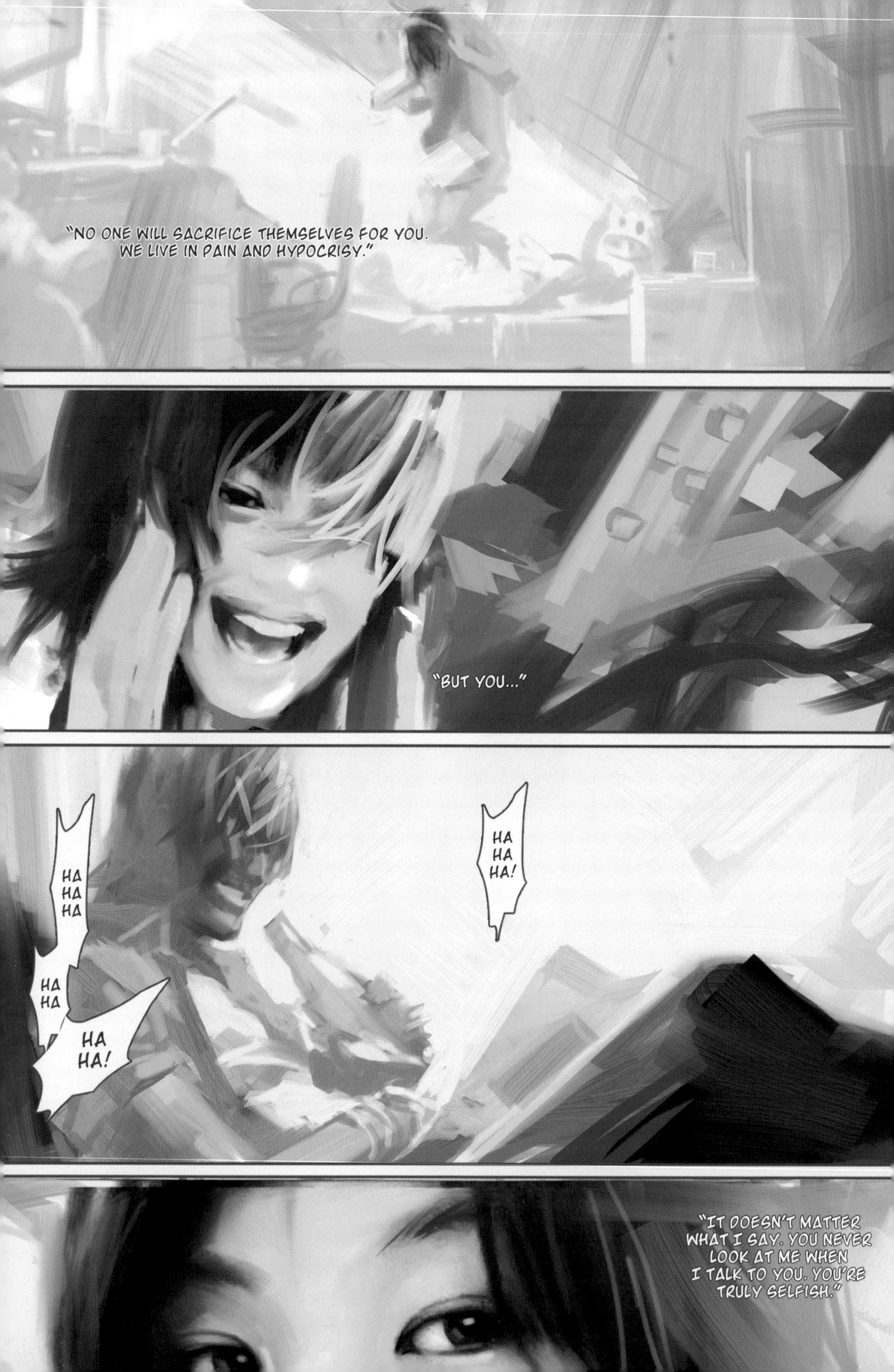
"NO ONE WILL SACRIFICE THEMSELVES FOR YOU. WE LIVE IN PAIN AND HYPOCRISY."
"BUT YOU..."
HA HA HA!
HA HA HA
HA HA
HA HA!
"IT DOESN'T MATTER WHAT I SAY. YOU NEVER LOOK AT ME WHEN I TALK TO YOU. YOU'RE TRULY SELFISH."

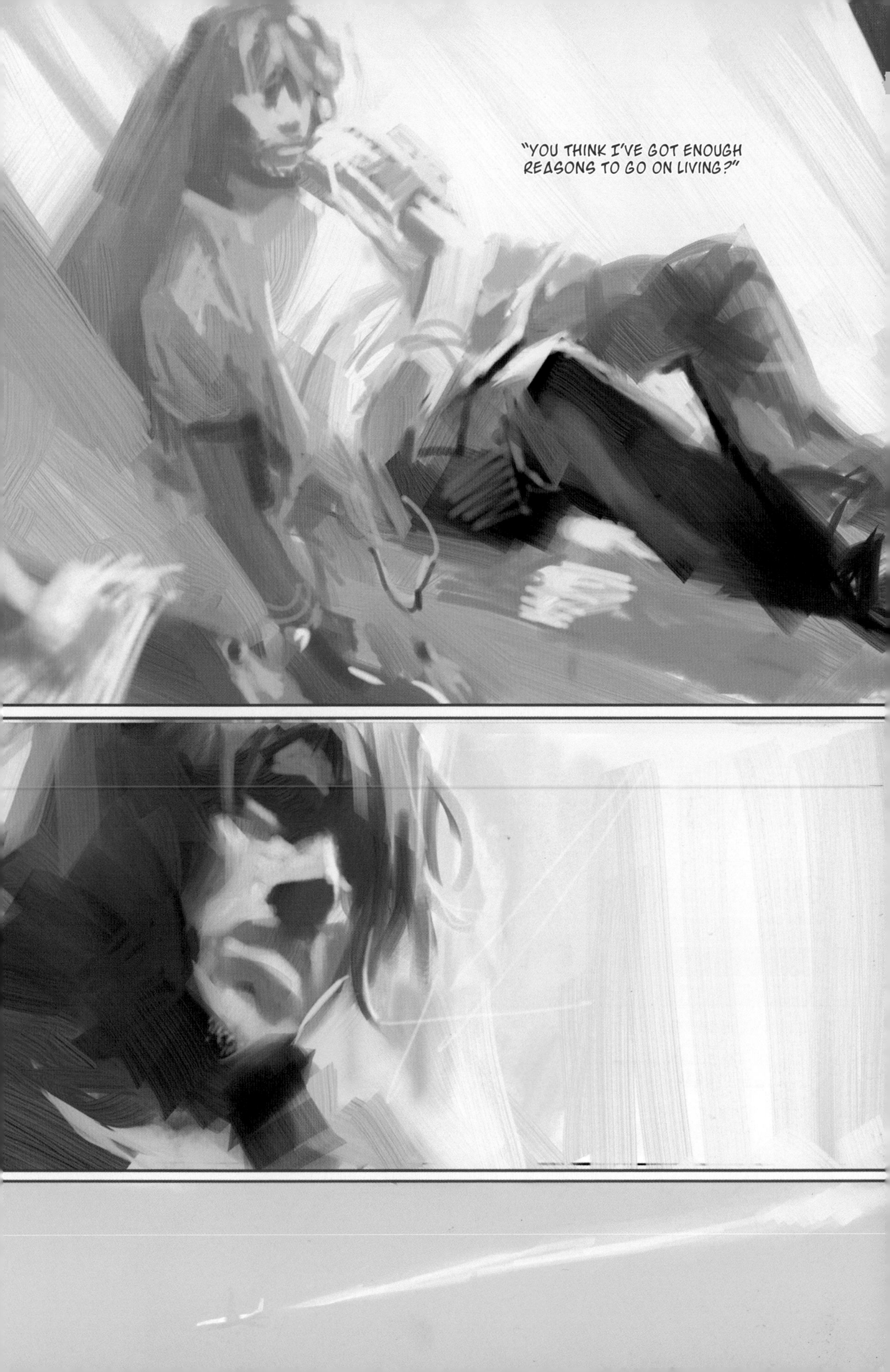
"YOU THINK I'VE GOT ENOUGH REASONS TO GO ON LIVING?"

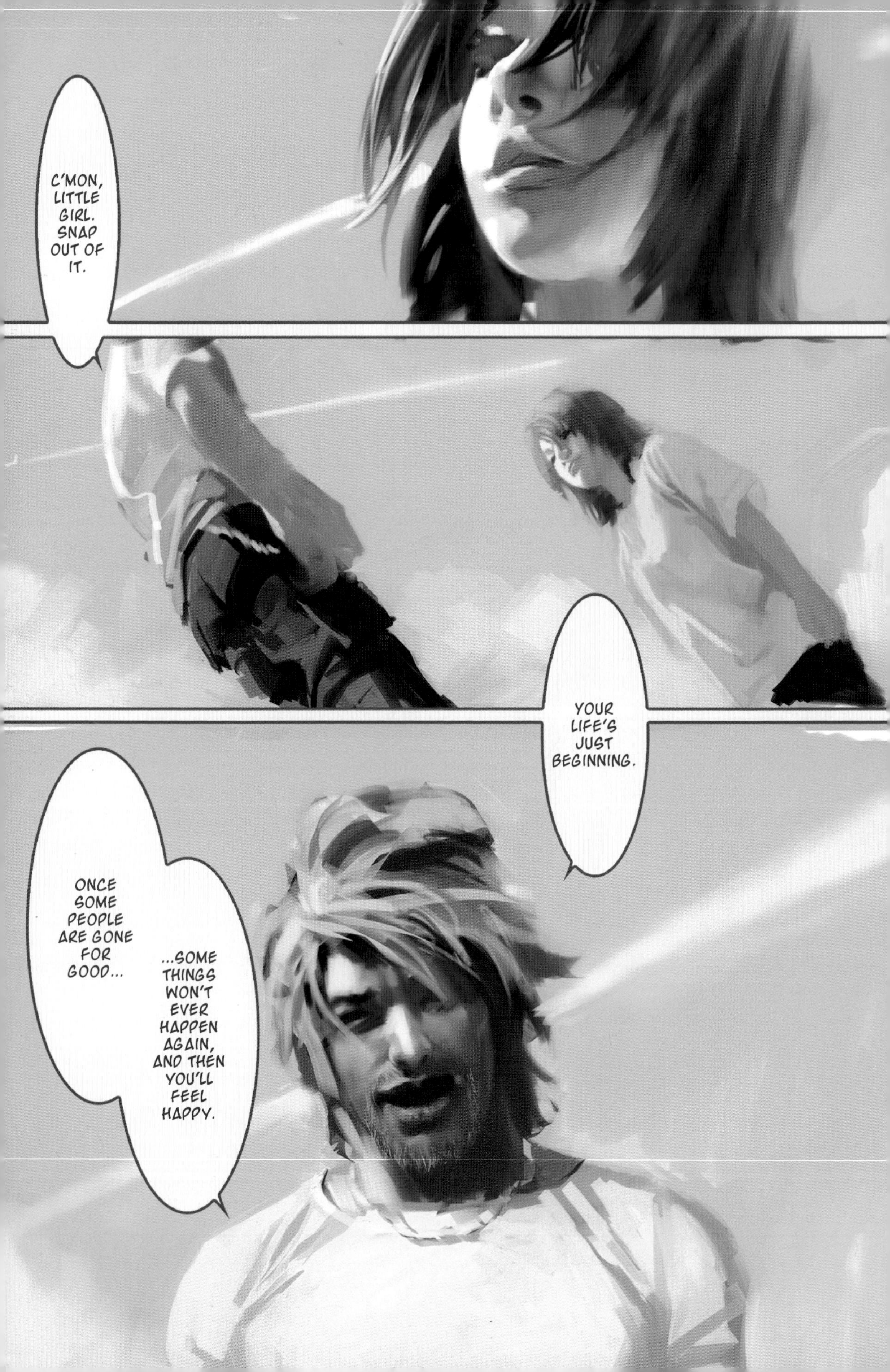
C'MON, LITTLE GIRL. SNAP OUT OF IT.
YOUR LIFE'S JUST BEGINNING.
ONCE SOME PEOPLE ARE GONE FOR GOOD...
...SOME THINGS WON'T EVER HAPPEN AGAIN, AND THEN YOU'LL FEEL HAPPY.

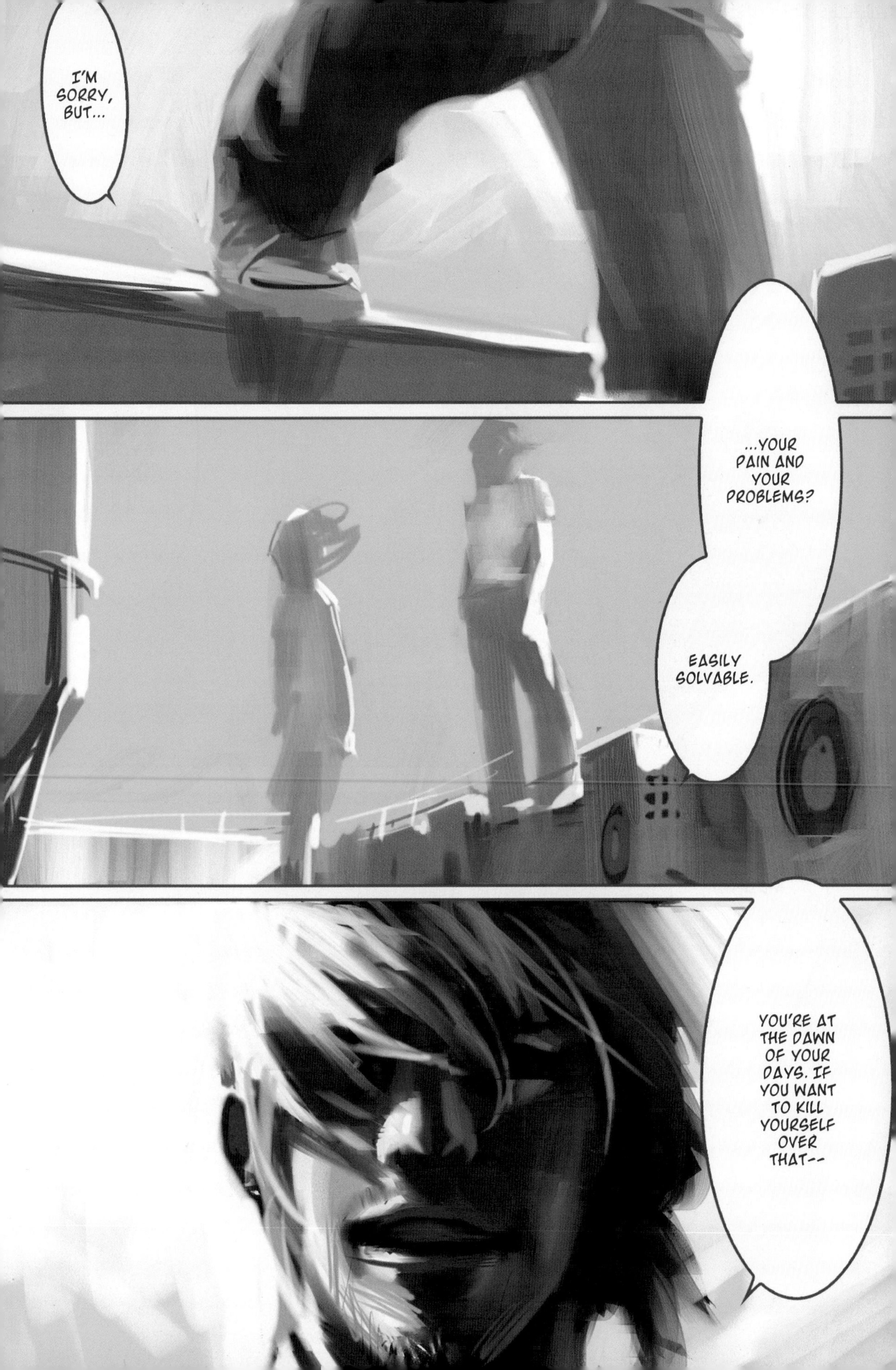
I'M SORRY, BUT...
...YOUR PAIN AND YOUR PROBLEMS?
EASILY SOLVABLE.
YOU'RE AT THE DAWN OF YOUR DAYS. IF YOU WANT TO KILL YOURSELF OVER THAT--

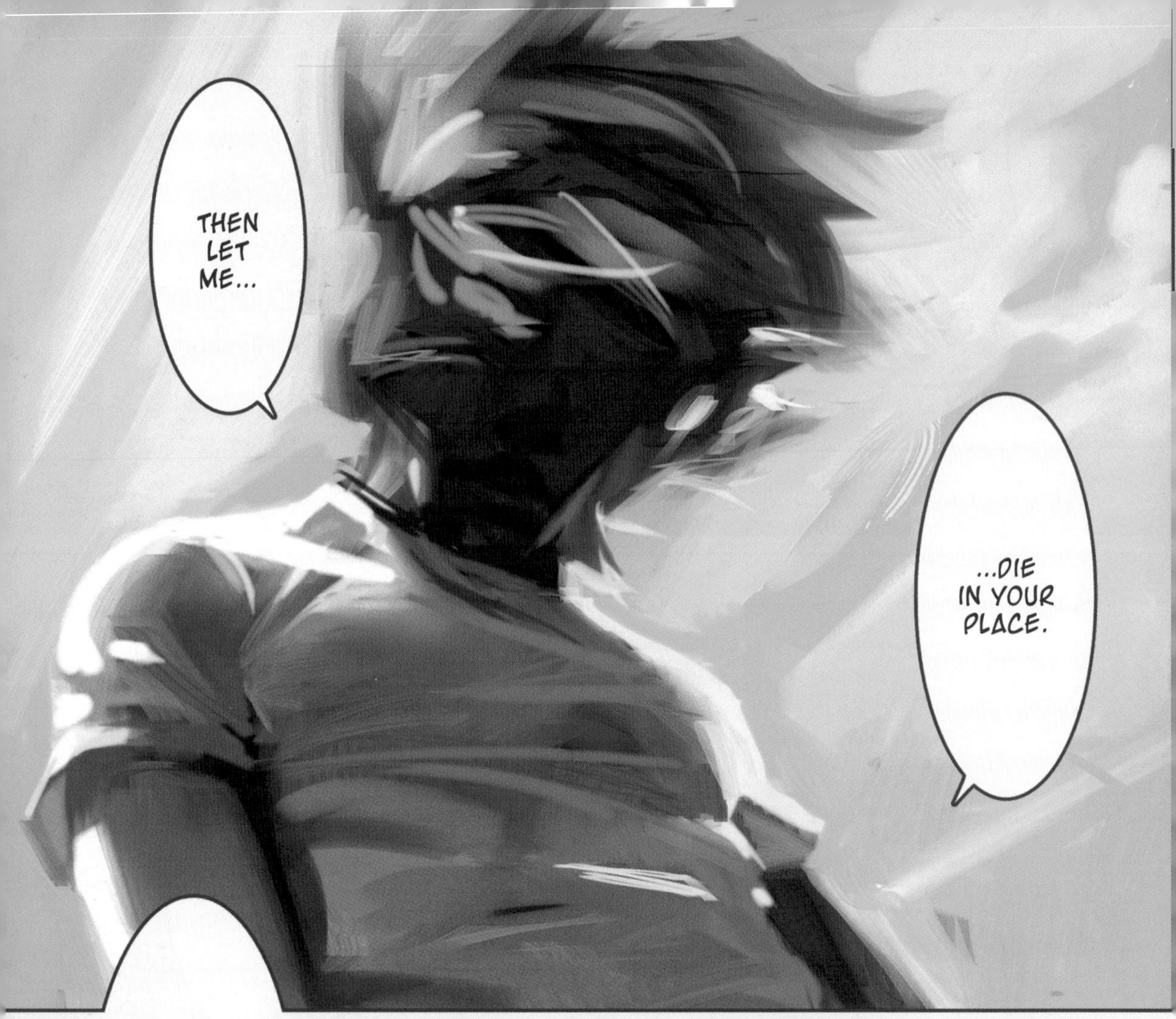
THEN LET ME...
...DIE IN YOUR PLACE.

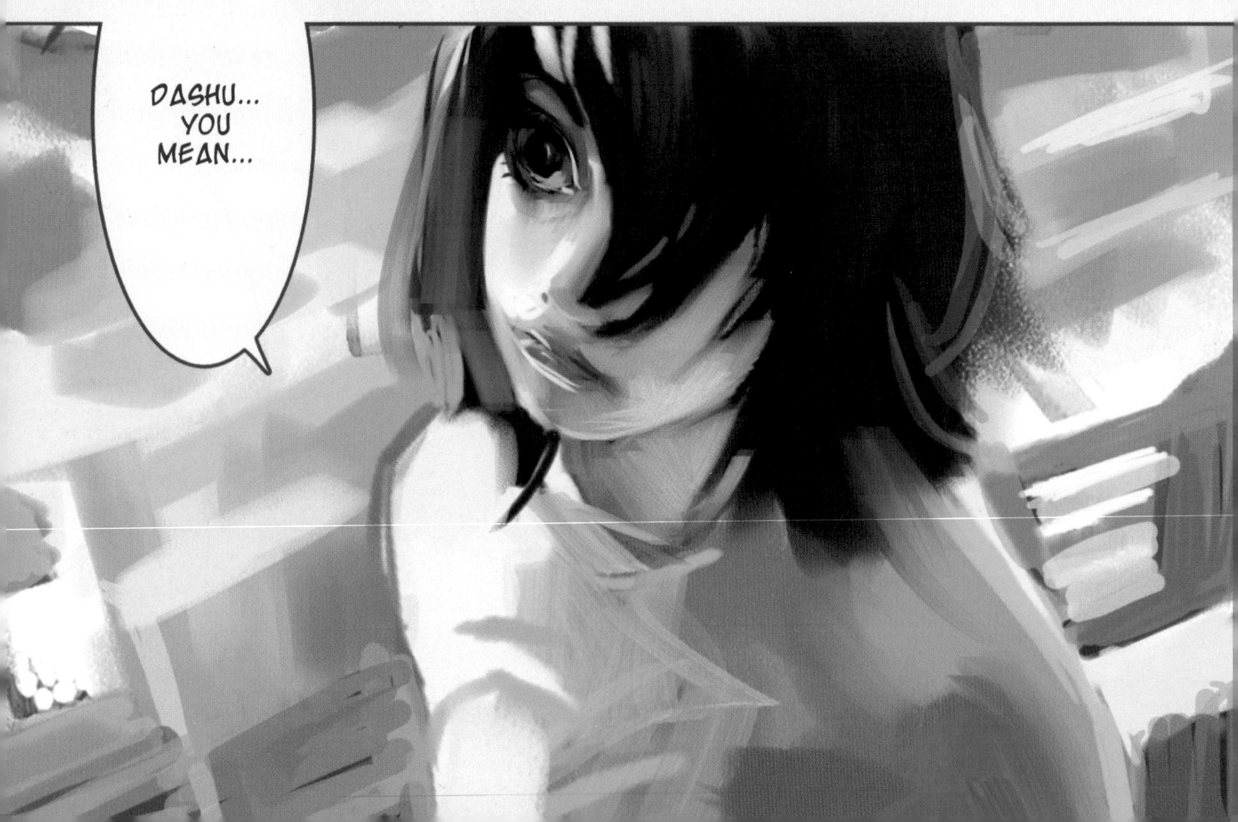
DASHU... YOU MEAN...

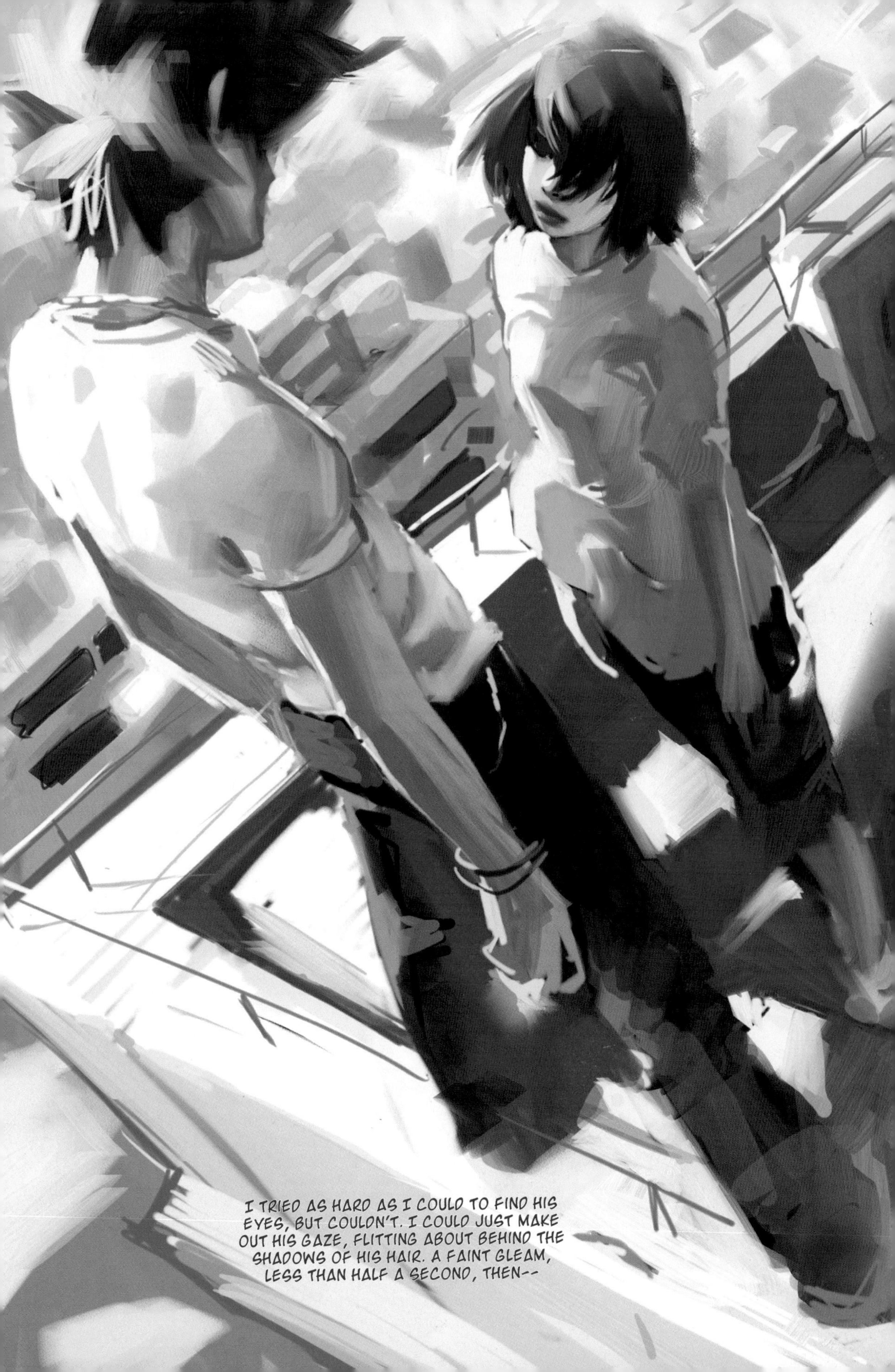
I TRIED AS HARD AS I COULD TO FIND HIS EYES, BUT COULDN'T. I COULD JUST MAKE OUT HIS GAZE, FLITTING ABOUT BEHIND THE SHADOWS OF HIS HAIR. A FAINT GLEAM, LESS THAN HALF A SECOND, THEN--

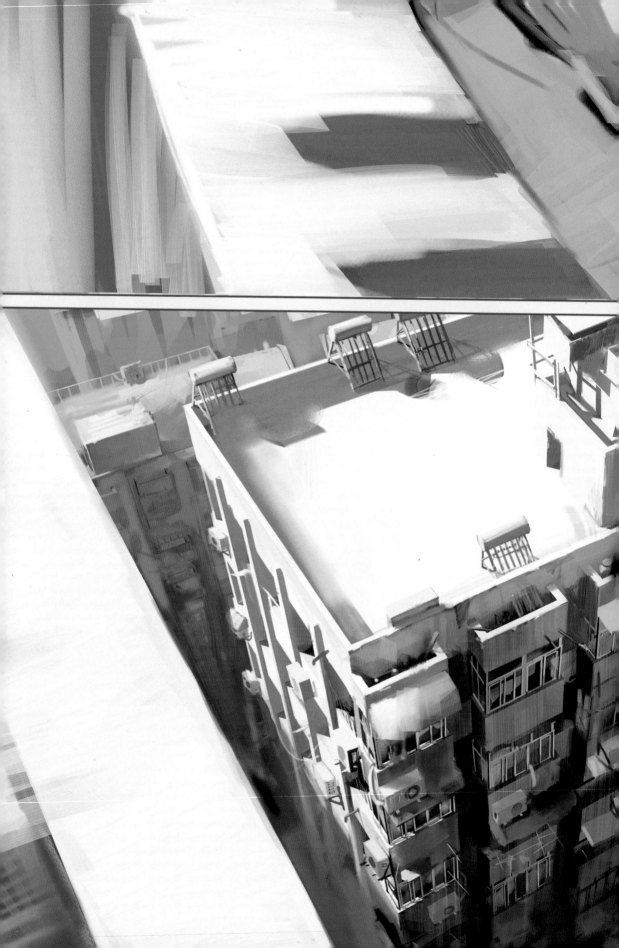

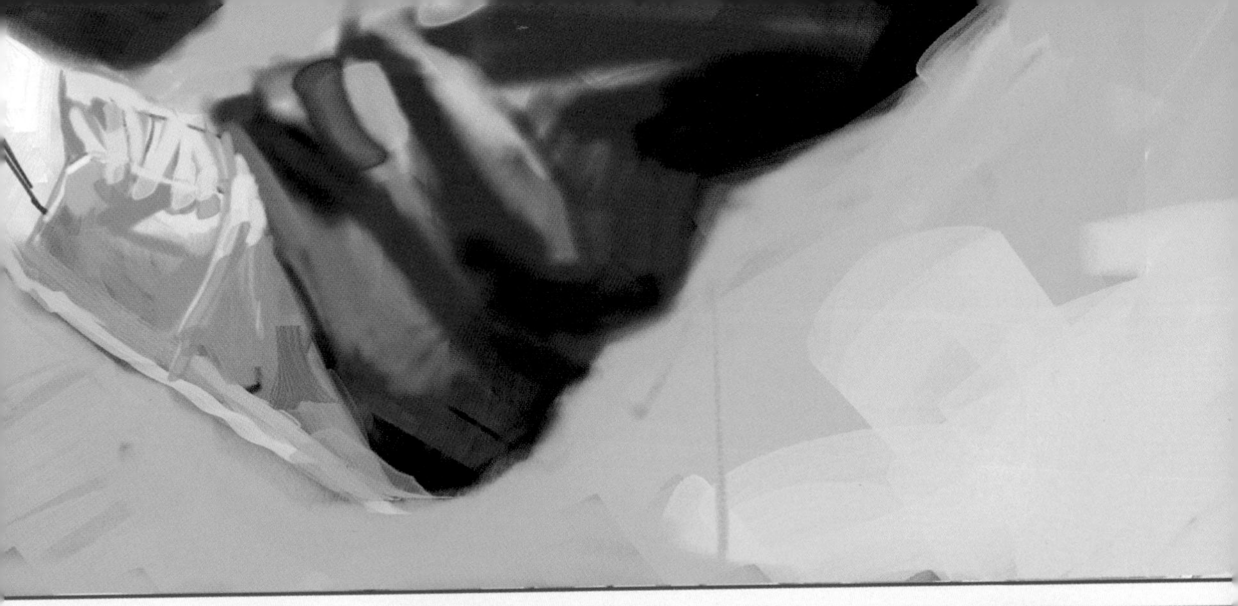
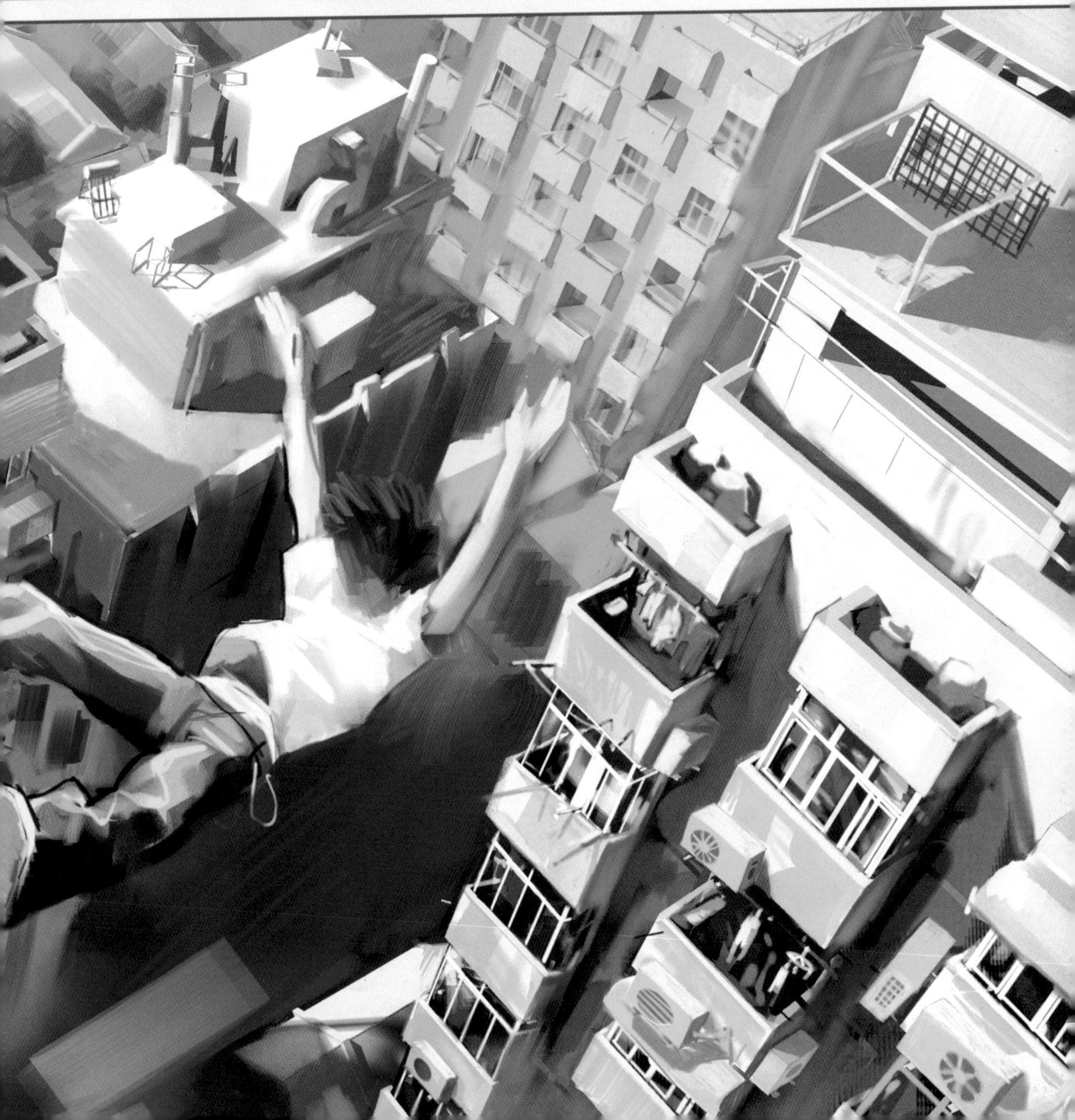

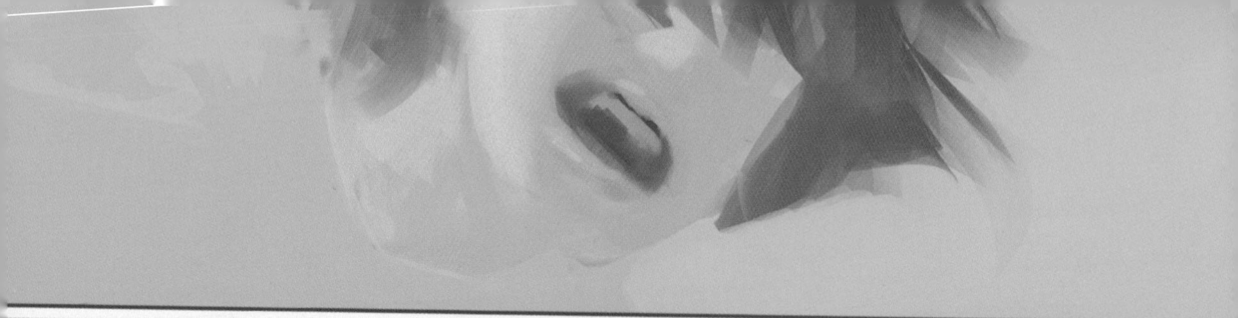

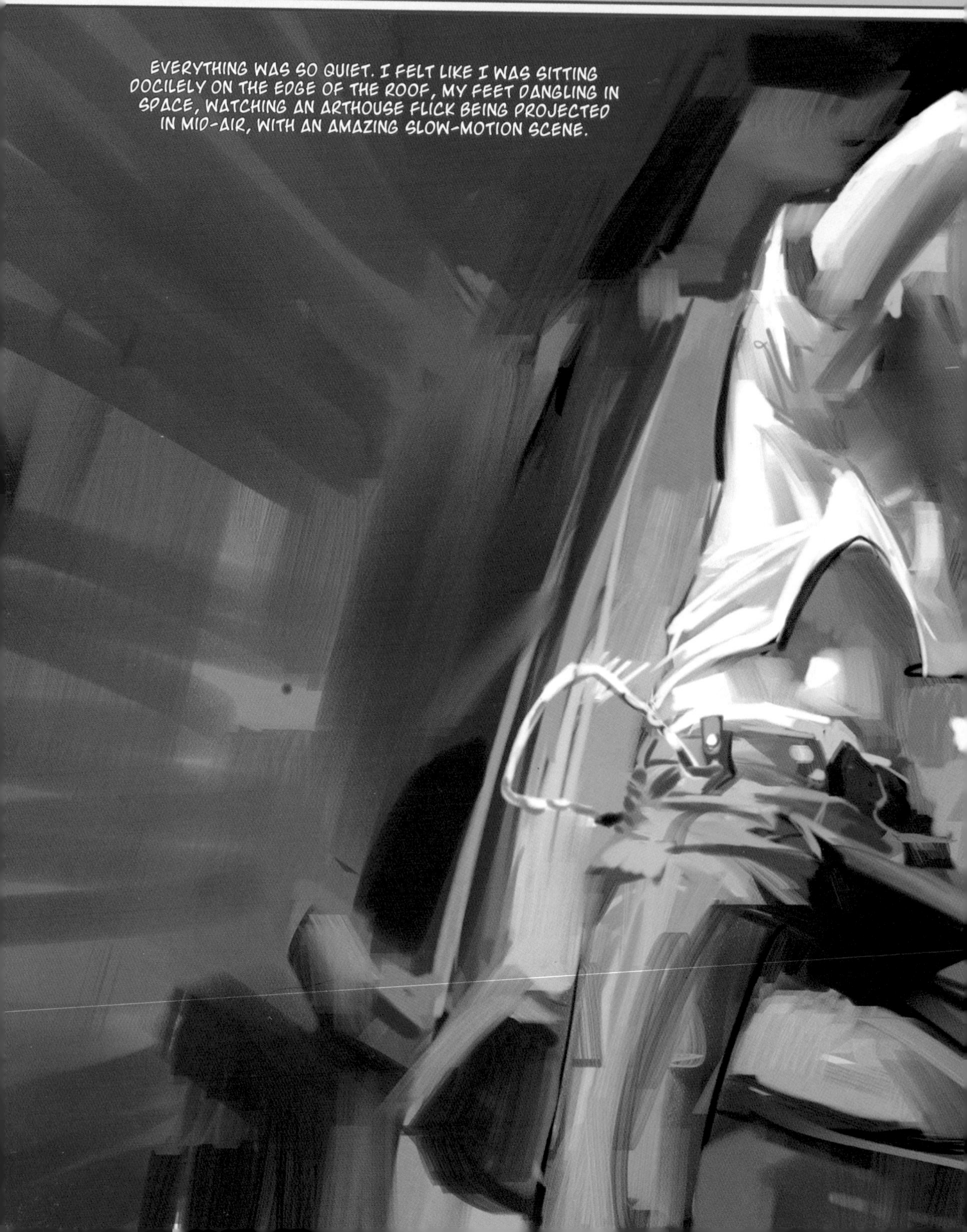
EVERYTHING WAS SO QUIET. I FELT LIKE I WAS SITTING DOCILELY ON THE EDGE OF THE ROOF, MY FEET DANGLING IN SPACE, WATCHING AN ARTHOUSE FLICK BEING PROJECTED IN MID-AIR, WITH AN AMAZING SLOW-MOTION SCENE.

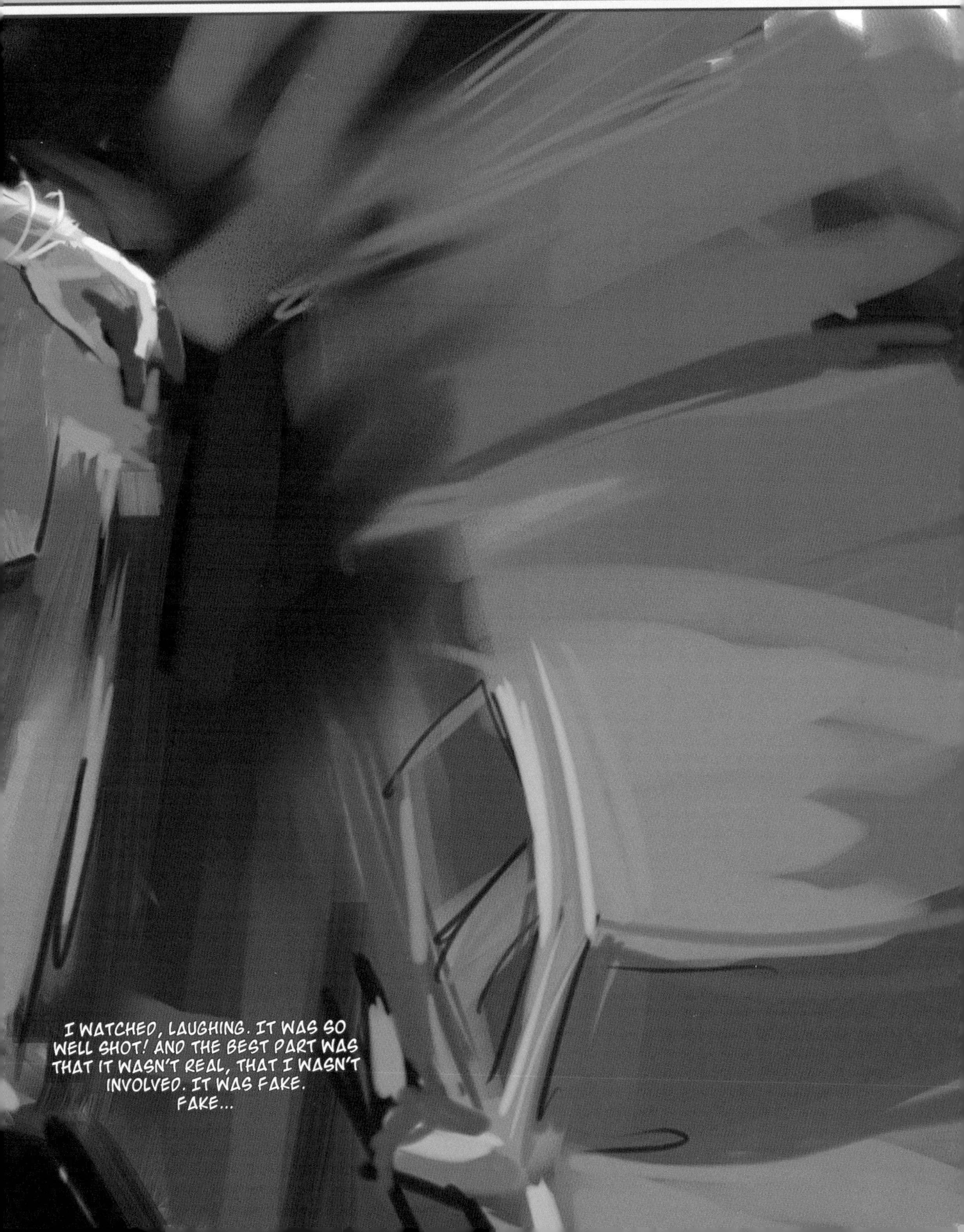
I WATCHED, LAUGHING. IT WAS SO WELL SHOT! AND THE BEST PART WAS THAT IT WASN'T REAL, THAT I WASN'T INVOLVED. IT WAS FAKE. FAKE...

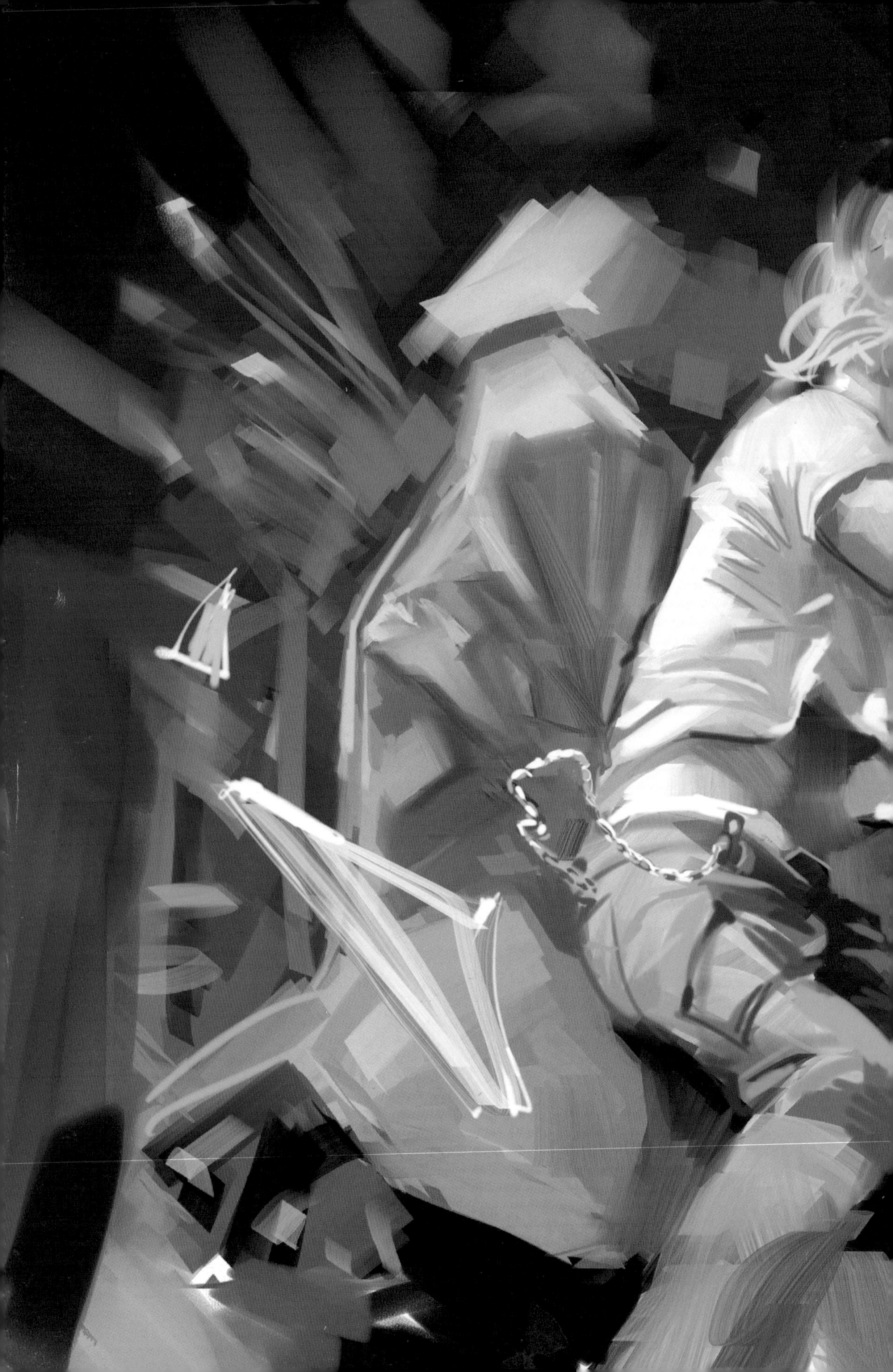

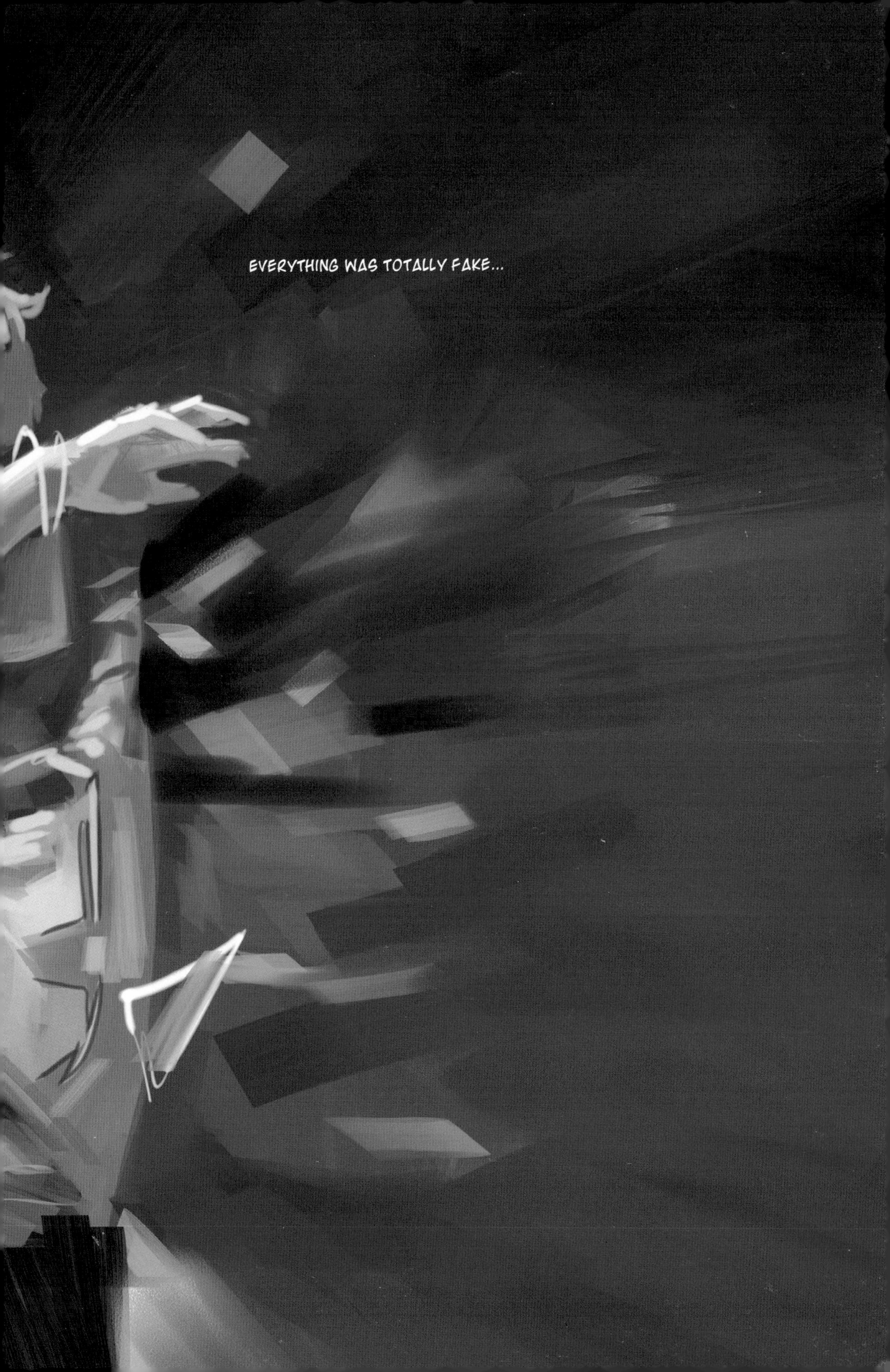
EVERYTHING WAS TOTALLY FAKE...

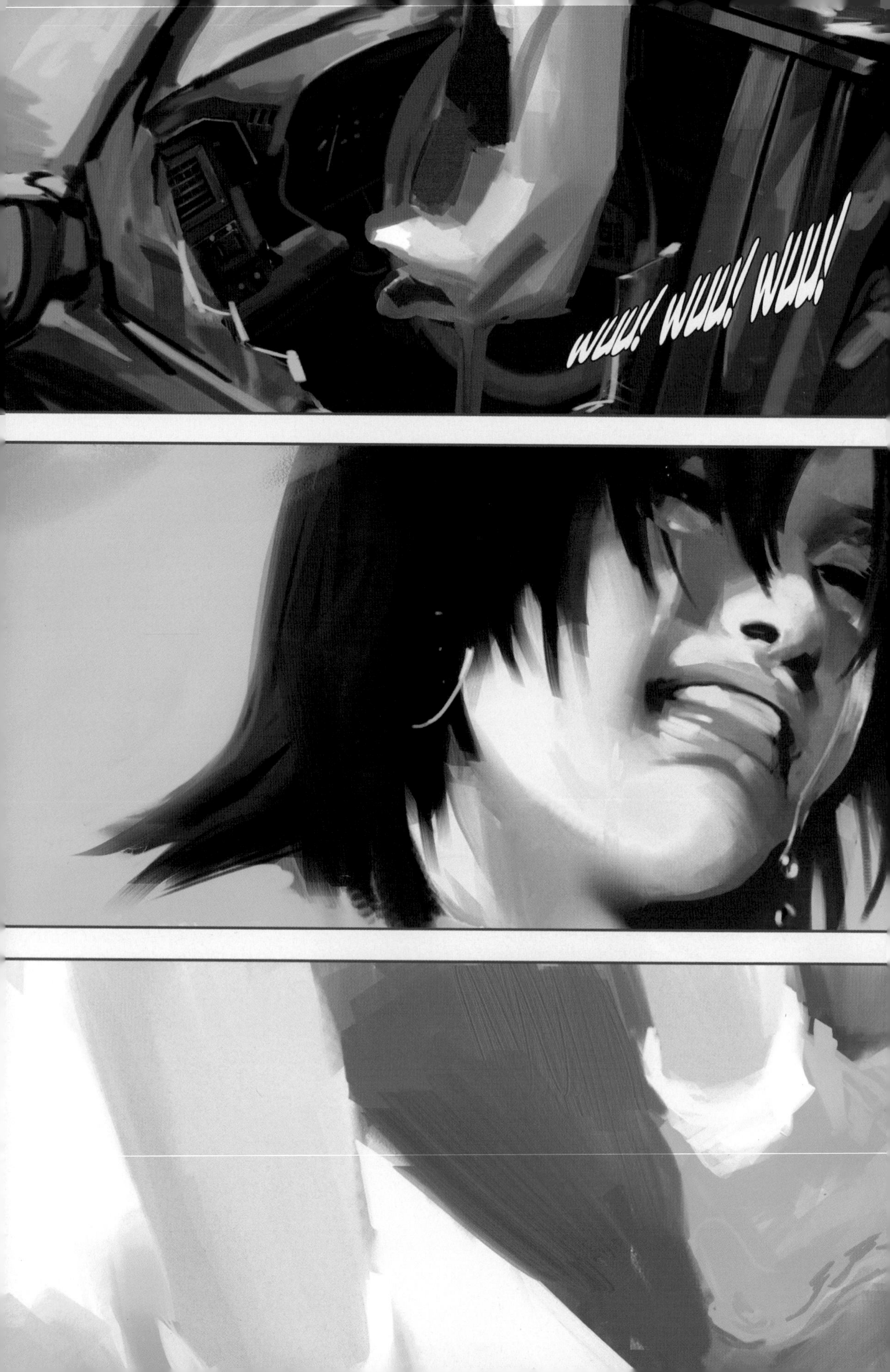
wuu! wuu! wuu!

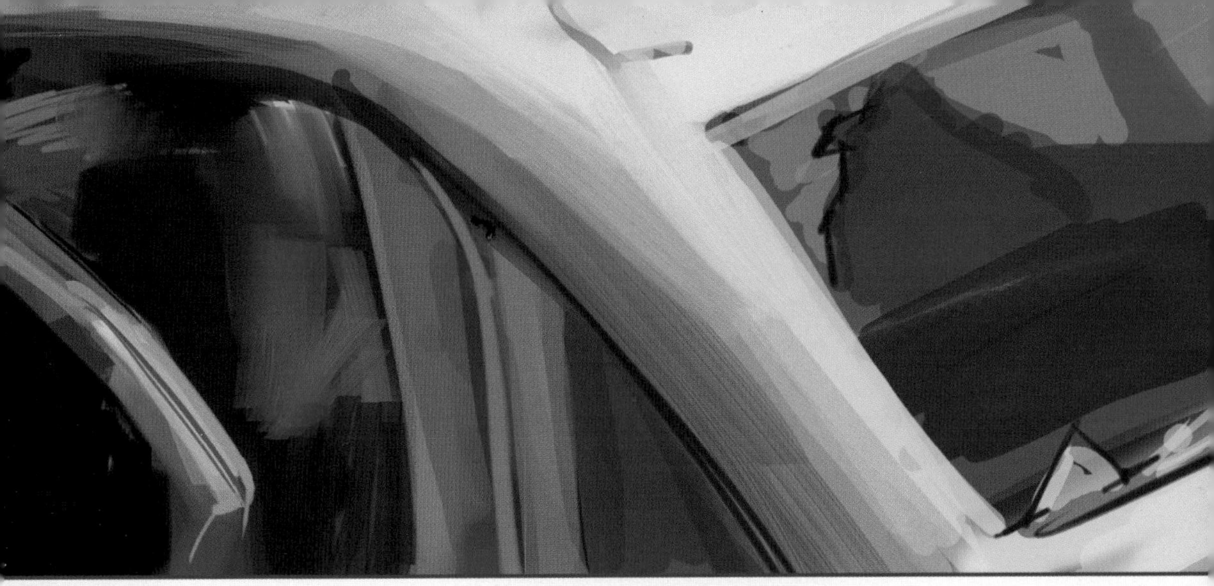

THE CAR ALARM KEPT BLARING AWAY.
I WAS WRITHING. WHAT HAD JUST HAPPENED?
WHY? WHY? I LOVE YOU SO, SO MUCH!

HE LEAPT WITHOUT LEAVING A NOTE.
I WOULD NEVER KNOW IF HE'D LOVED ME.

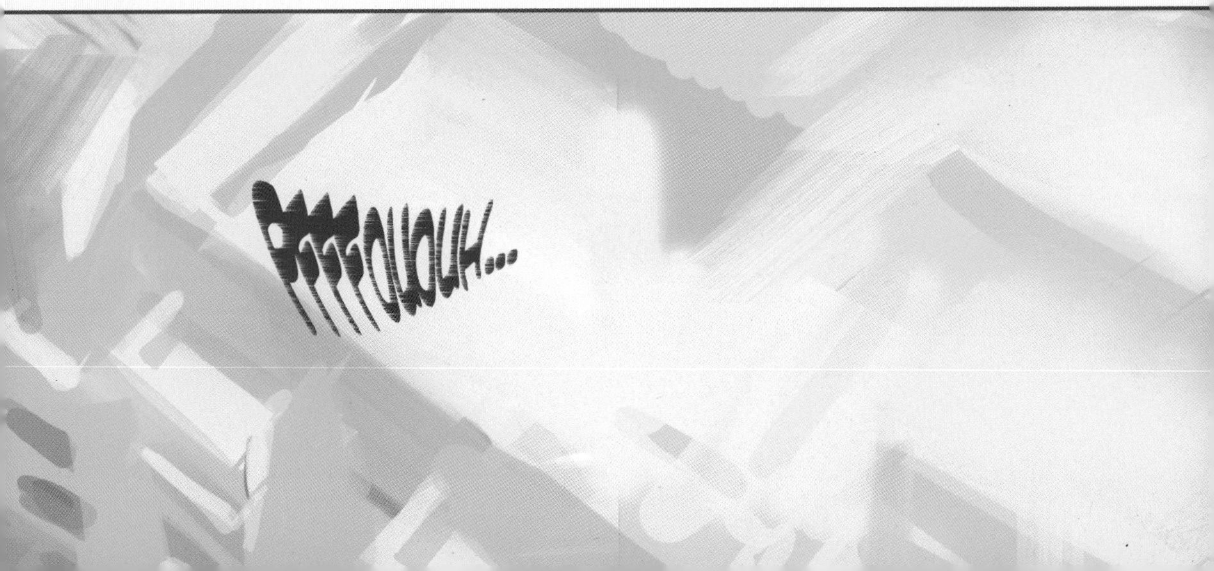
PFFFOUOUH...

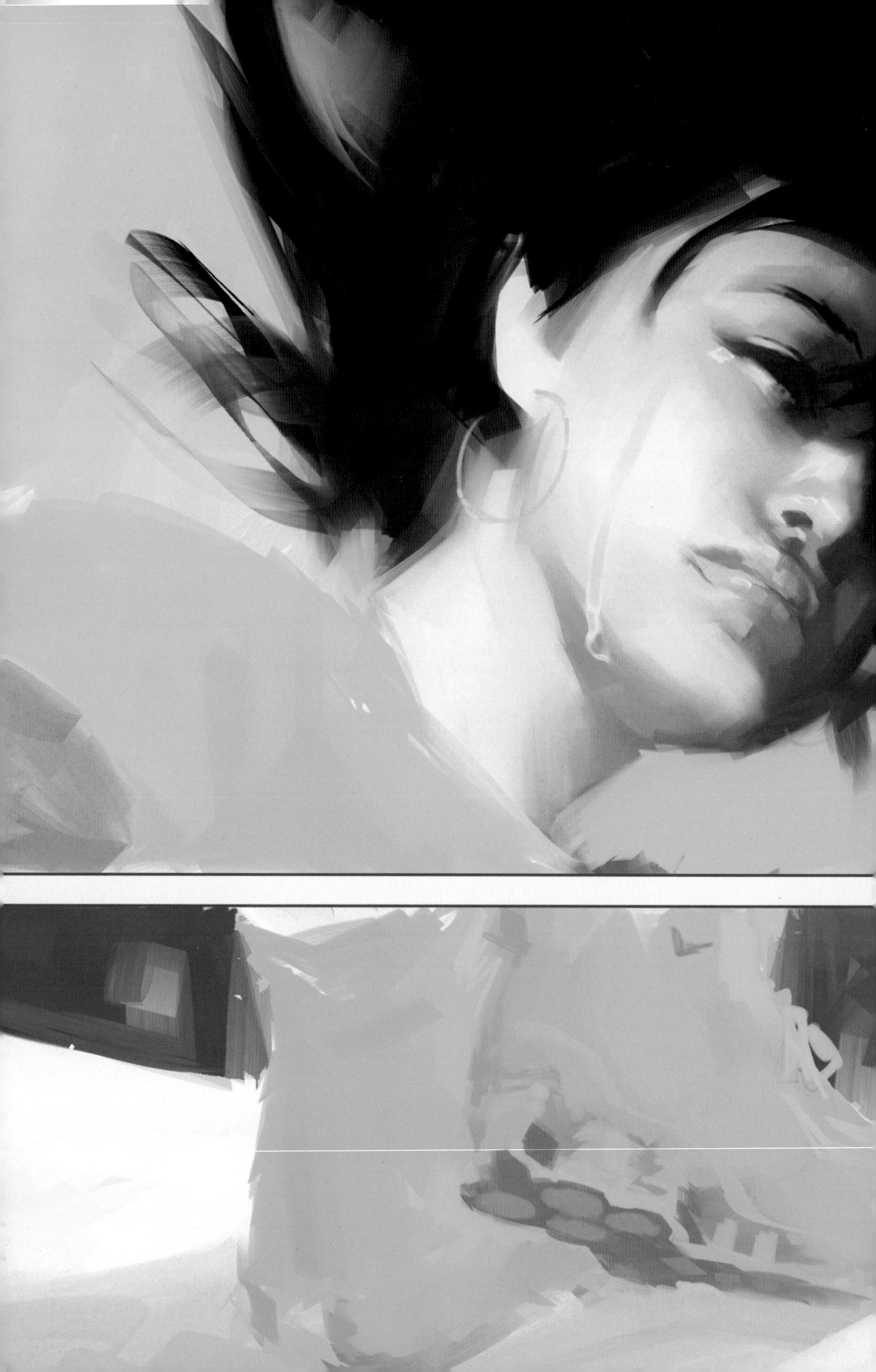

I DON'T UNDERSTAND... THERE ARE SO MANY BEAUTIFUL THINGS IN THIS WORLD. WHY DO GROWNUPS HAVE TO TORTURE THEMSELVES SO MUCH OVER EVERYTHING?

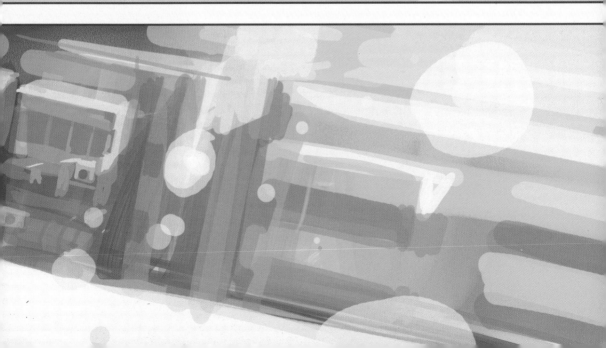

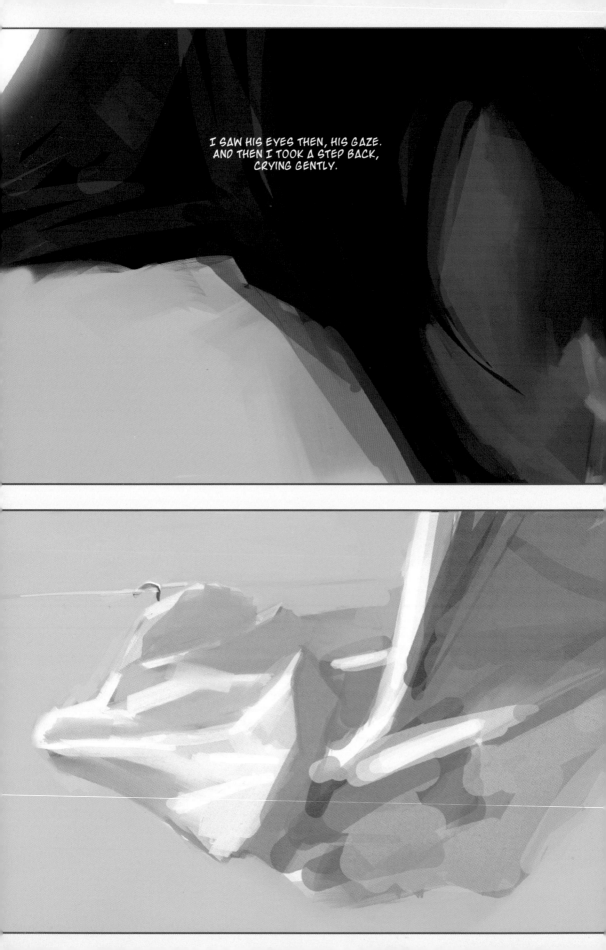

I SAW HIS EYES THEN, HIS GAZE.
AND THEN I TOOK A STEP BACK,
CRYING GENTLY.

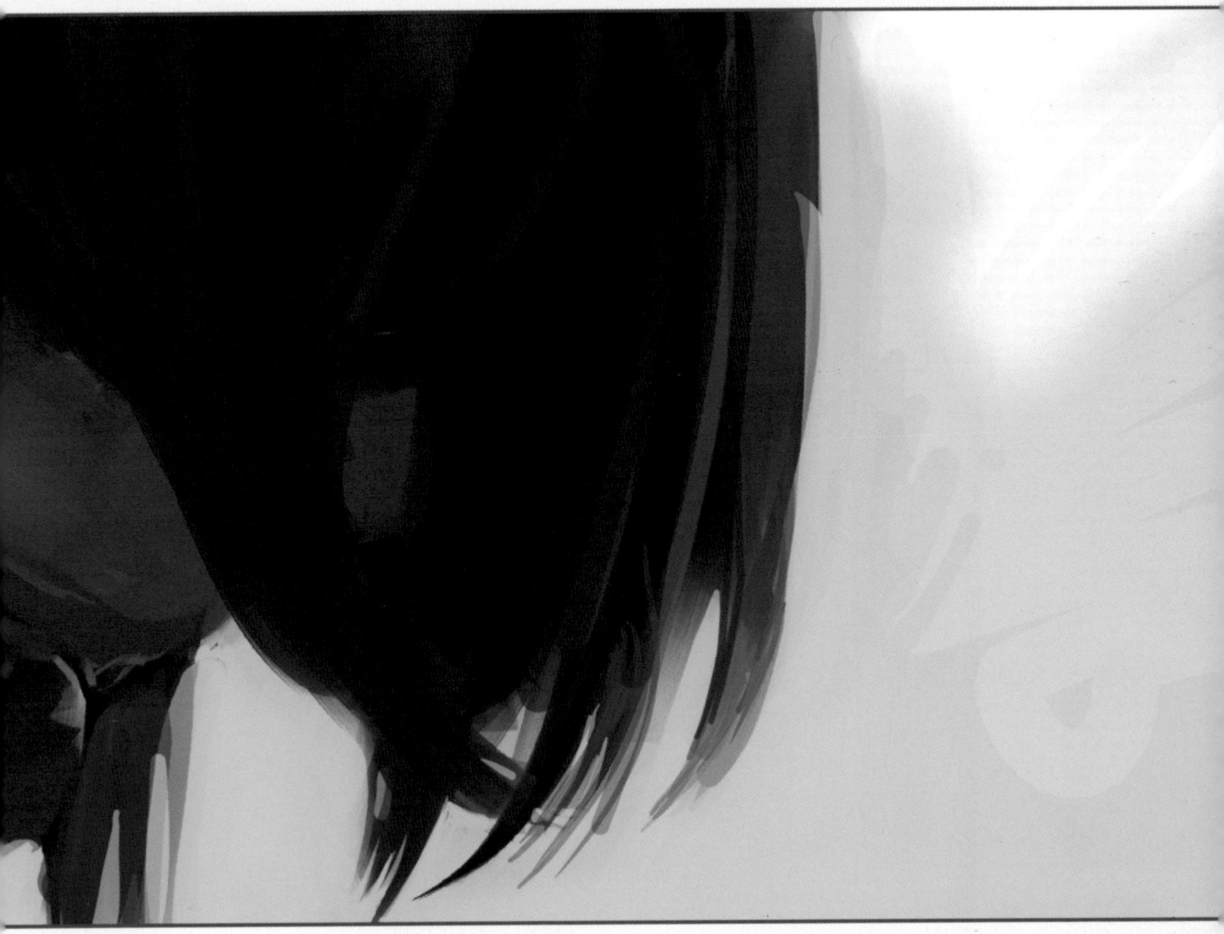

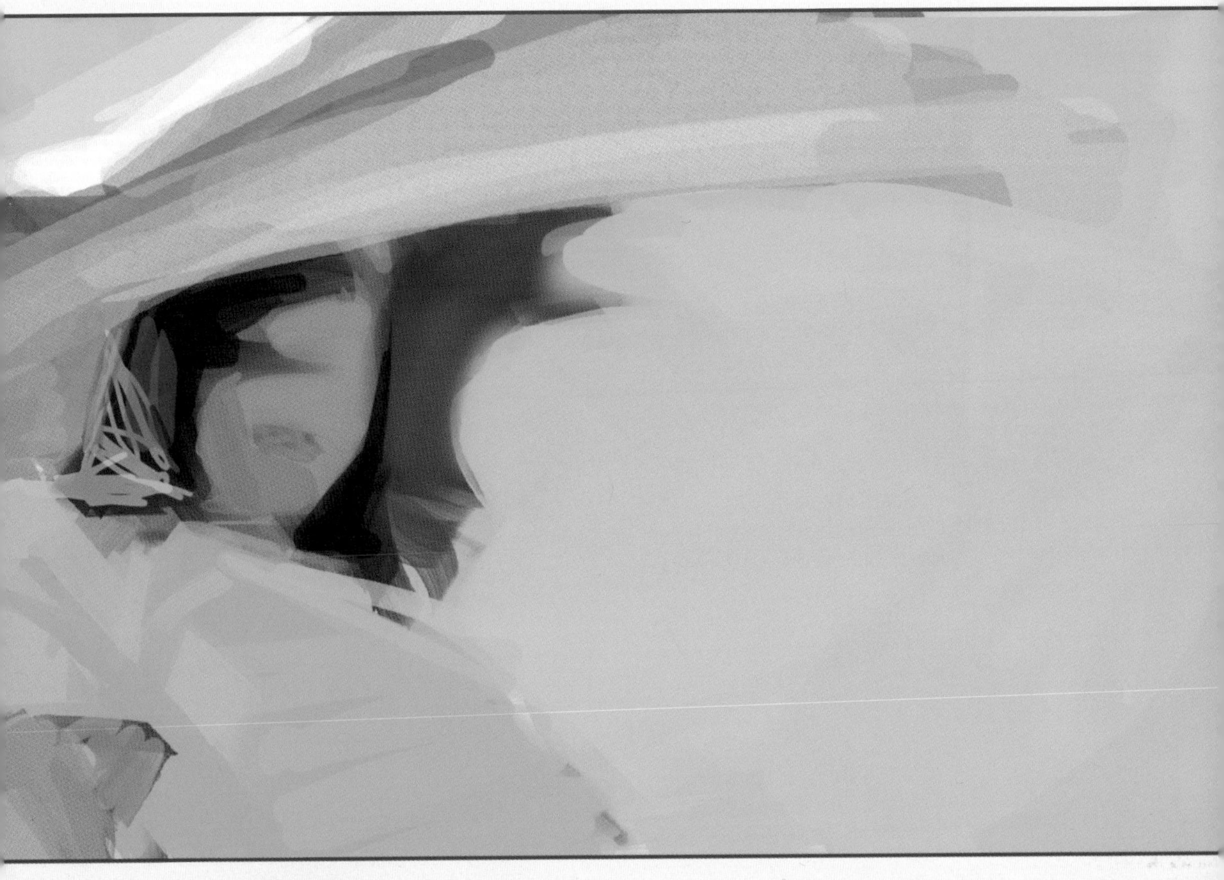

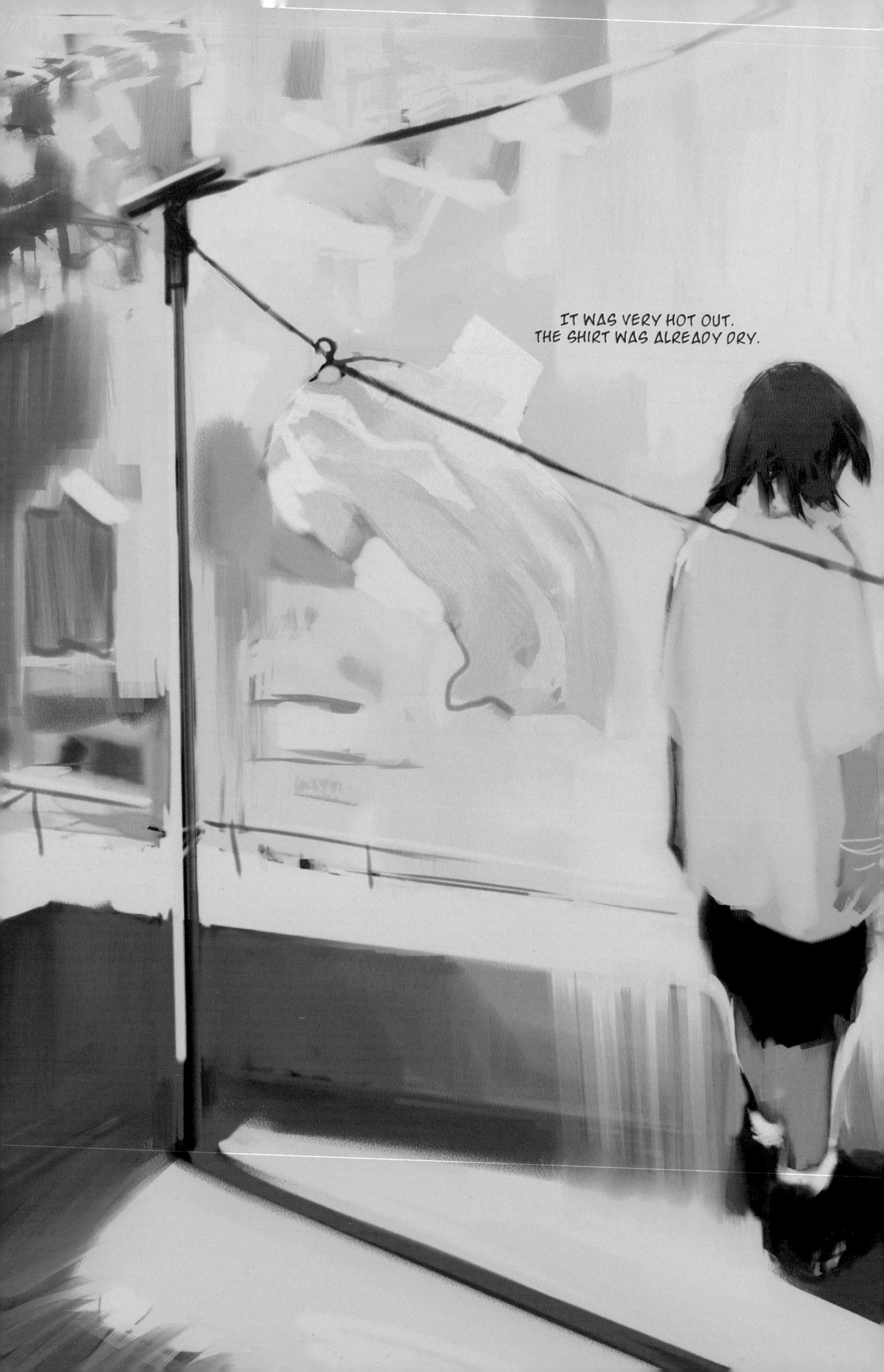
IT WAS VERY HOT OUT.
THE SHIRT WAS ALREADY DRY.

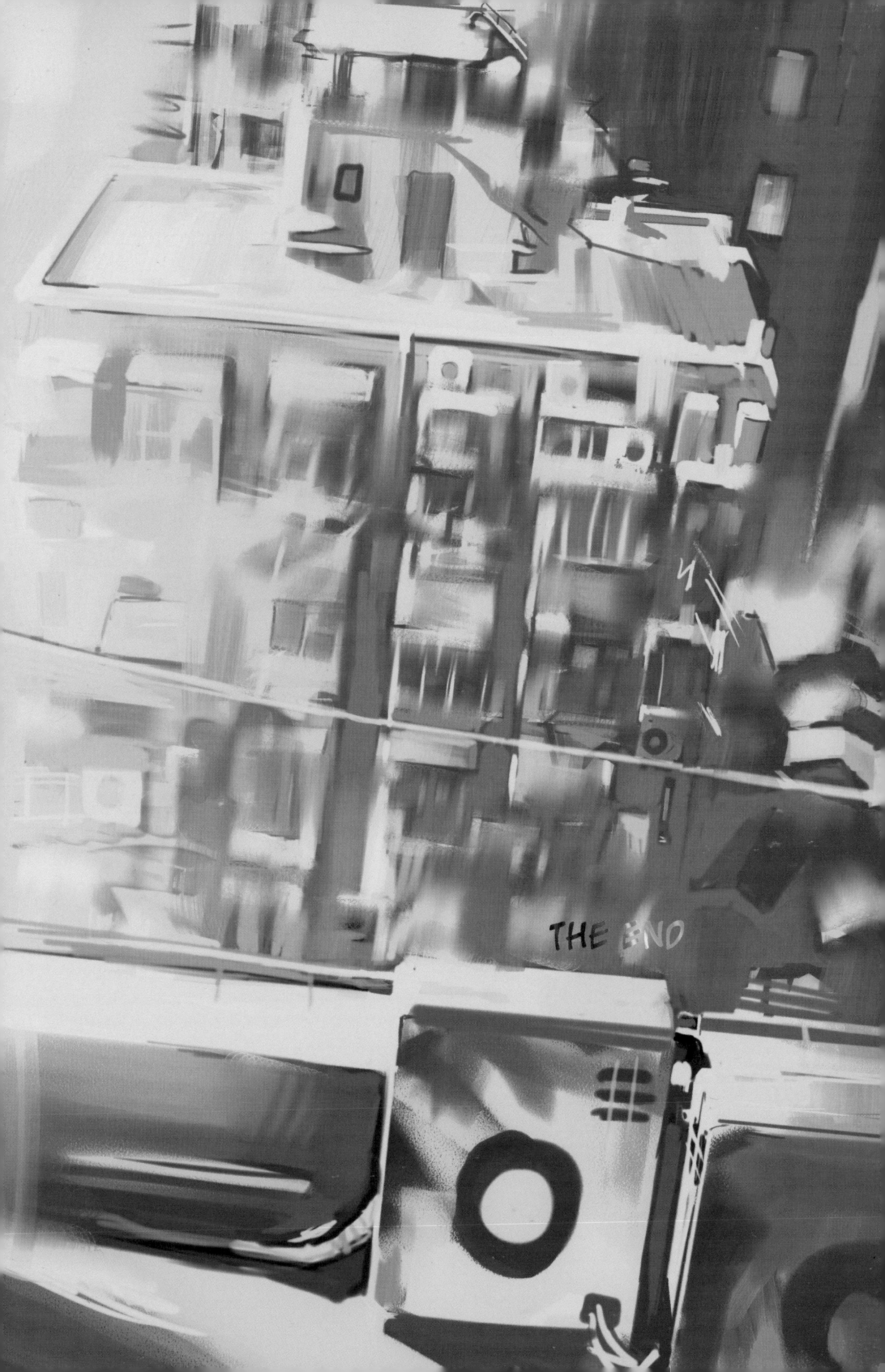
THE END

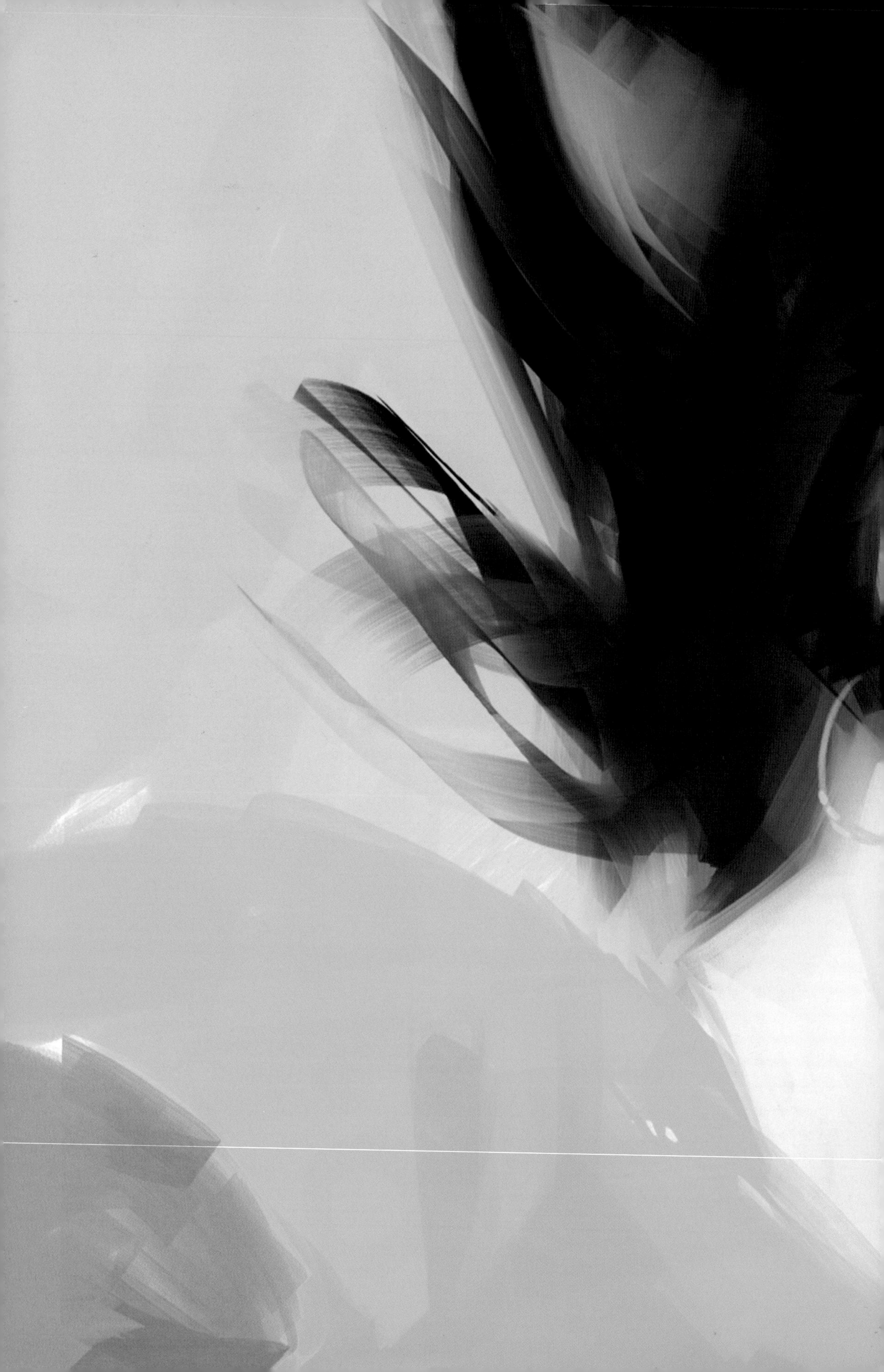

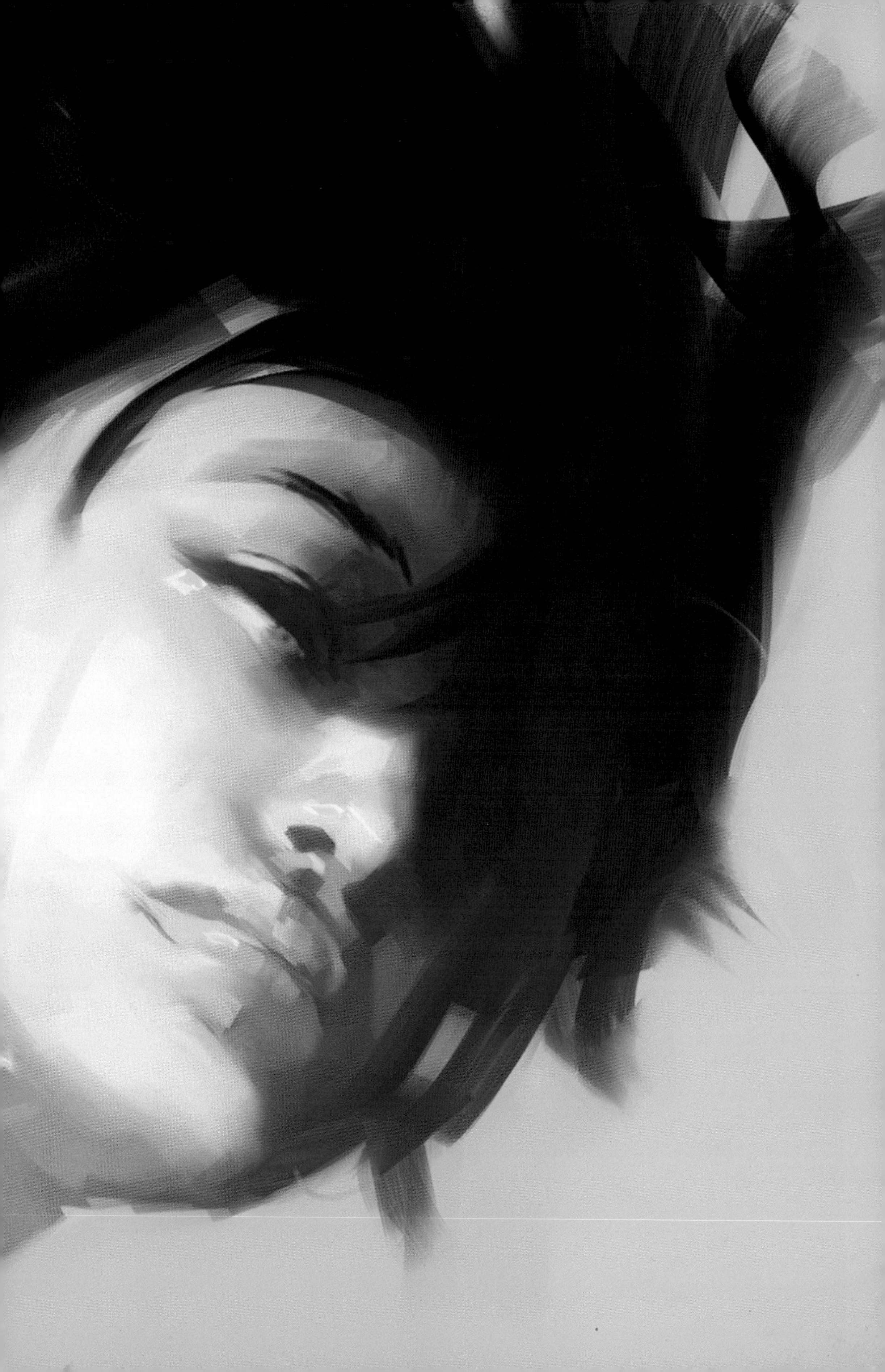

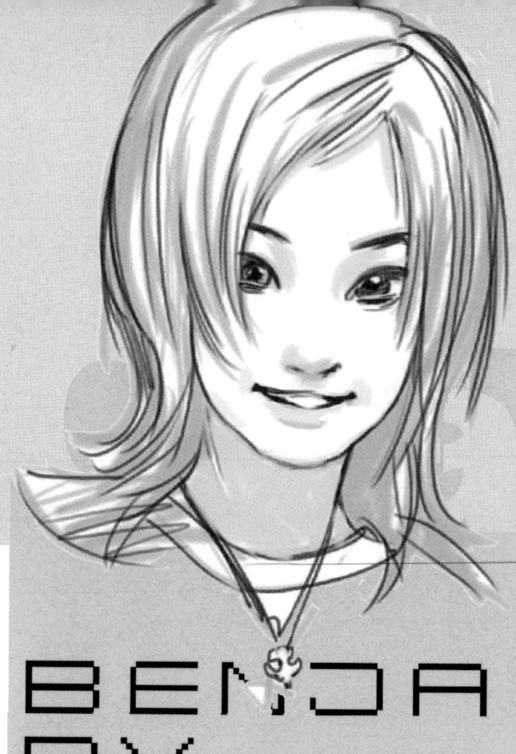

# BENJAMIN BY 2006

When I finished drawing *Orange*, it'd been a long time since I'd written a script. I was typing away in the morning light. Every last sunbeam seemed to be bringing me its final caress. It took me one day and one night of straight typing to finish this story. Afterwards, I went to sleep.

Reading a book you love is like taking a course with a famous professor who teaches you what's beautiful and what's evil in life, everything you didn't know yet.

In this book, how much was planned and how much a gift? I don't know. There were a hundred pages already drawn, that were going to be published. That was all. I didn't know what I'd drawn. All I knew was that I was sad. If I'd had a gun, I would've blown my brains out after drawing this story. If I'd been brave enough, I would've turned the gas on to fulfill the wish of seeing myself transfigured by flames. But I didn't have a gun, and I wasn't brave. I had no ideals, and I wasn't gifted. I wasn't a fighter. Right now, today, I don't even have any more feelings, I don't go out with girls, I don't sing anymore, I don't earn any more money, I hardly eat, I don't buy new clothes, I don't even send text messages. At night, I play stupid games online. And I'm afraid that one day I'll end up not even liking to draw anymore.

I was told my hero was poor, even though today she's known all over China. Despite tireless pursuits that have made her millions, made her a star, she still has no car. She's still "pitiful." I was so happy to find that out. A real hero, better than all the rest of us. All you others are rich, but not my hero. You've got a wife and a handsome car that gleams, but not my hero, and you won't pity my hero what she hasn't got.

My hero was confronted with a problem that drove her to try to kill herself. She couldn't write music anymore. I love you, hero mine, I love you--you who never stooped to the vulgar, who never gave in.

All right, fine, books fall under the category of quality literature. *Orange* was rejected three years ago. Three years, since I drew it, without being published. The reason? "Too depressing." I don't know exactly why it finally got published. Until the moment I finished drawing and writing, I didn't know if I could get it published or who would do it. Which, of all the companies I worked for, was I going to put on the cover as publisher? Whoever it was, I needed to thank them. Three years later, I took up this old book and redrew it. Young girl of three years ago, where did you go?

Did you grow up? Do you still want to die so much? I can't enter your heart to comfort you, I can't dry your tears. I can't even tell you what I'm drawing. I can't send you a text message or call you. I've changed my number. You can't call me at night, drunk. I loved you so much. I couldn't give you anything but suffering. If ever, from sheerest coincidence, you read this book, remember that if I hated you, it was because I loved you so much. The most important thing is that you not let me down. Don't give up, don't give in, don't dirty or debase yourself. You wouldn't be the girl I loved. You wouldn't be the one all those people have read about. You've got to keep on rockin' and never give up. I can't sacrifice myself, as I haven't finished you yet. The world changes too fast. I don't know anything anymore. In the middle of the street, I feel like I'm from another time. There was so much love before. Who'd I give it to? My head's empty. I have to get drunk to remember. In my head, there are so many of you, and I doubt that, in my drunken exhilaration, my memory will return.

The most important thing is still happiness. Why don't I aspire to happiness? Why am I the only person to be wounded by happiness? Always a vale of tears. When, late at night, I think of you, I always come up with various ways to avenge myself, and wind up injuring my hands. No matter how savage I get, no matter how sincere, I can't resist a few lies, a few pretty promises. Lost, all is lost. Ideals lose out against happiness, bravery against love, honesty against the need for security--because happiness is the most important thing, because I love you.

I no longer sleep or eat. I've conquered work, I've conquered weakness, I've conquered exhaustion and the limits of my physical endurance. I've even conquered time and what people might say. But I've lost it all–to you.

Human beings are terrible and end up breaking your heart.

POSTSCRIPT

The heart is like a fierce tiger.
The heart is like a deep forest.

# The Film Poster for *Seven Swords*

This poster, which took a great deal of work, finally turned up far in the background of a photo, a vag
backdrop behind the actors.

The handful of great classic Hong Kong *wuxia* films I like were all directed by Tsui Hark. When, as a b
I watched his movies, I stayed glued to the screen with a foolish grin on my face. I never thought that one d
I'd do a poster for one his films. I realize now that, among the people I know in the art world, even the m
well known, like Ma Rongcheng or the great director Tsui Hark, most are very warm human bein
That's the difference between people who are full of talent and people who aren't. Like those little st
who only exist because we sing their praises, or agents who have no balls.

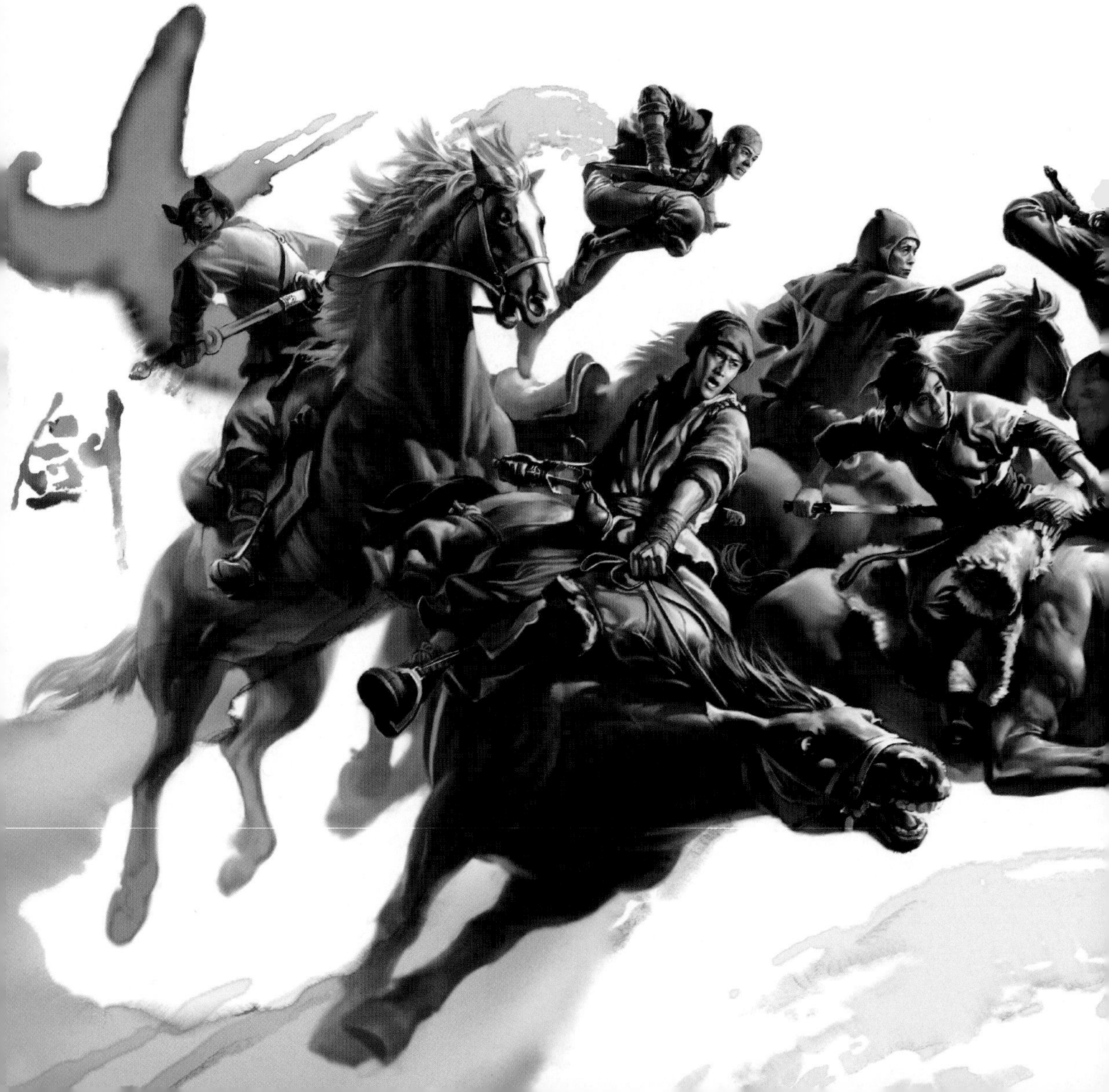
劍

ɔple who have talent don't need to prove themselves by putting on high airs. People with talent are sy creating and don't have time for crap like that.

i Hark can also draw. That surprised me a lot. I asked him, "You've made so many movies. Wasn't t hard? I've been drawing for a long time, and each piece is harder for me." Laughing, he answered, o, filming good guys beating bad guys is really great! I like drawing, but the hard part is not having time. After a day of shooting, I'm exhausted. Once everyone's gone, I can go to bed, but I can't fall eep because I finally have a little time to draw. Seeing you draw all day long really makes me envy u, you know!"

i Hark is happy to have a bit of time to draw, but as for me, drawing isn't what makes me happy. this rotten era, my happiness comes from knowing great men, real heroes. I'll work hard and imitate se men, my idols, in order to be able to win and lose just like them, to stake my life on things, yet not e things too seriously.

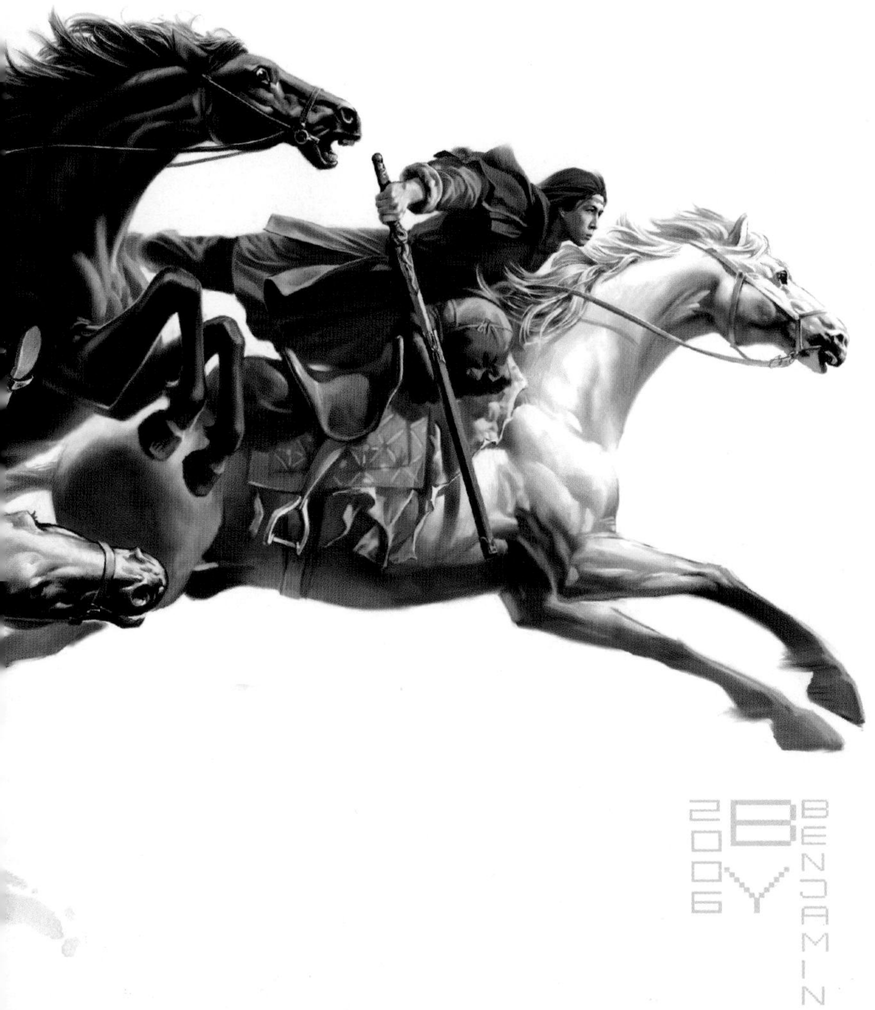
2006
BY
BENJAMIN

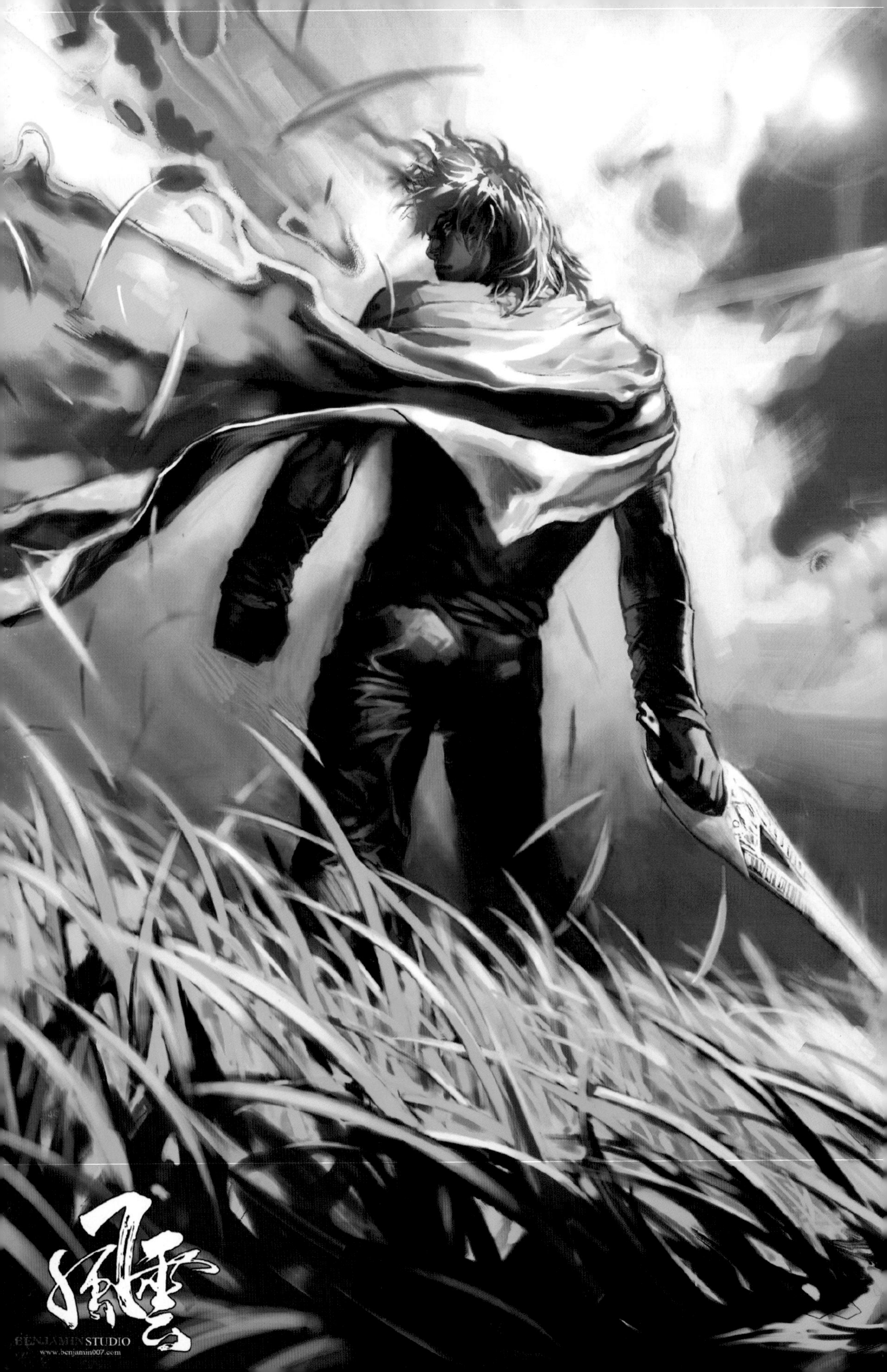
風雲
BENJAMIN STUDIO
www.benjamin007.com

# Poster for *Fengyun**, a Hong Kong manhua

Ma Rongcheng is one of the people from the generation before mine who has influenced me the most.

His high standards for his images and his love of drawing inspire me a great deal. I hope that one day, when I've made it, when I have assistants who do a lot of work for me, I'll still feel, like Ma Rongcheng, the same pleasure in drawing. This joy surpasses all others: fame, the industry, business. I want to be an artist always engrossed in the pleasure of drawing.

••• BENJAMIN

* Translator's Note: "Fengyun" literally means "wind, cloud"; here, "situation" or "circumstance."

# The Sword of Xuanyuan*

Poster for an online game

Nowadays we're busier than ever, with less and less time to envision an ideal future. I got this gig from a friend who no longer works for this online gaming company.

Before, he loved drawing, like me. Then he started working and shelved his dreams. One hot summer night last year, we walked around half of old Beijing like a pair of teenagers, talking. At the Princess' Tomb**, we sat on the sidewalk to have a Coke and watch the cars and people go by. I had a sudden feeling of déjà vu. Ten years ago, we'd talked all night long about our hopes and dreams with a bunch of friends in the middle of the street.

The night before last, this friend showed up again to tell me that he'd been fired, and that he wanted to seize the rest of his life: at the age of 30, he was going to take another shot at his dreams!

BY 2006 ...

* Translator's Note: surname of the Yellow Emperor, a legendary ruler.
** Translator's Note: a place in the western part of Beijing, near the third beltway.

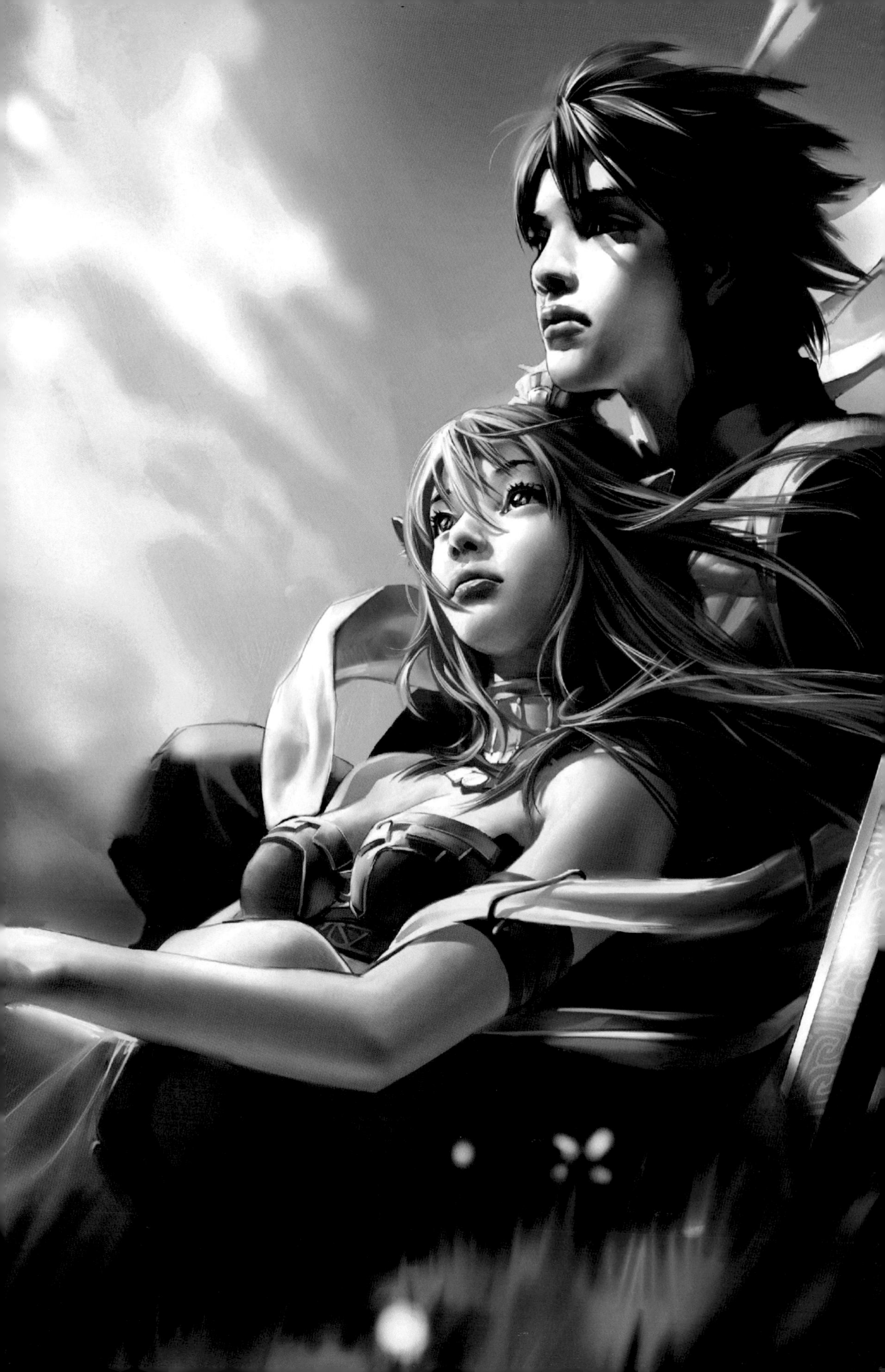

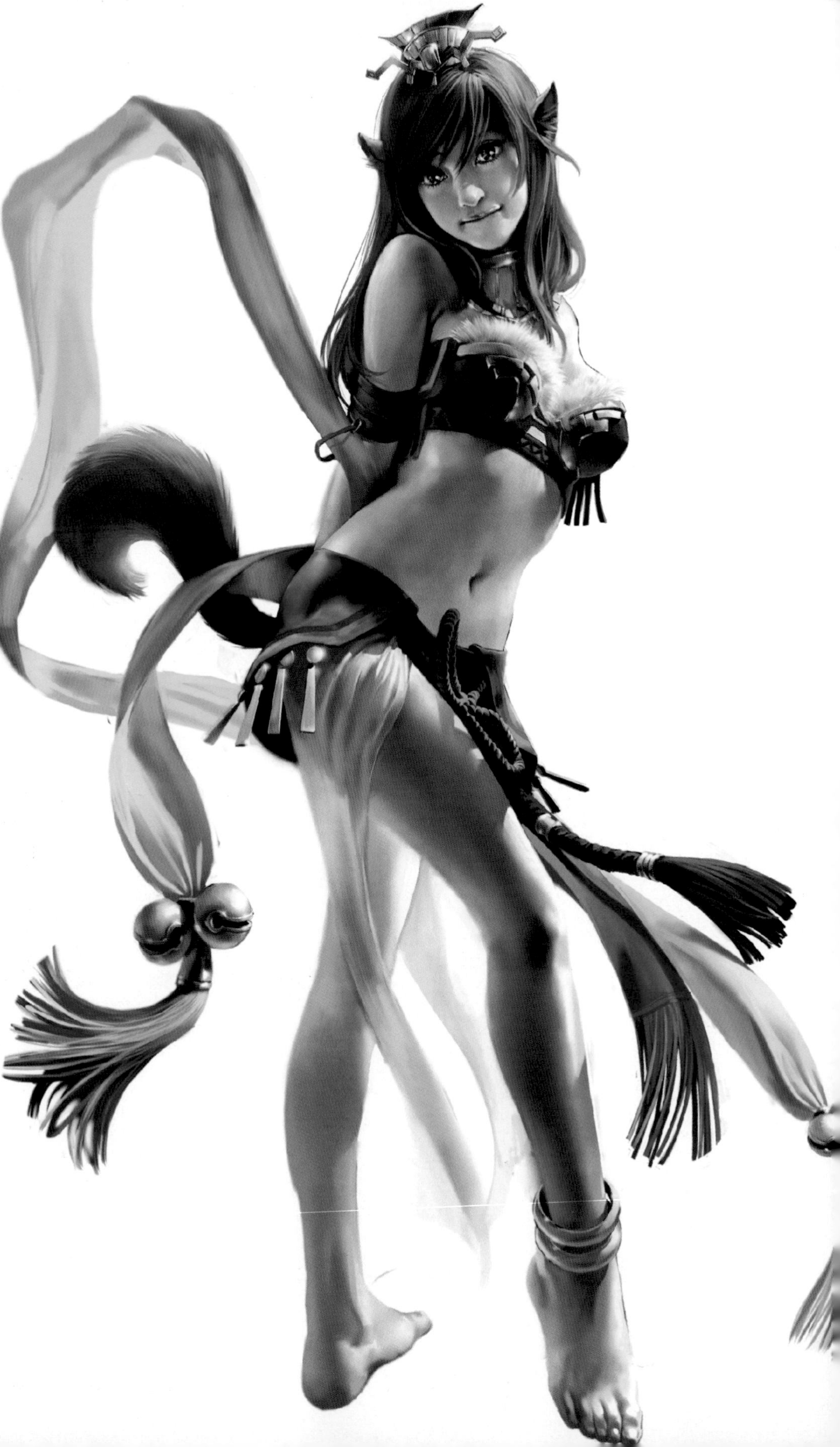

1

For the story of *The Sword of Xuanyuan*, my client wanted really young girls. I didn't know that. I'd drawn a simple and approachable young woman. Not in the high-collared style of most Chinese women, but one of those girls who makes the world a nicer place.

While drawing, I fell asleep at my computer. At the time, I didn't sleep much. I was like a man possessed, and I spent a lot of time on things that really weren't worth it. That's all in the past now, and I can let go of it all. By spending my time drawing without sleep or love, seeking profit and glory, I'd almost forgotten who I was.

2

Nazha*

My only drawing of a character who isn't real. In this instance, I sent the editor packing because she was impolite to the writers and wanted to play hardball harder than I liked. A long time ago, as a young art fan, I'd sworn to myself that if I became famous one day, I'd be nice to everyone and never be mean. But sometimes you have to play hardball to be respected.

Kid, if you want me to play with you, don't bug me.

* Translator's Note: Nata in Sanskrit, a very powerful demon king from Buddhist mythology.

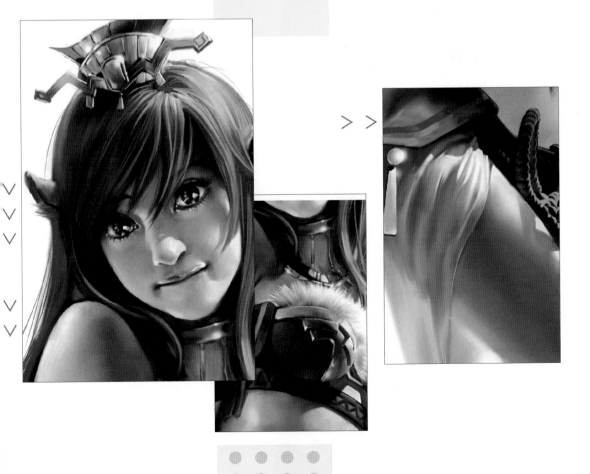

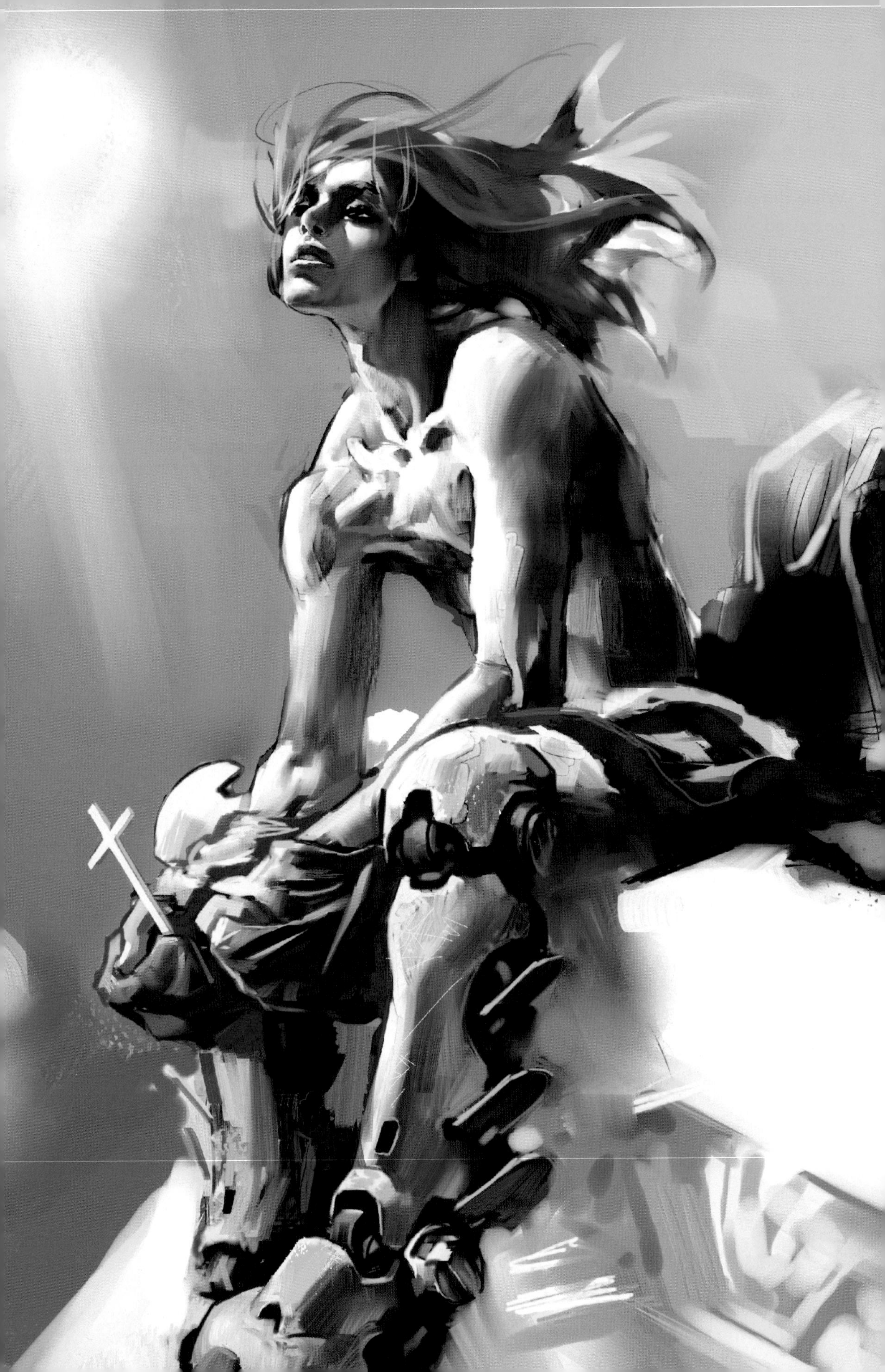

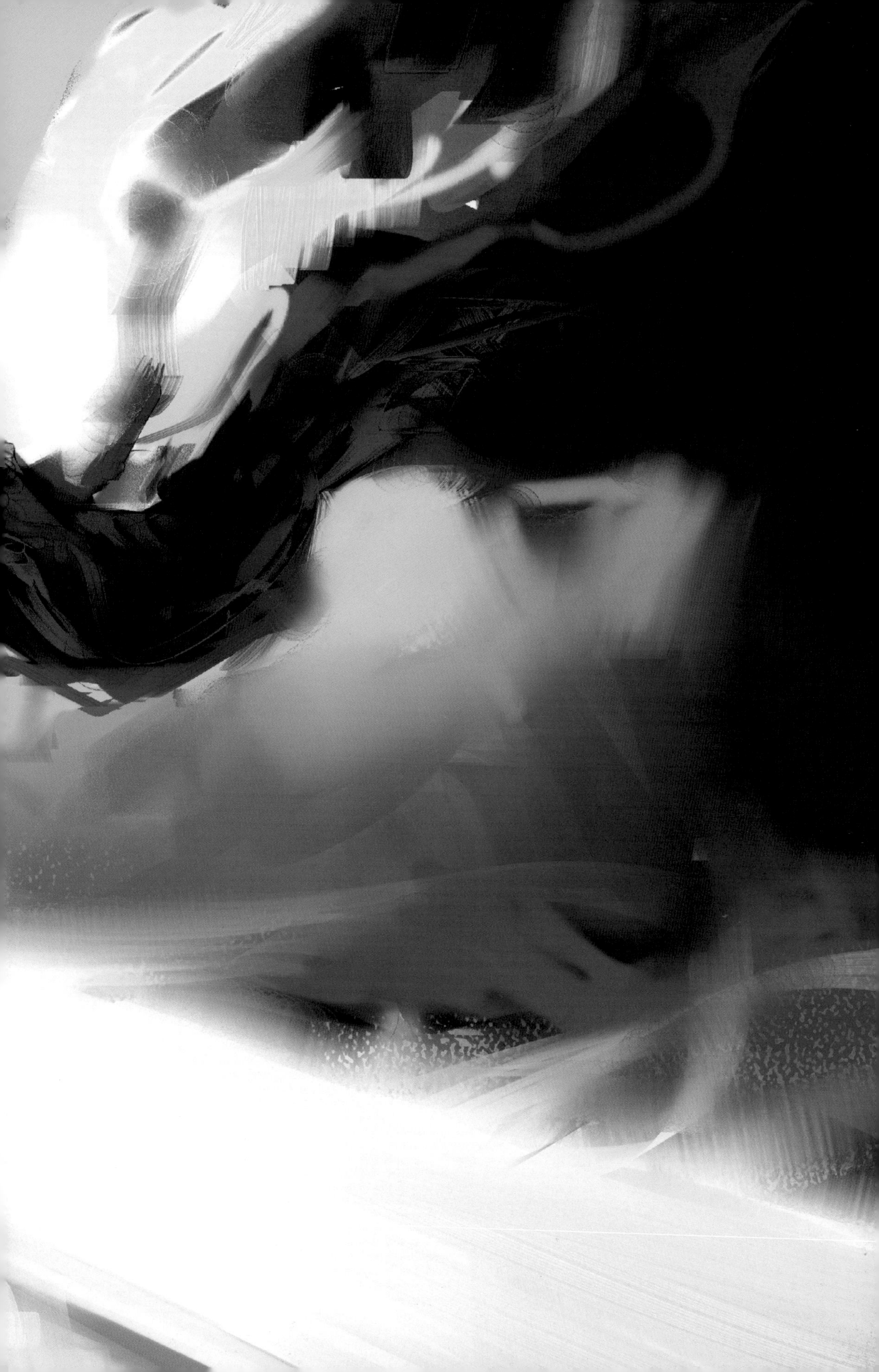

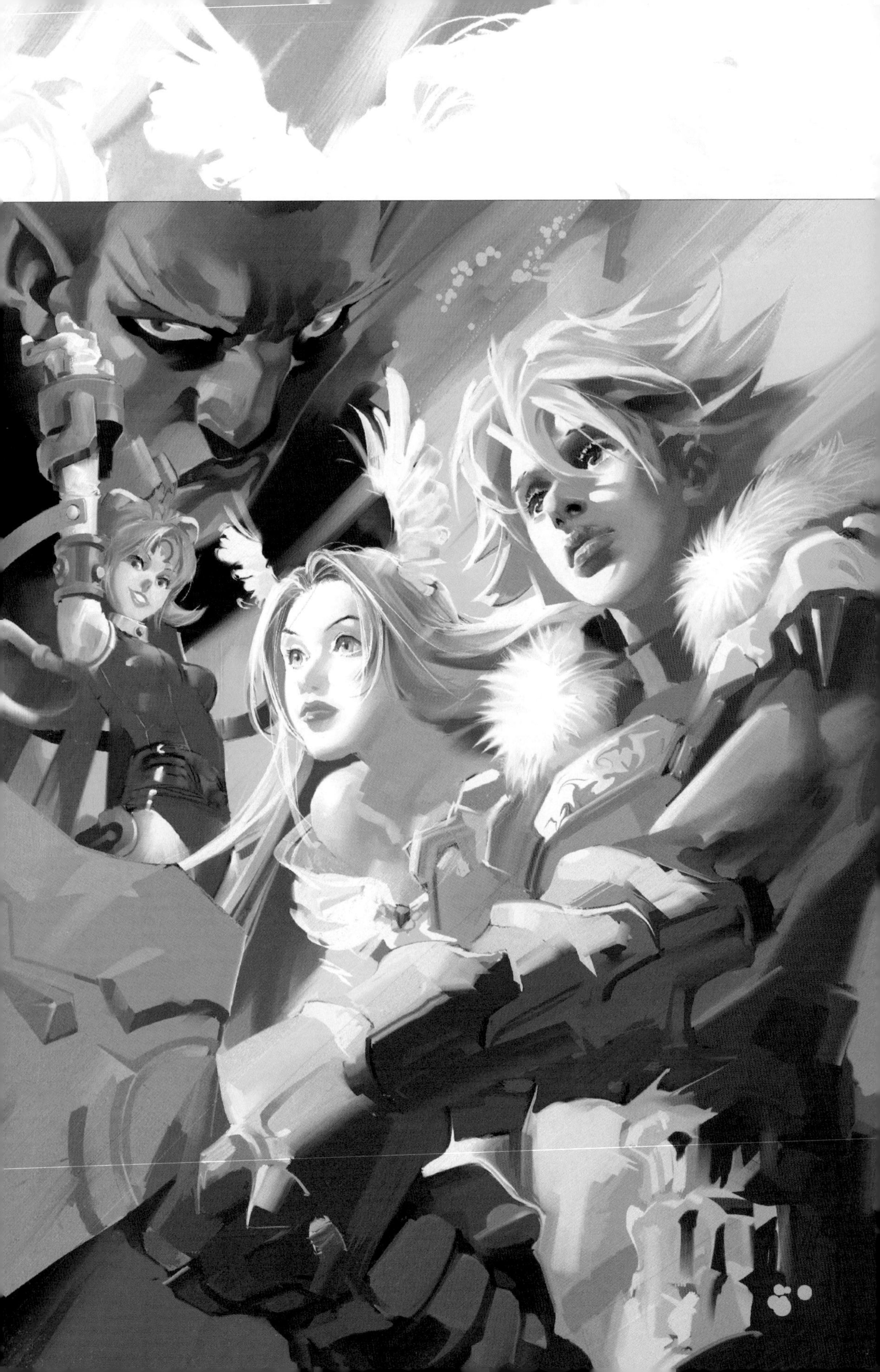

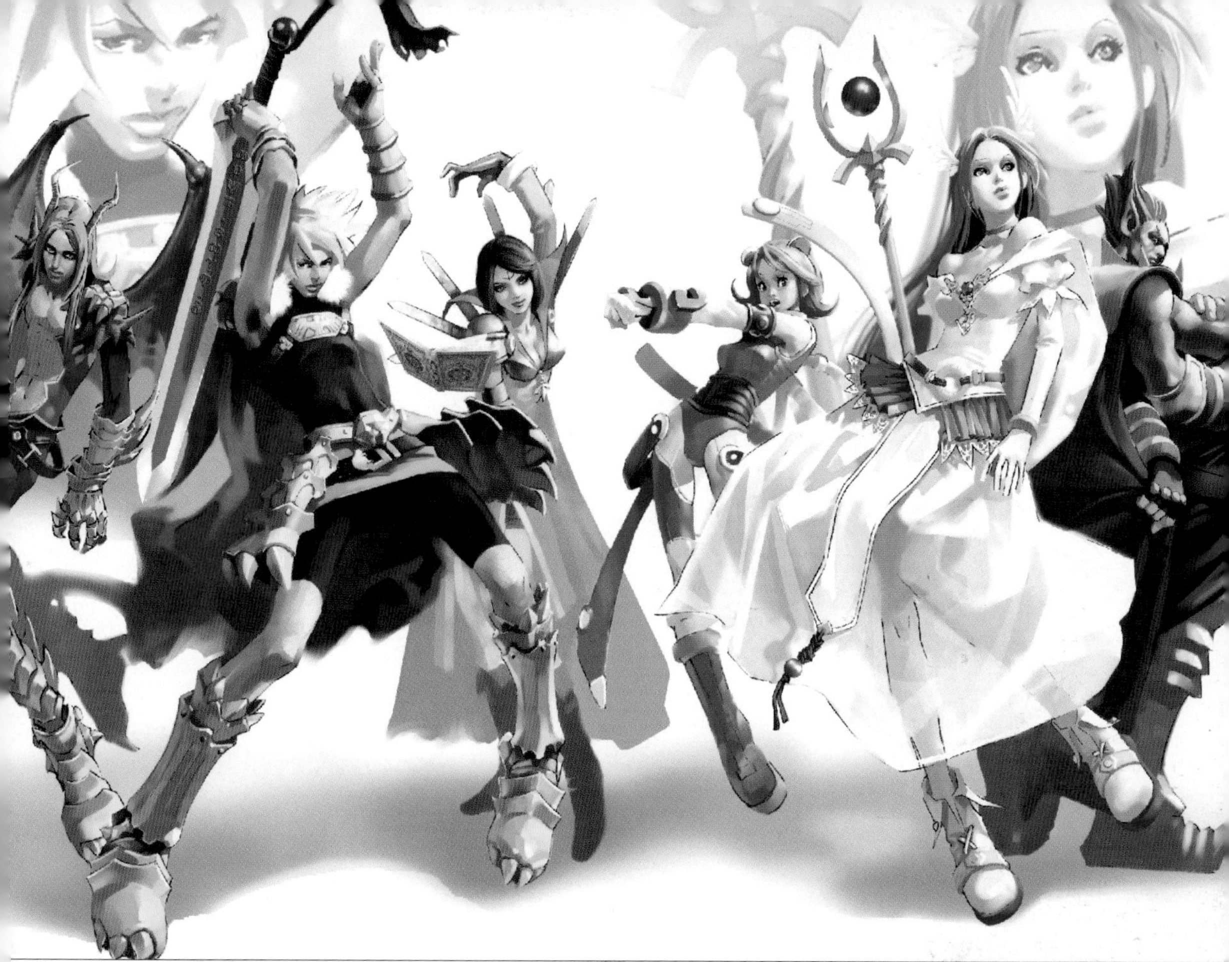

Another poster for a game that didn't last long. Too bad. To make this drawing, I went to where the game was manufactured, in Nanking. I spent a month being called "Professor*" in that gloomy, rainy town, and wore out a pair of pants. That was four years ago already. I remember the flock of crows on the road to the airport. They flew off noisily when cars came by, chased away by splashes. They circled in the air, then came down to land again. A time of friends, in a sad city.

*Translator's Note: a colloquial way of addressing a young person who is a specialist in their field.

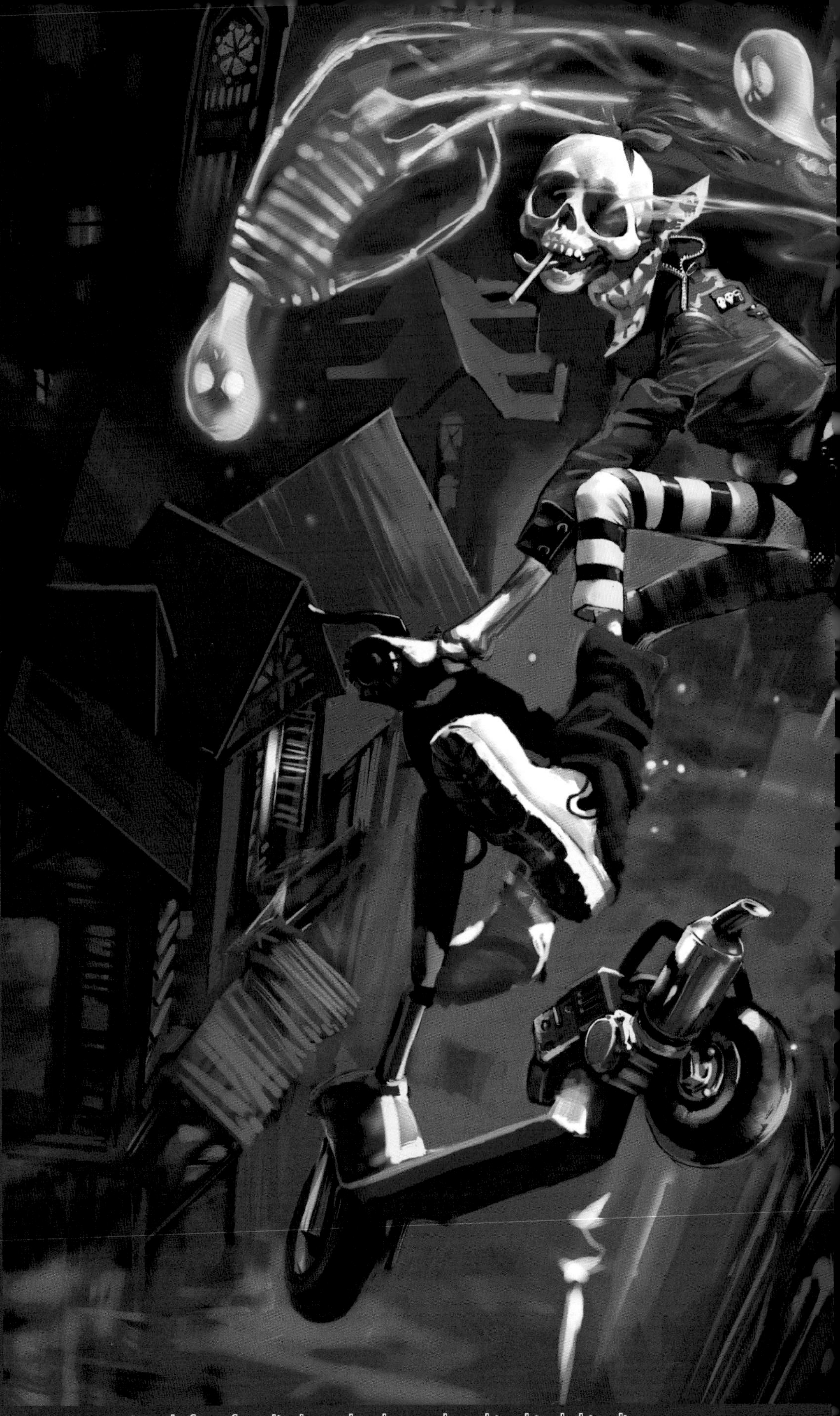

Here is a poster I made for a friend's shop when he was launching his clothing line.

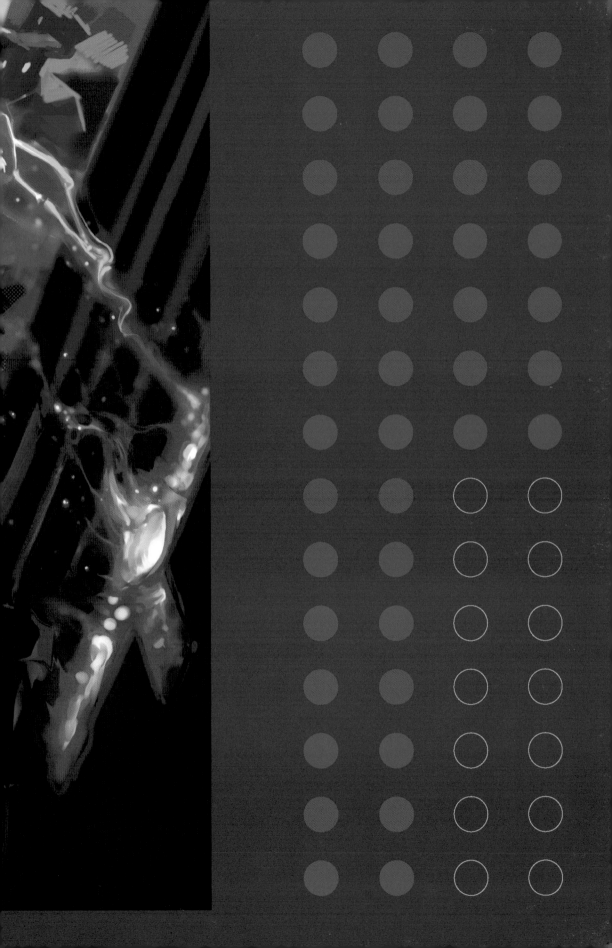

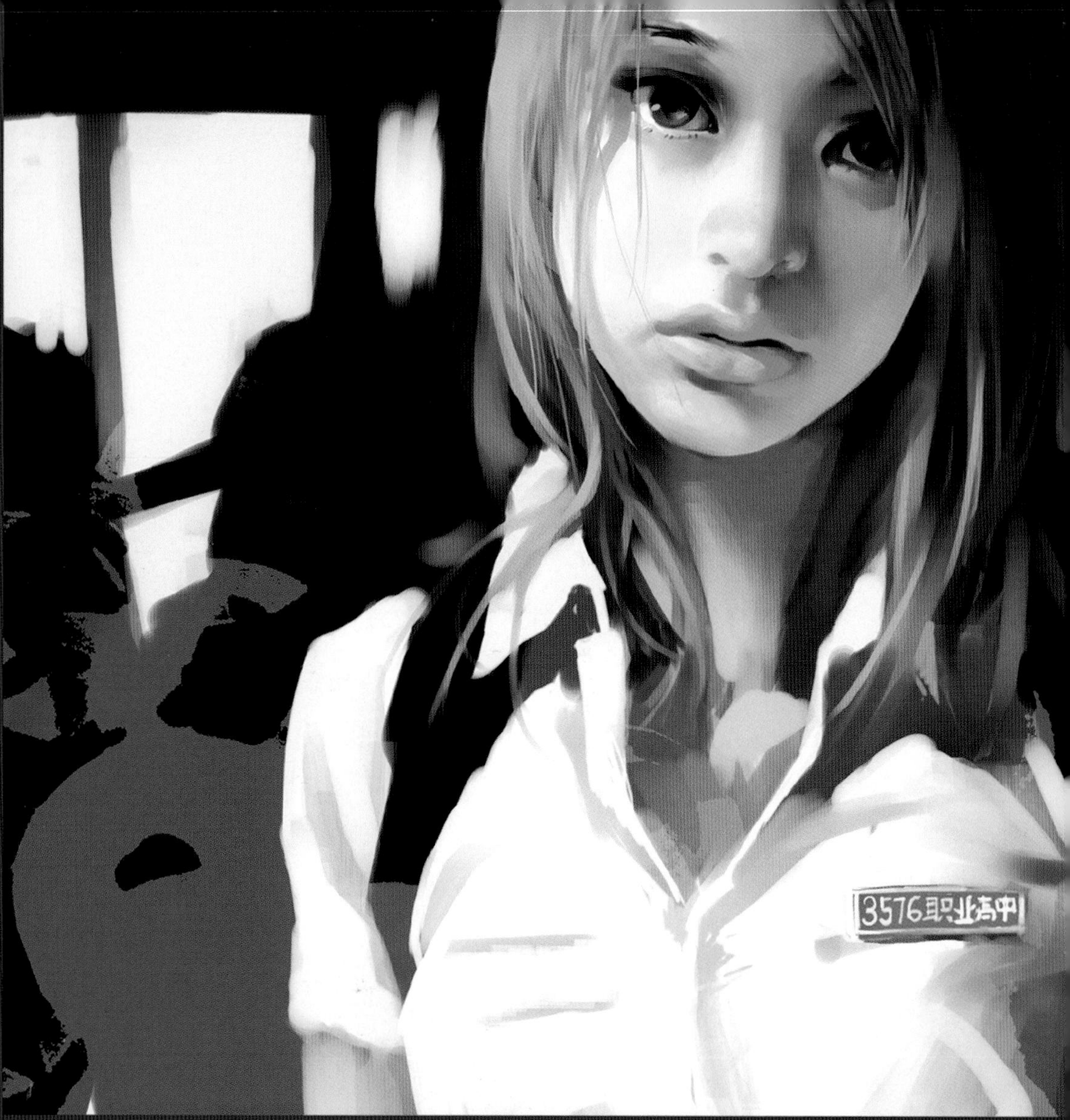
3576

This is the girl from *Basement*, my first novel. My only novel for a while, in fact. Though now there's also *Wher*
*We Going?* I'm not a professional writer, but I hope to be able to keep writing as well as drawing. Making manhu
me to write reviews of manhua. These reviews won me the trust of editors, which then led to me writing short st
I was asked to turn my short story "Basement" into a novel. That's how, little by little, step by step, I was able to re
my mother's dream. I thank those who've helped me. But that's not the most important thing. The most important th
that I was finally able to find a way to pour out my resentment. Those who like sentimental stories will be disappo
Those expecting a sweet love story will spit blood. Sorry, but I can't lie. There's always a moment when I betray m
and that is in the desire to commit murder.

We poor artists, unfairly treated--don't make martyrs of us. Instead, understand that whether we're making music o
we're slaving away after an ideal. Not for money or women. We're slaves of the art we love.

[redacted]
My second novel was called *Where Are We Going?* In retrospect, I find my point
[redacted]
of view in it a bit extreme. I was feverish, elated while writing it. Perhaps I was
[redacted]
unbalanced because the story was very close to my own experiences.
[redacted]
At least I described a strange life with great sincerity. Critique it all
[redacted]
you like, it's a true story. Even if the book's no good, I put my heart
[redacted]
and soul into it, and took a little time from everyone else, too.

[redacted]
Sorry, but I can't explain why the story's like this and not that, why the girl's
[redacted]
like this and not that, why the guy's like this and not that. What I mean is,
[redacted]
it doesn't matter much who the book is about, boy or girl: the important
[redacted]
thing is that the character has real feelings, just like in drawings.

[redacted]
Life is a funny story. At the beginning, you don't understand a thing, and then, in a
[redacted]
flash of lightning, you become intelligent and get it all. Today, even with all I've been
[redacted]
through, I'm really exhausted, but I realize that I don't understand anything yet.

[redacted]
Whether writing or drawing, what I do is nonsense. I let my hand move freely without
[redacted]
knowing what I'm drawing. I feel stupid. All youth's aspirations are shattered. How can
[redacted]
I find them again? It's so hard. I live as though my brain were locked in a glass bottle.

[redacted]
I don't want anything. I just want to create ever-better books, make things
[redacted]
that are more beautiful than women, than food, than life itself.

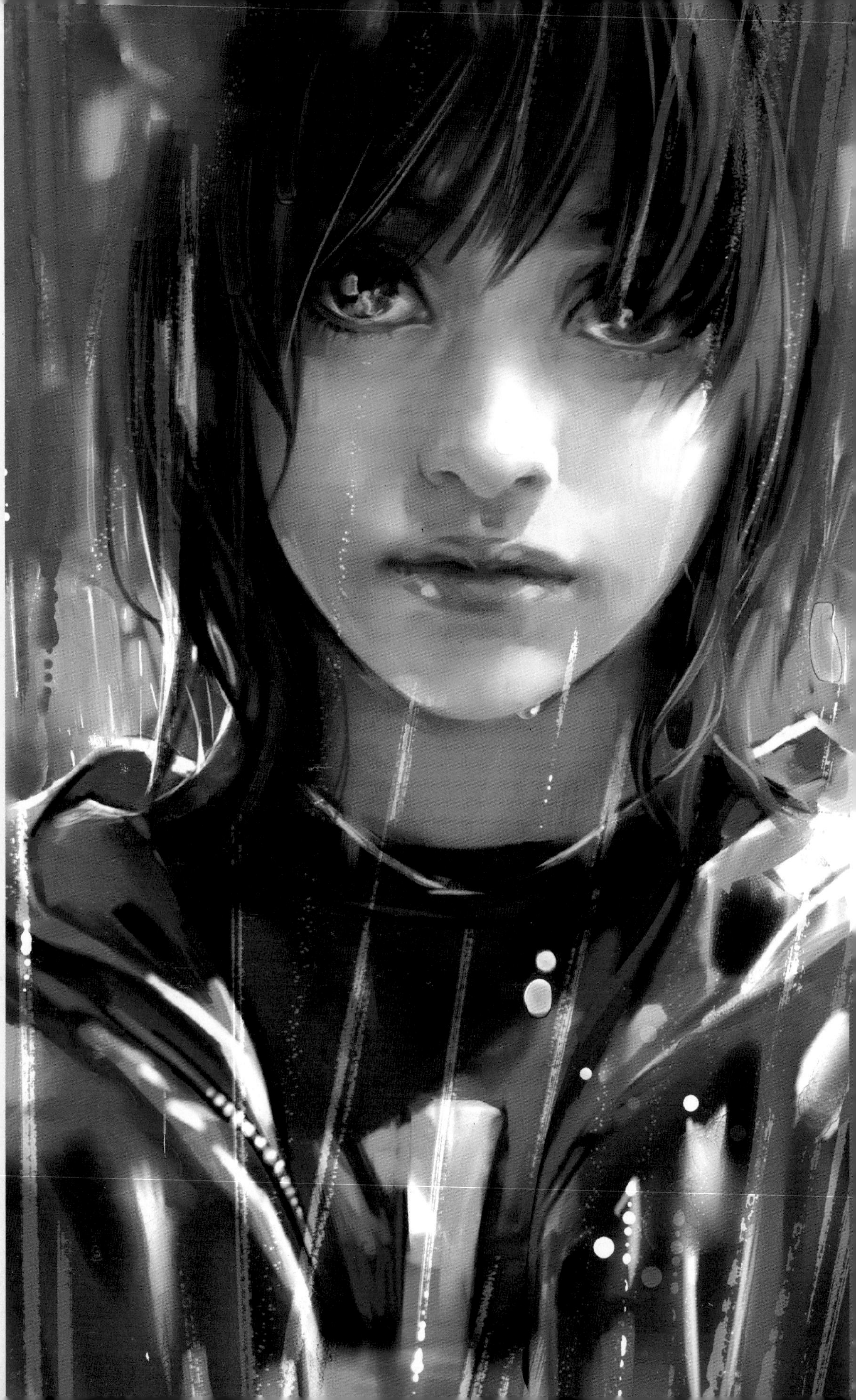

A girl with a piercing stare in a dark bathroom. An image from *Basement* that came to me too late for publication and got left out. I like this picture, but not my friends, who say: "I can't have that at my place, my mother'll have a fit."

Who is she? She's the one we fall in love with just like that, for a moment. I can't manage to fathom what's going on in her eyes: love or sarcasm?

Creations are sometimes terrible omens, without the poor creators knowing any better. One of my friends has a band. His most beautiful song was about despair in love. He wrote it in the middle of a great relationship. Everything he described in the song happened to him six months later. He hadn't suspected a thing. At the time, he just kept sighing and saying he didn't understand how he could've written such a sordid story when he was so happy.

A similar thing happened to me with this drawing. Even though I was happy, it seemed to presage a present that I hadn't expected. I'm convinced that, in the depths of the shadows, the god of artists plays with us, giving us talent but not beauty. We accept in good faith the complications of existence, that great script.

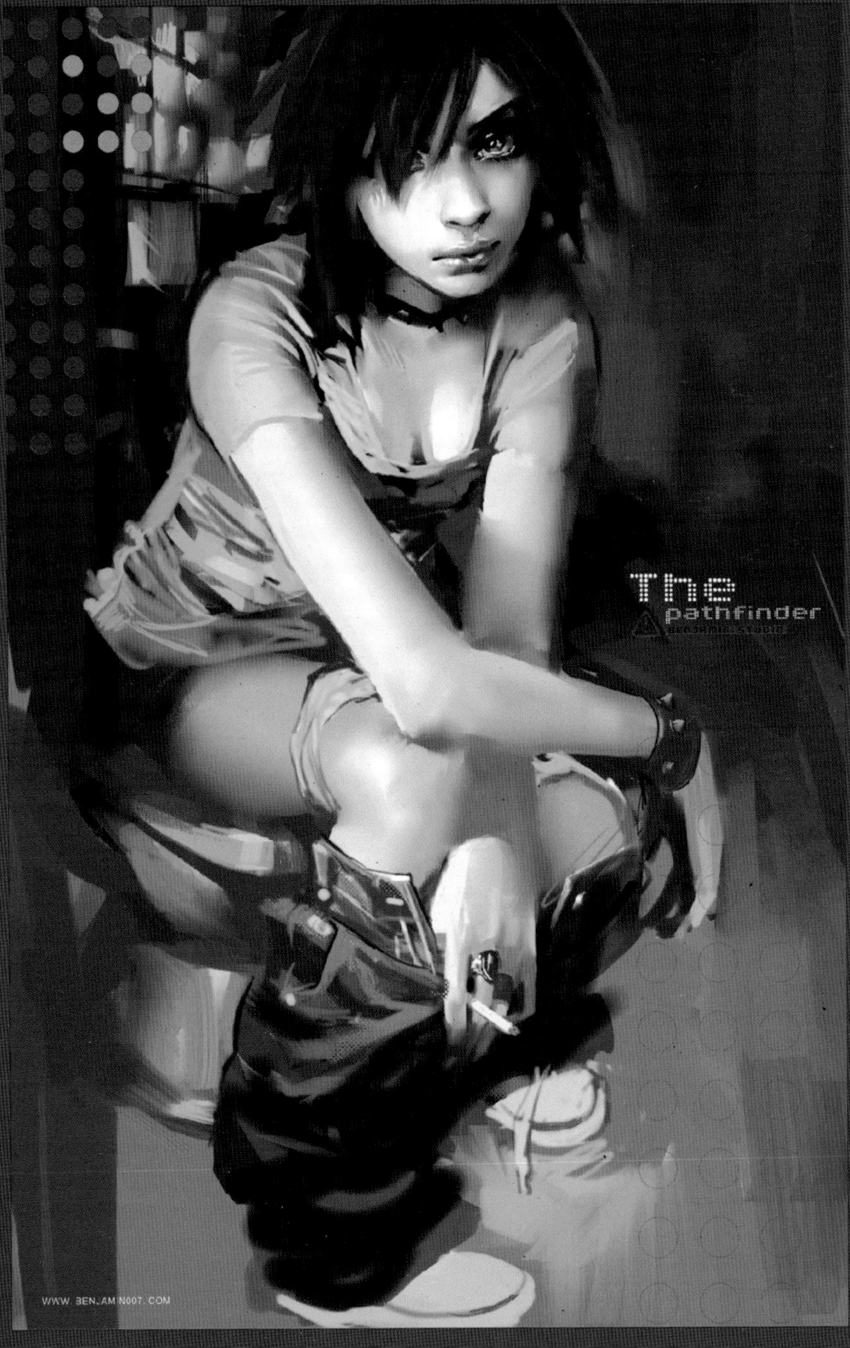
The
pathfinder
WWW. BENJAMIN007. COM

The Toilets from *Basement*

When I created Orange, I was in love with her. Maybe it wasn't love. It doesn't matter. This book took me three years to do. I can't believe it. Spending so much time on a simple little book. The people who were working with me at the beginning have moved or changed, some quite a while ago. I was still fragile at the beginning; I've lived through many hard times. Now I'm more like a real artist. From pickling my brain in toxic liquids, I learned to behave oddly in public. Now I can laugh openly; I know what I can and can't do. Now if I'm normal during the day, I have nightmares at night. Now I know how to draw fast, but the quality of my drawings no longer improves. Now I no longer get drunk when I drink.

Some things are contagious. For three years, when I was working on *Orange*, I was infected by her sadness. I felt either lost or depressed. When I was finishing up at the beginning of the year, I seesawed between depression and suicide. Luckily, I held on, and not only did I finish *Orange*, but I wrote an even more depressing novel, *Where Are We Going?*

Three years ago, I would've said something like this: "Artists! Stop pretending at despair!" Five years ago, I would've said: "What's the idea, lying around waiting to commit suicide, you bunch of incompetents?" Ten years ago, I would've said, naively, "Guys, you should go get your heads checked at the hospital. It might be a brain hemorrhage due to meningitis."

During those three years, I lived as a recluse in my little room, drawing. More and more people wound up coming by to see me, until they formed the big family I have today. My associates, my collaborators, my friends--I love you. Thank you, my irreplaceable assistant and designer, Dazhuozi. Thank you, my friends and loved ones. Luckily, you supported me. I'll be okay, you'll be okay, we'll all move forward.

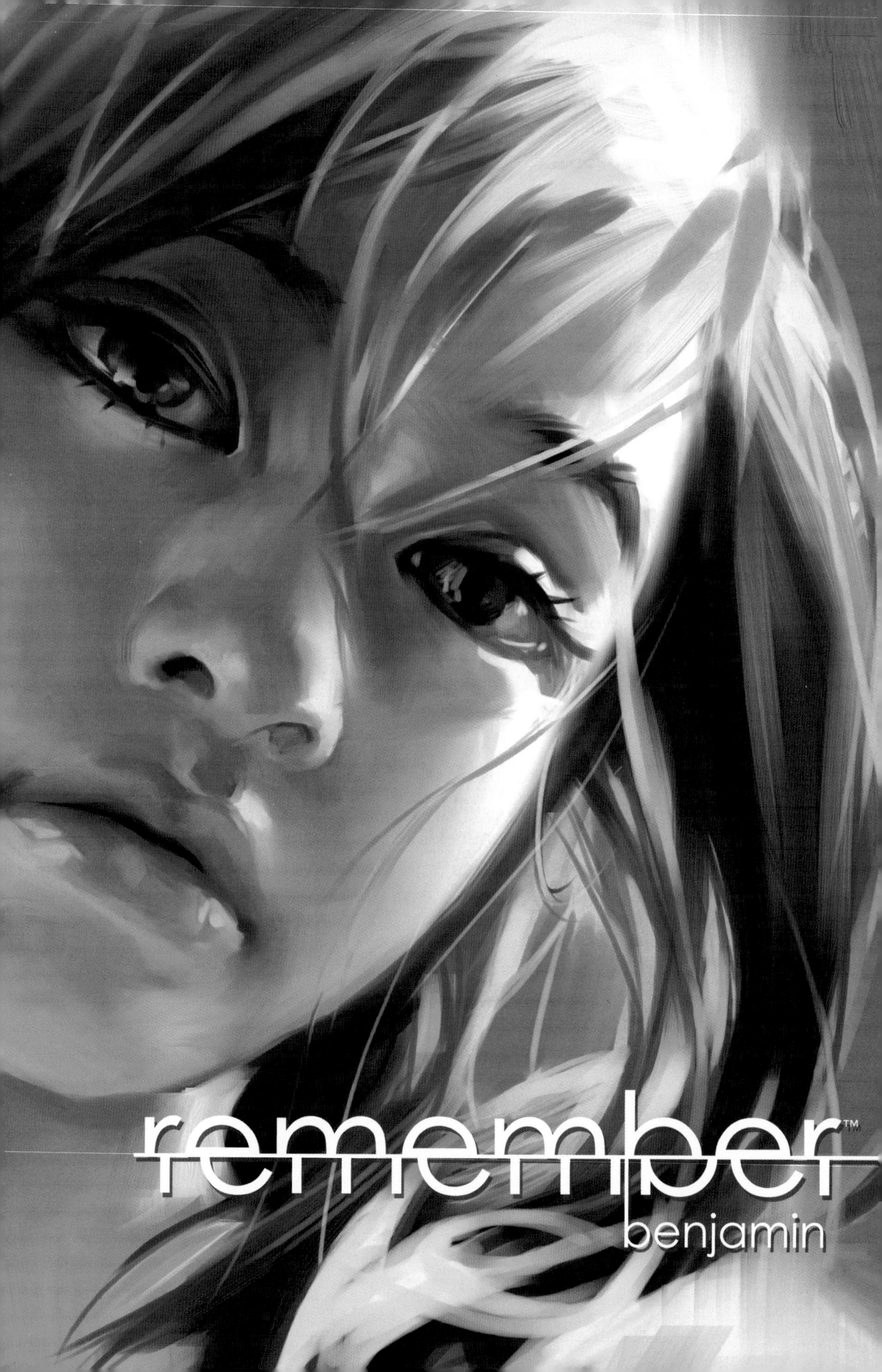
remember™
benjamin

TOKYOPOP
is proud to present
an early preview of
selected artwork
from the
upcoming
graphic novel
REMEMBER
by Benjamin

Available June 2009

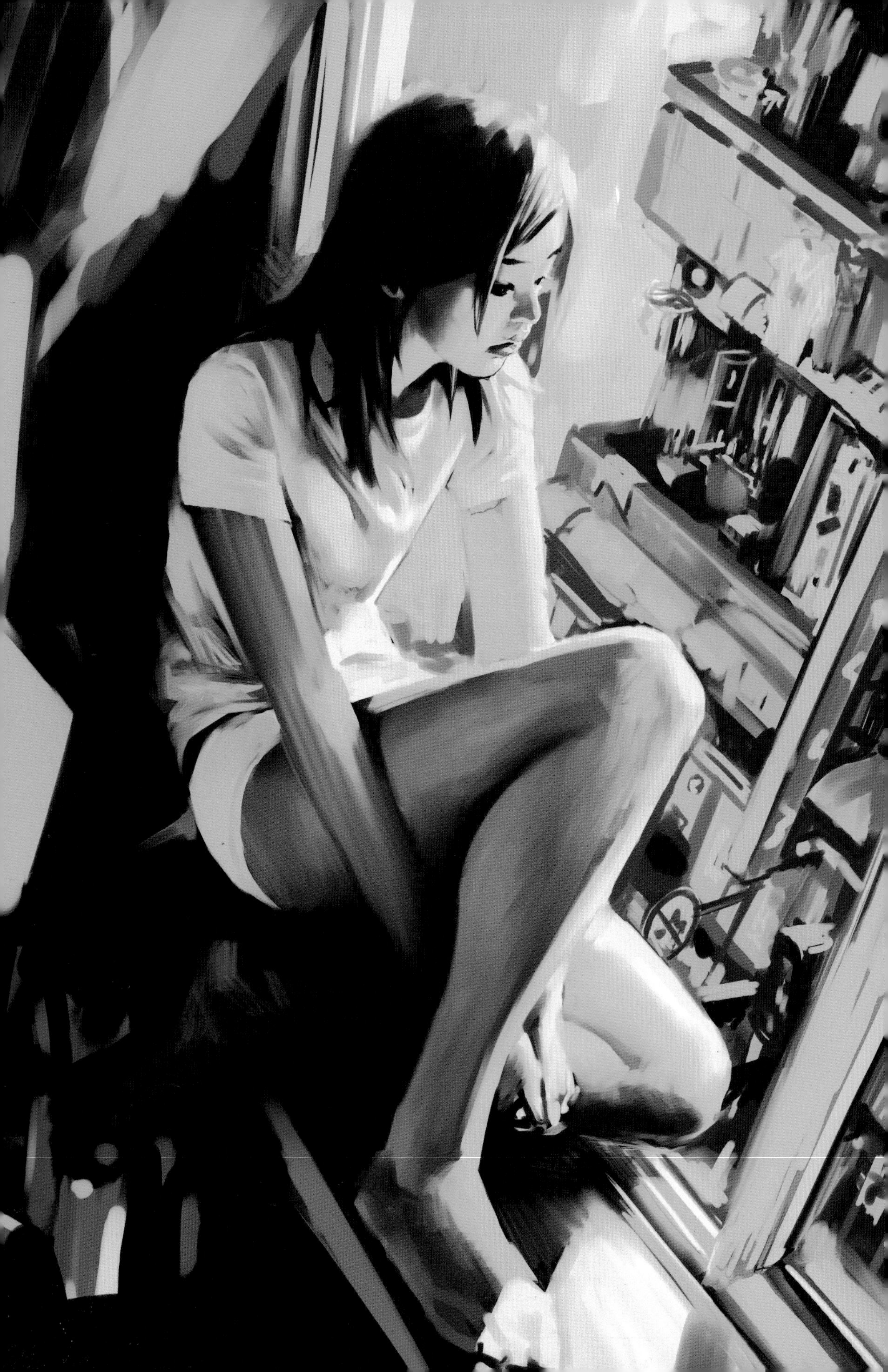

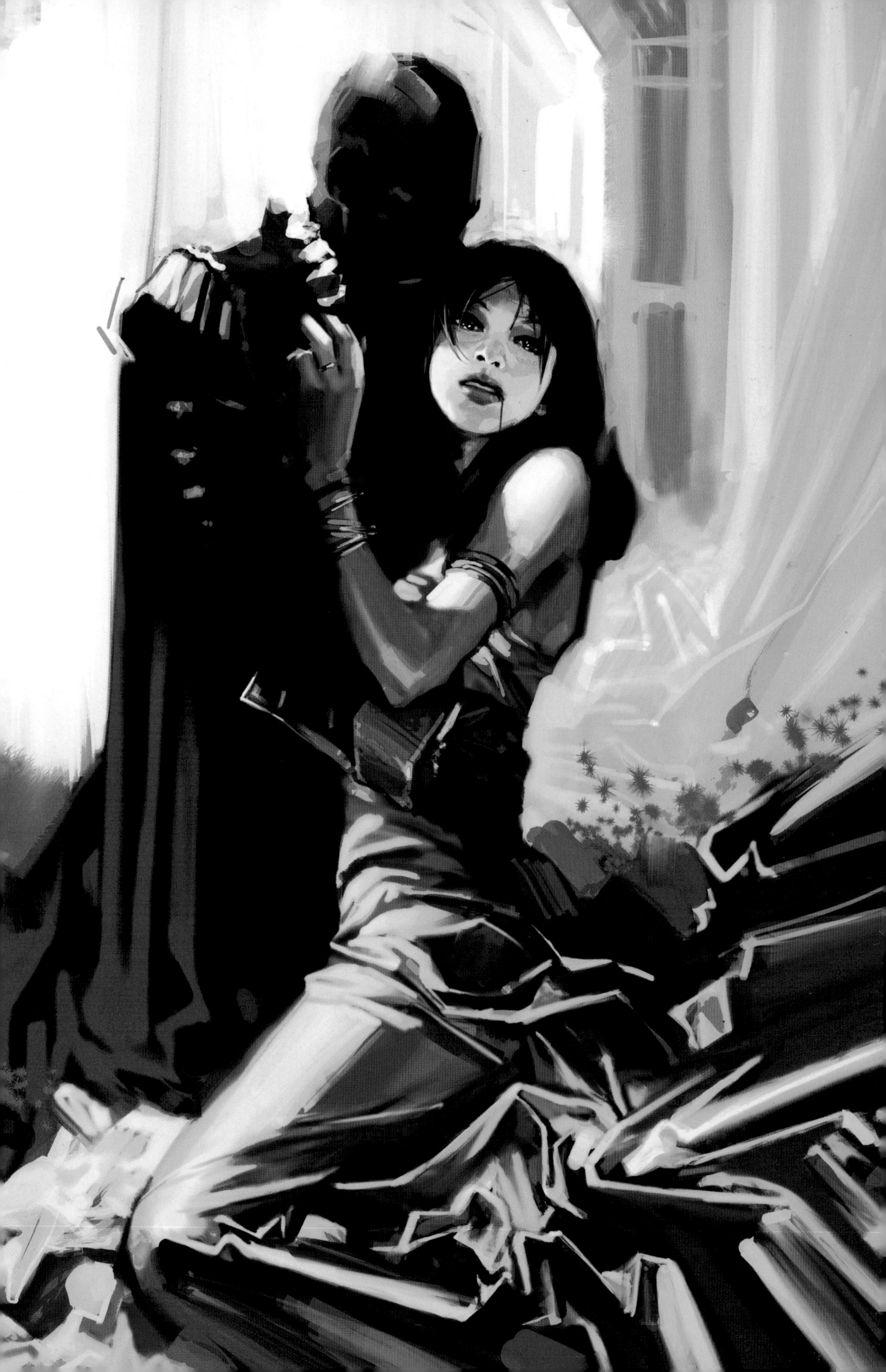

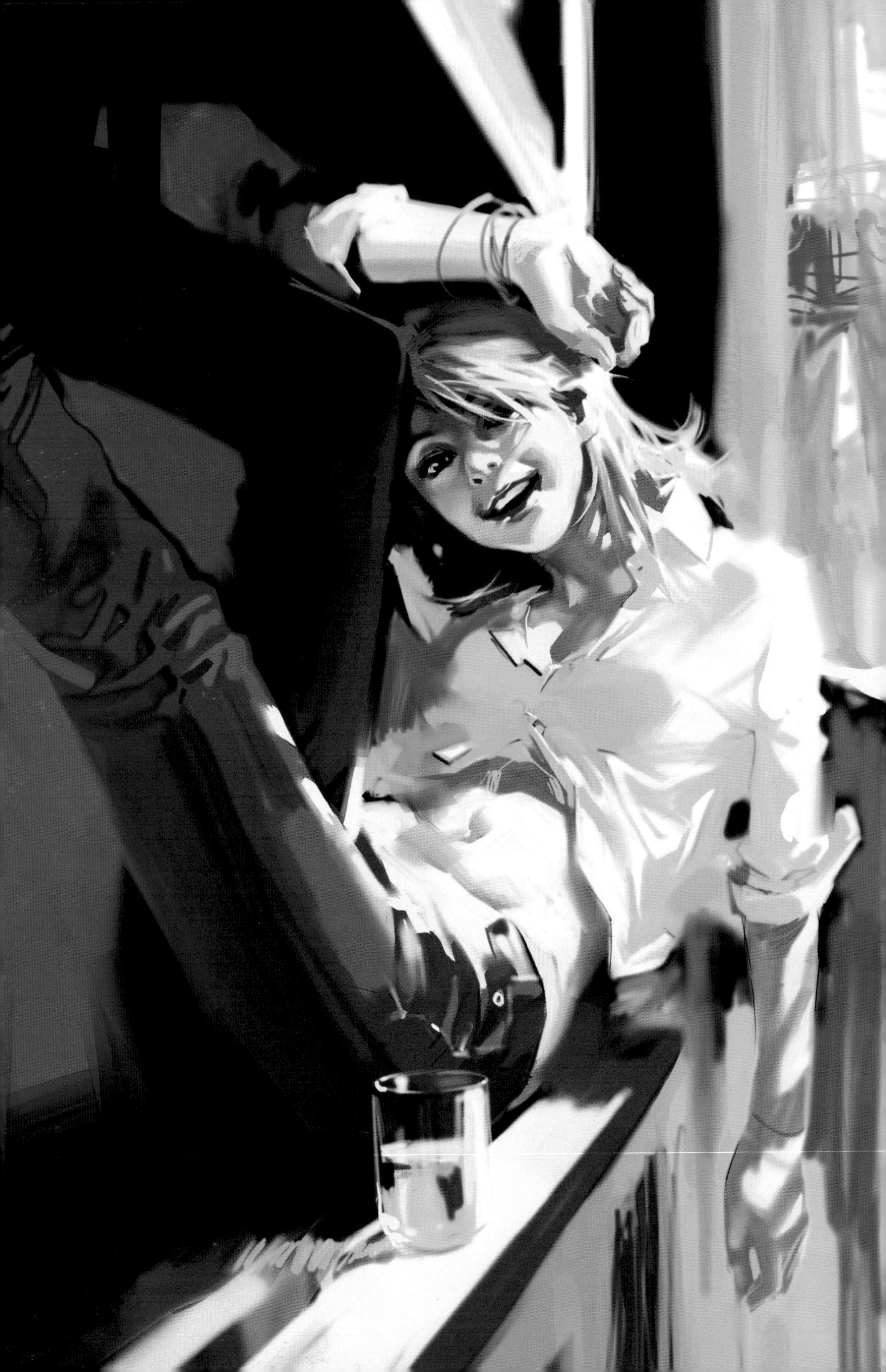

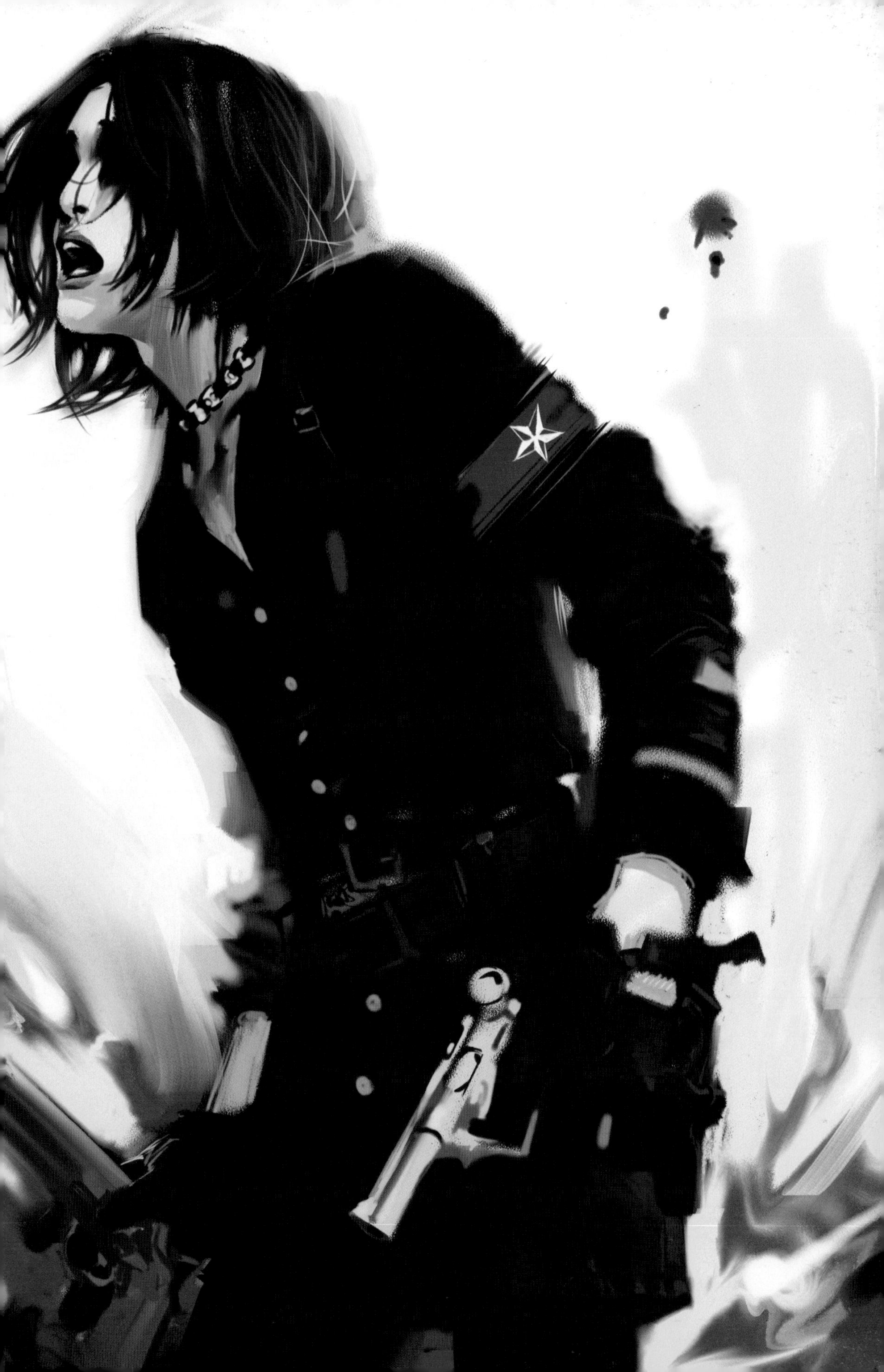

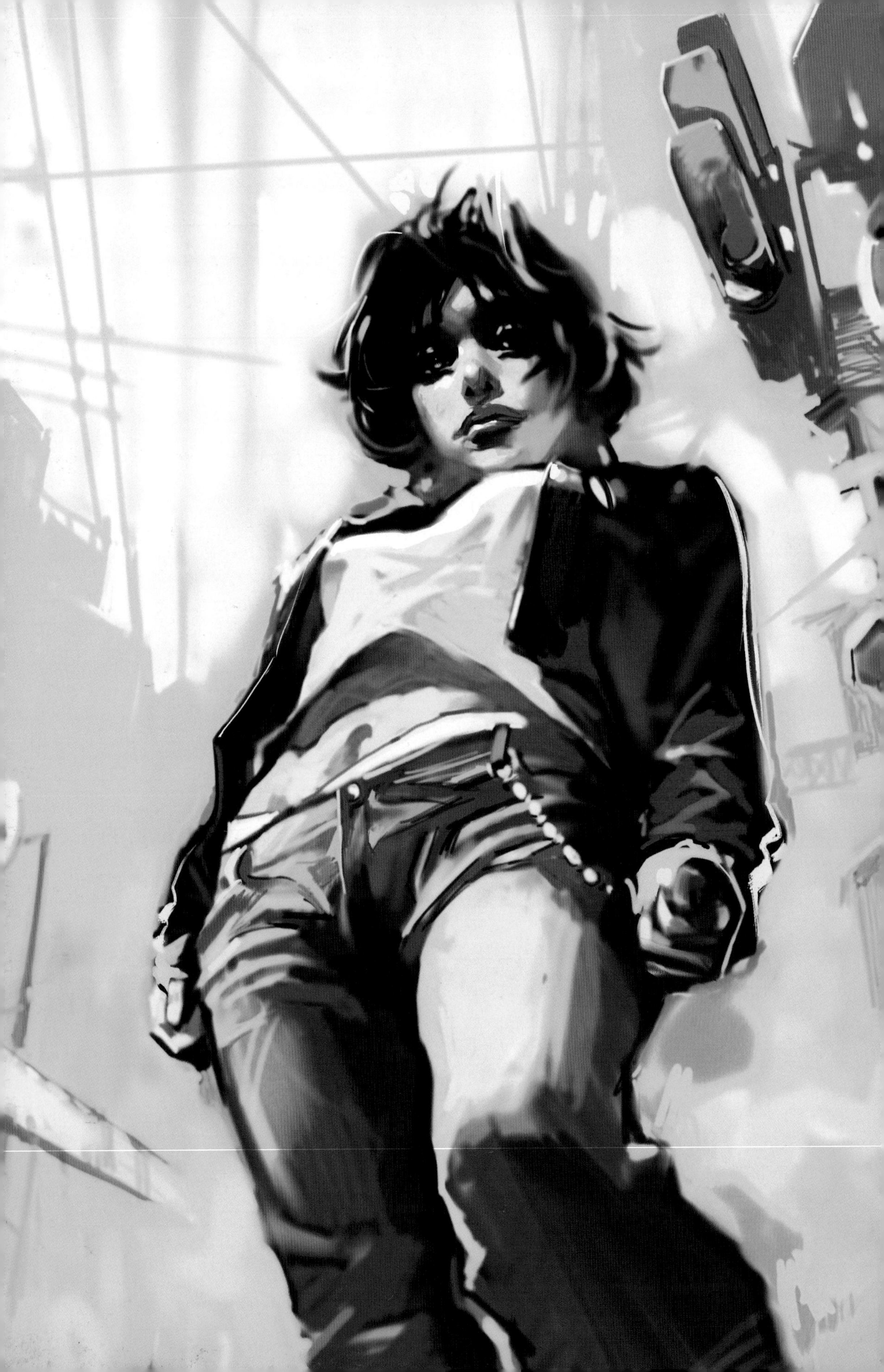

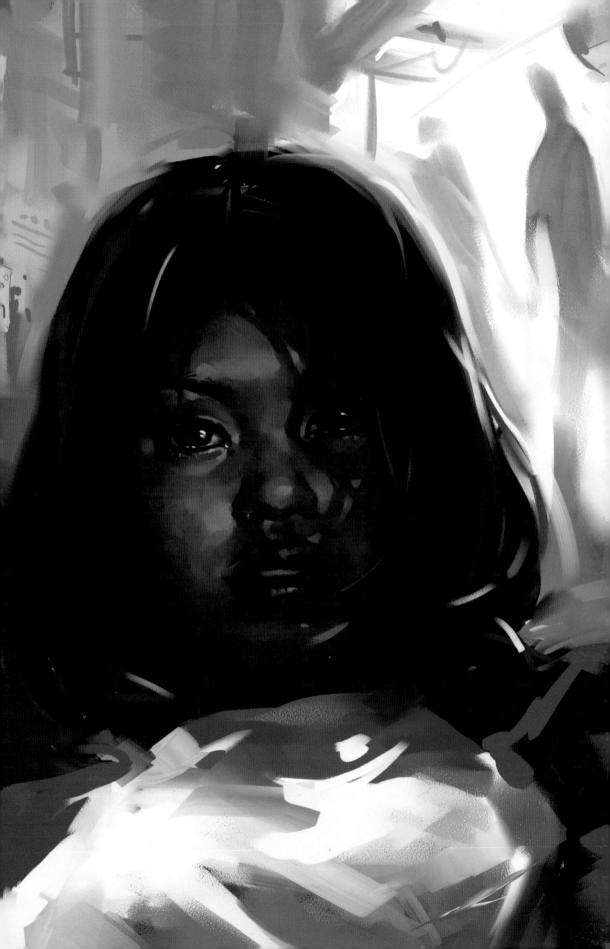

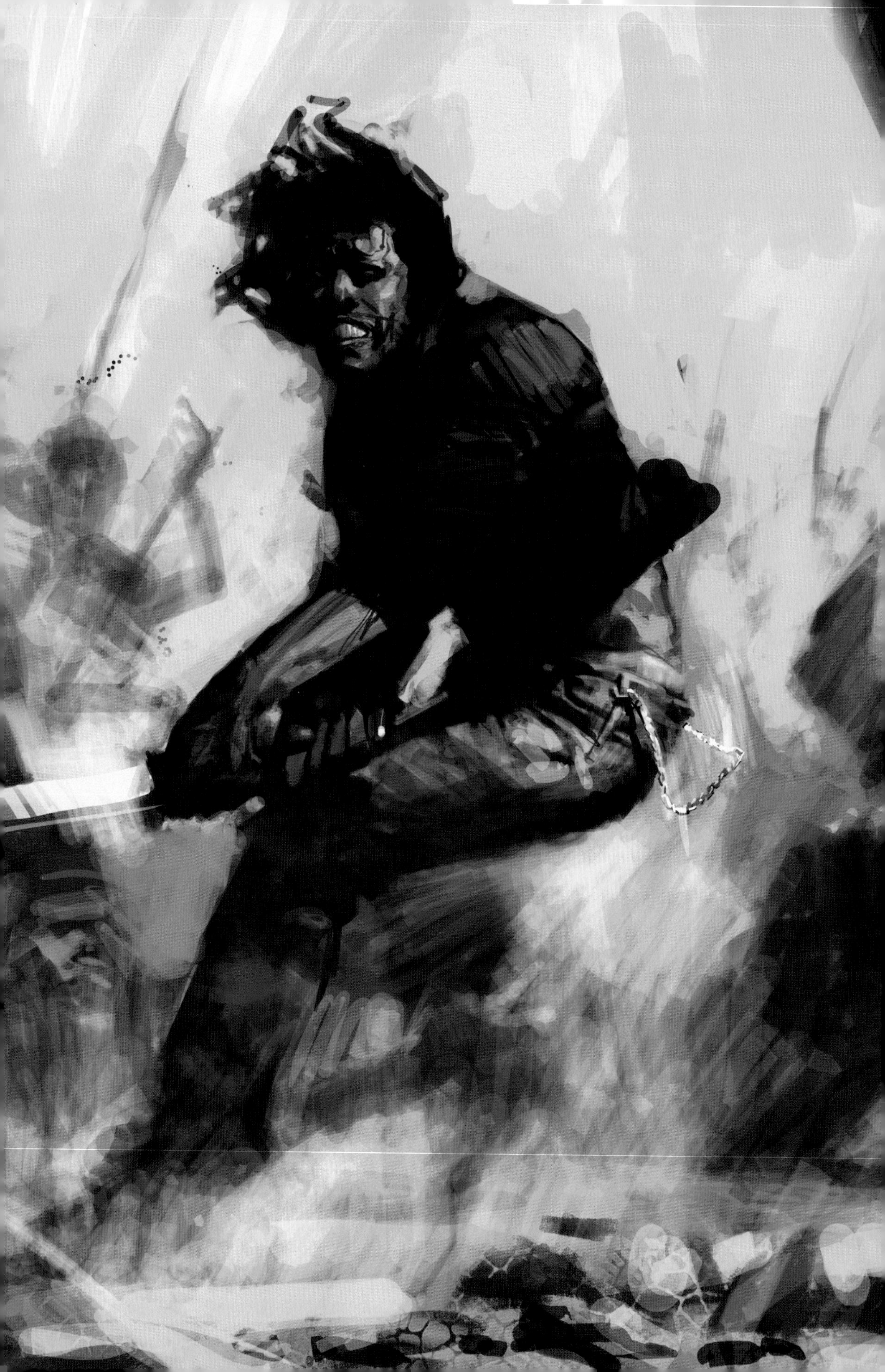

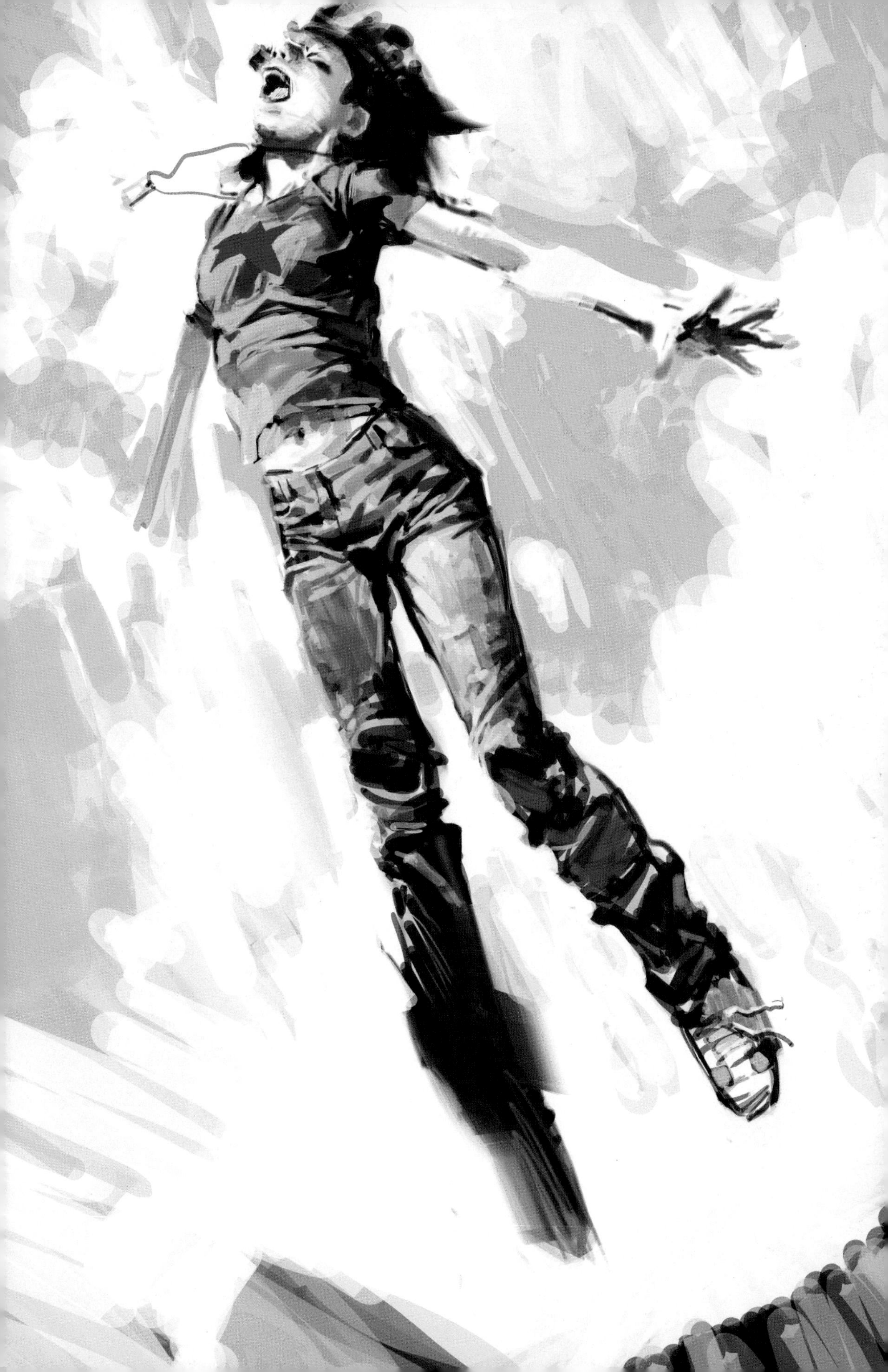

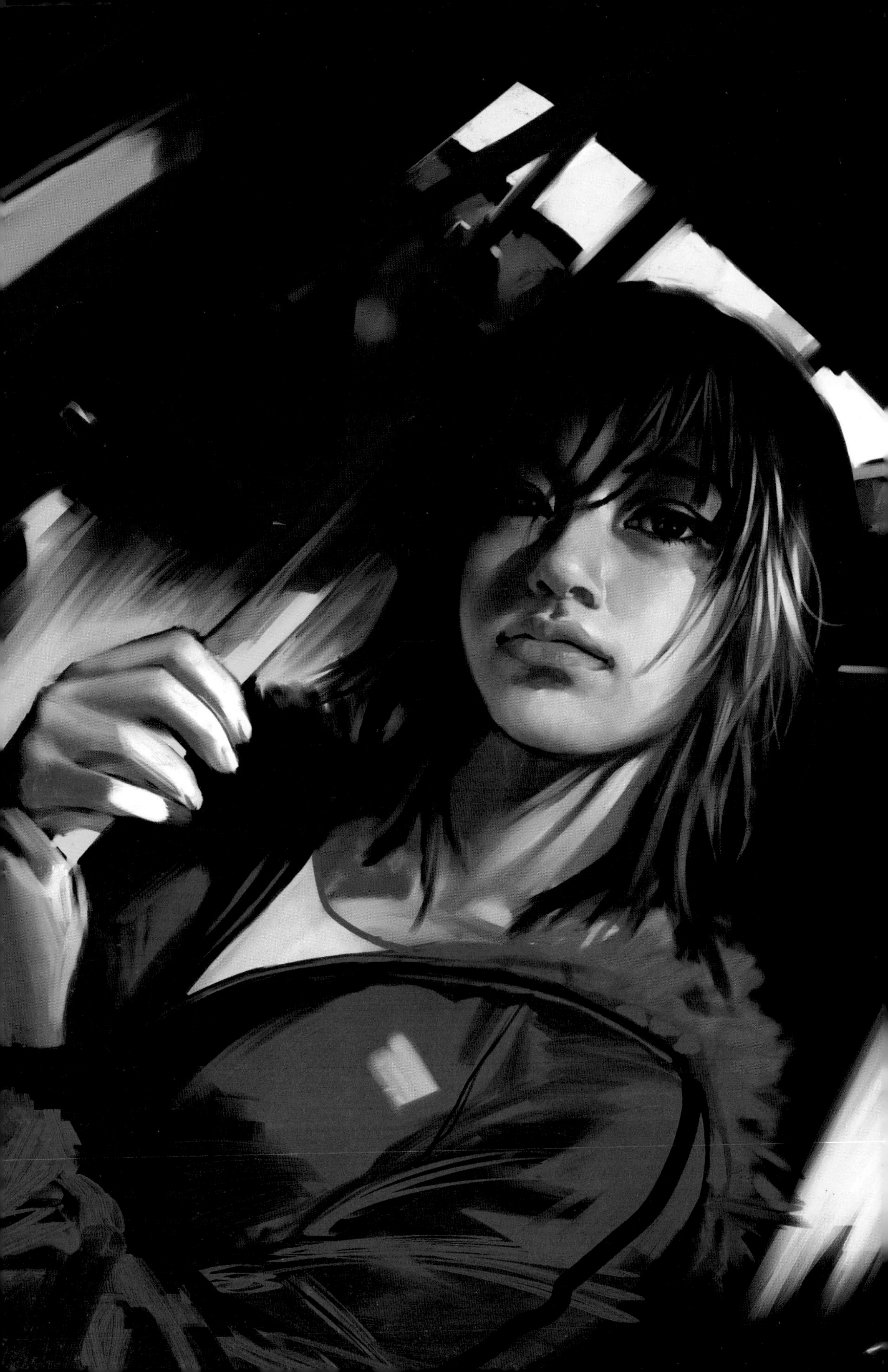

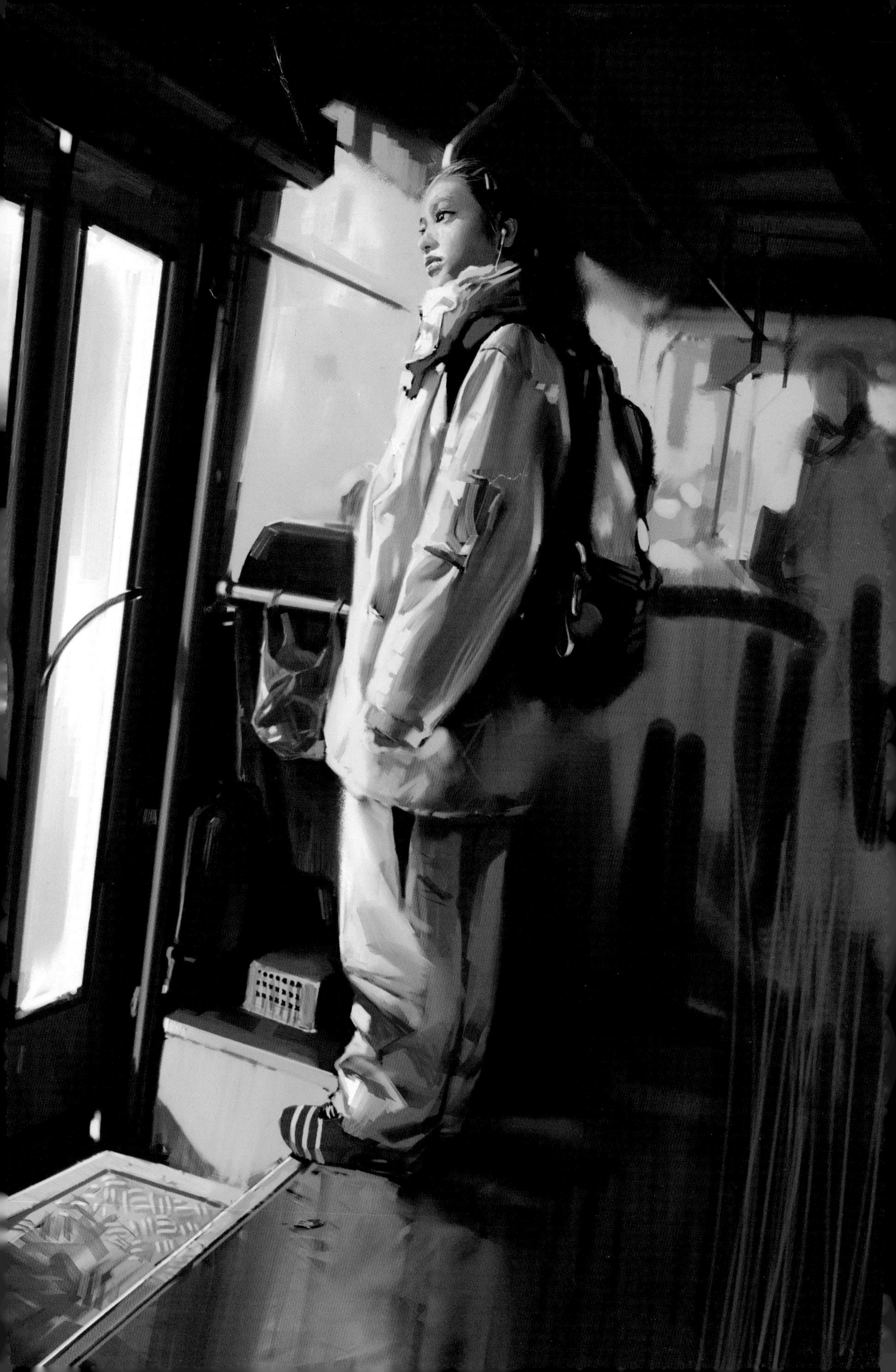

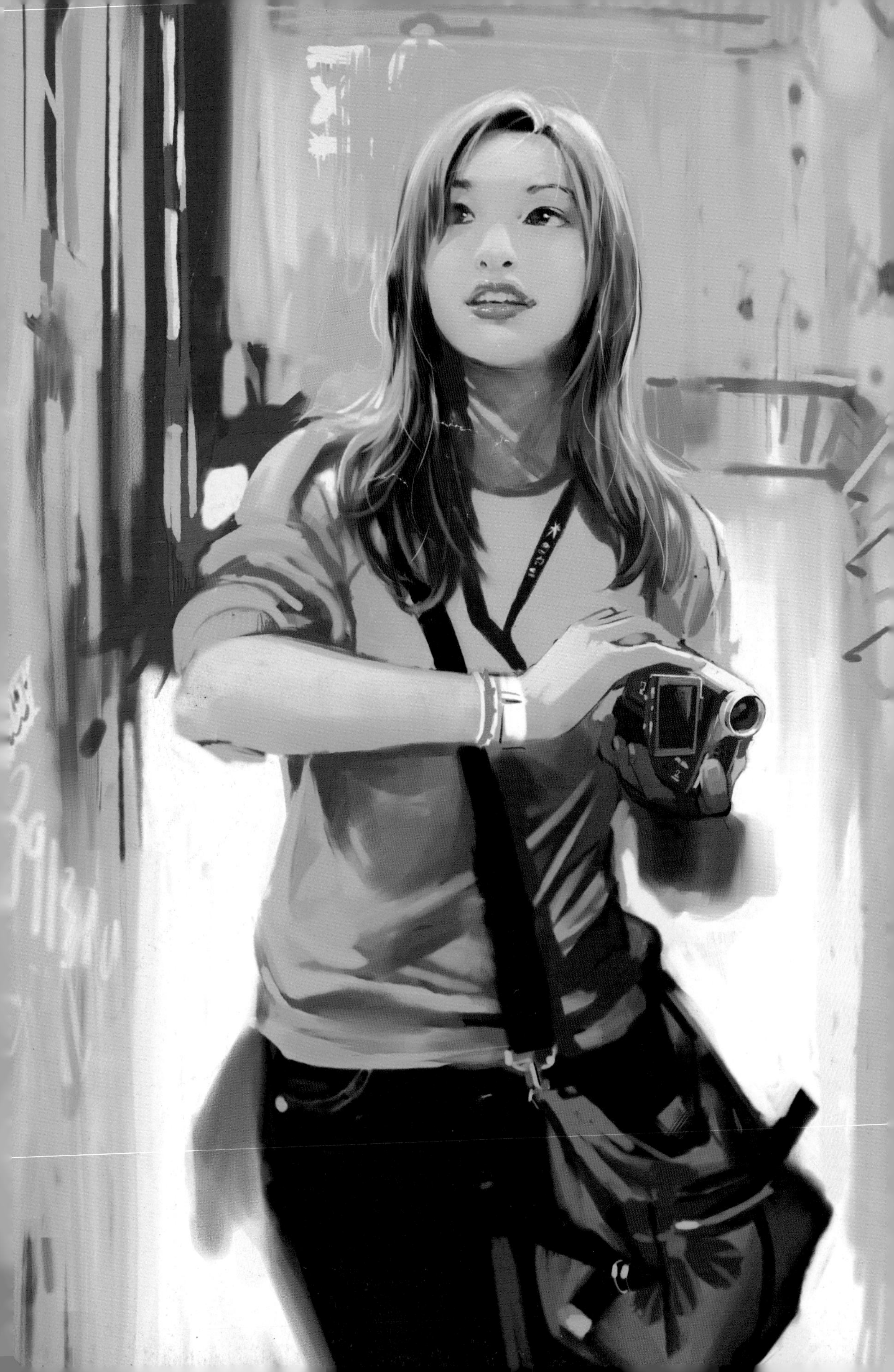

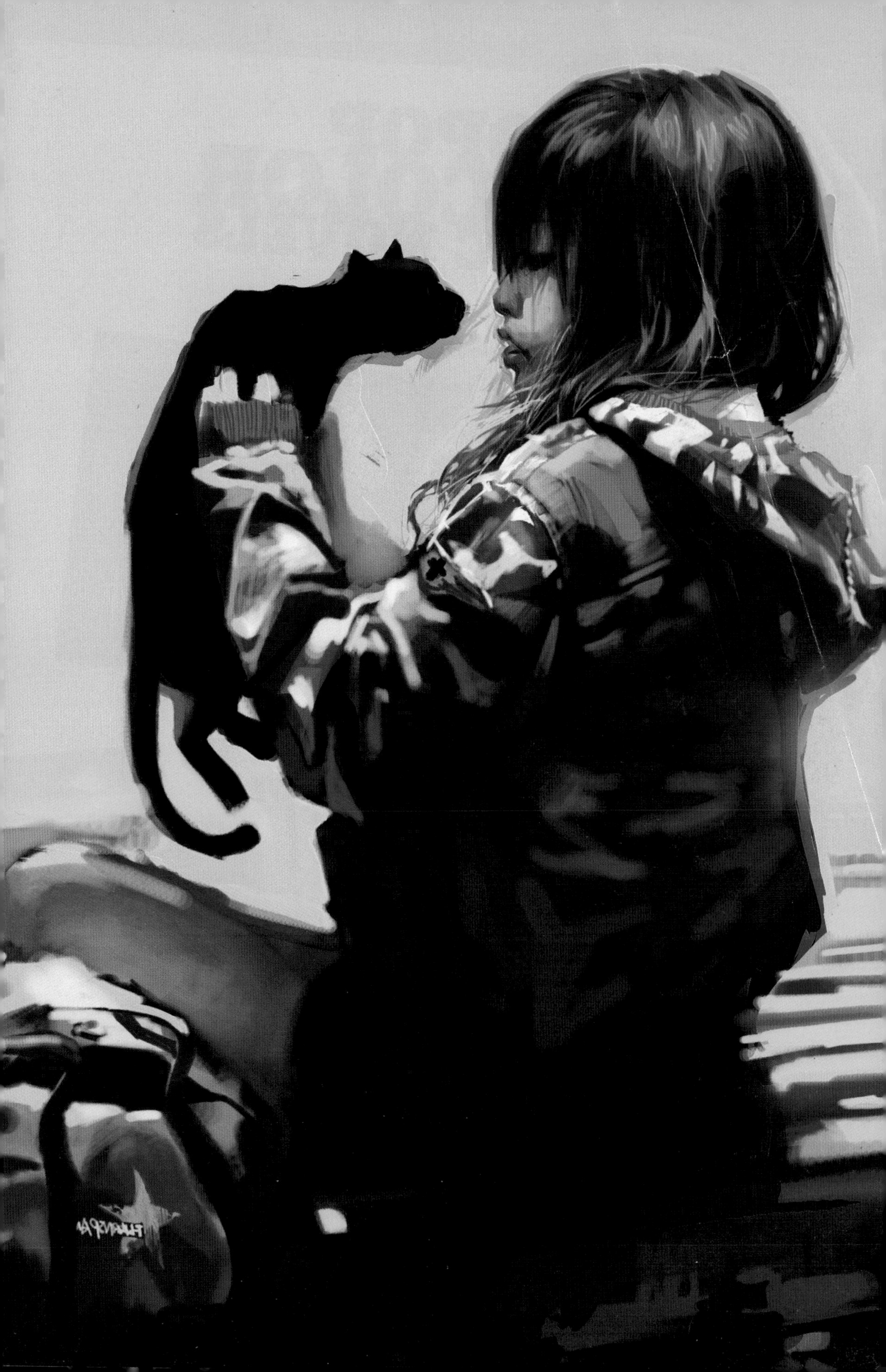

# TOKYOPOP FULL-COLOR GRAPHIC NOVELS

Read TOKYOPOP graphic novels on www.TOKYOPOP.com

*Everyone deserves a little more color in their life*

## Pixie

The mesmerizing voyage of a young prince and his thief friend as they cross the limits of time and imagination

## Luuna

Luuna, a member of the Native American tribe the Paumanoks, is sent out to find her totem spirits, only to discover what it means to be truly alive